GUIDEBOOK OF

FREE CASH & BENEFITS FOR 50 AND OVER

Charles C. Grant

Additional copies of this book may be purchased directly from the publisher. To order, please enclose $26.95 plus $3 postage and handling. Send to:

Book Distribution Center
Post Office Box 747
Walnut, CA 91789

Printed in the United States of America

0 9 8 7 6 5 4 3 2 1

FREE CASH & BENEFITS FOR 50 AND OVER

Table Of Contents

Chapter 7
Miscellaneous Free Cash And Benefits

Chapter 8
Special Bargains On Government Property

Chapter 9
More Free And Low Cost Travel For 50 Or Over

Chapter 10
Late Addition: 50 More Federal Money Programs

Chapter 11
Free Stuff For Seniors And Their Grandkids

Appendix

Introduction

Uncle Sam Has Something For You!

That's not an ominous warning from the IRS or the draft board. It's the good news that the government has millions of dollars in free cash, benefits, discounts and information set aside exclusively for senior citizens.

If you're 50 or older, your fair share of this government windfall could be $15,000 free cash to fix up your home, free college tuition, free world travel, or even a $15 an hour part-time job. This isn't a government handout either. The truth is, the free cash and benefits are yours to start with. You worked hard all your life and paid for it with your taxes. Now it's time to collect your fair share— perhaps up to $500 a month or more in extra money.

There's only one problem in claiming your fair share of this government money and benefits—

Uncle Sam is not going to contact you. The free money programs, the government benefits, services, free advice and information are not advertised. Government bureaucrats don't particularly like to answer questions, and they certainly don't volunteer information. You have to find what's available and then stake your claim. This edition of "Free Cash & Benefits For 50 Or Over" will help you do just that.

There are literally hundreds of federal and state government agencies and most of them have programs and services designed especially for seniors. There's free cash for homeowners and renters, free cash for home winterization; free cash for the art, music and crafts you do in your spare time; free legal services; free tax advice; free prescription medicines; free hospital and health care; free medical and nutrition advice; free and low-cost travel programs, and much more. But very few people have the time, patience, and know-how to search through all the government agencies and red tape. As a result most Americans have never collected even one dime of what is rightfully and lawfully theirs.

With "Free Cash & Benefits For 50 Or Over", we've done the searching and compiled page after page of government programs designed especially for senior citizens. With the information provided in this book, you're sure to find a government source of free cash and/or benefits that can help you secure your future and live in comfort.

MAKING CONTACT

When contacting any of the government sources listed in this book, you should keep a few things in mind. First of all, whether your initial contact is in writing or over the telephone, always be polite. Government bureaucrats are much more likely to be receptive and cooperative to your questions and requests if you're courteous and friendly rather than aggressive and demanding. After all, government bureaucrats are human beings too.

You also should be honest. Most government programs have certain restrictions and requirements. Don't lie about your circumstances and your needs. Explain as clearly and as succinctly as possible the information you need. And once you receive the information you request, make sure you go over the guidelines for a government grant or benefit program before you submit an application.

Finally, you should keep in mind that things change. While every effort has been made to ensure that the information in this book is up-to-date and accurate at the time of printing, some telephone numbers and/or addresses may have changed, or some programs may no longer exist. For example, due to recent cuts in funding, the National Endowment for the Arts (NEA) has been forced to eliminate a number of free money programs. If you contacted the NEA for information about its Arts in

Education Program, Visual Arts Program, or Folk and Traditional Arts Program, you would find that those programs have been cut and no longer exist.

However, you shouldn't be discouraged. Whenever a program has been changed or eliminated altogether, the administering government agency may be able to provide you with information about additional or new programs for which you may qualify. The same is true for informational publications distributed by many government agencies. Publications become dated or go out of print. When that happens, a new or similar publication may be available. Be patient.

The government programs and services listed in this book are presented as information only and are not intended as guarantees that any reader 50 or older automatically qualifies for specific free money and/or benefit programs.

Chapter 1

Free Cash From The Government

Imagine getting free cash and discounts on a variety of goods and services just for making it to the relatively young age of 65. Or how about receiving thousands of dollars in free cash to express your hidden artistic talents. It's all possible, thanks to the generosity of your Uncle Sam.

Senior citizen status provides many perks. Just ask the seniors in Alaska who receive monthly checks from their state just for being 65. And every state has government funded programs that provide free cash in the form of grants and fellowships to promote and support individuals in their artistic endeavors. Regardless of your age, there's a government grant waiting to reward your talents as a painter, sculptor, musician, dancer, storyteller, designer, or illustrator. You even can receive thousands of dollars for the crafts you make in your spare time.

As Grandma Moses proved, you're never too old to unleash your creative talents. And as the information in this chapter shows, Uncle Sam has a number of grants and fellowships to reward your artistic endeavors.

$150 FREE CASH EVERY MONTH, JUST FOR BEING 65

Its weather may not be ideal, but the state of Alaska can warm up its senior citizens with a "Longevity Bonus" of $150 a month. Alaska's Longevity Bonus Program provides a monthly check to seniors 65 and over who have lived in the state for one year. The program is administered in Juneau, Alaska, and is supervised by:

Karen Phillips,
Administrative Assistant II,
P.O. Box 110211;
(907) 465-4416.

Not all states have a Longevity Bonus Program, but all states do have other programs that provide older Americans with special senior discounts and tax benefits. Of course, 65 also is the "magic" age for a number of senior discounts in every state. For example, persons 65 and older can:

* Get discounts of up to 15% on groceries in some stores in Ohio;
* Save 1% on sales tax in South Carolina;
* Save as much as $100 on hearing aids in New Jersey;

Senior citizens also can get free hunting and fishing licenses in most states; pay discounted admission at many major league ballparks; discounts on admission to state parks; senior discounts on meals at many restaurants; discounts on travel and accommodations; and much more. To find out what programs your state has available for senior citizens, contact your state Department on Aging listed in the Appendix of this book.

$10,000 FREE CASH TO HELP YOU DESIGN, LANDSCAPE AND DECORATE YOUR HOME

Many states offer grants and fellowships to individuals who work in the fields of interior design, landscape, architecture, graphic design, and other related disciplines. For example, the Alabama State Council on Arts awards fellowships of $5,000 to $10,000 to individual artists in architecture, fashion design, graphic design, interior design and landscape architecture. Any artist who is a resident of Alabama and who has lived in the state for two years prior to application, may apply under this program in Alabama.

If your state offers such a grant or fellowship program, and if you qualify, you could get thousands of dollars in free cash to design, landscape, and decorate your home. To find out if your state offers such a program, contact your State Art Agency, listed at the end of this chapter.

$6,000 FREE CASH TO MUSIC LOVERS

All that singing in the shower may finally pay off. If you're in fine singing voice, you may be eligible for a grant from your particular state. Most State Art Agencies offer grants and fellowships for excellence in music performance and music lovers can cash in on their singing talents or other musical abilities.

In Maryland, the State Arts Council awards individual artists $1,000 to $6,000 for artistic excellence, and that includes solo musical performances. Your State Art Agency most likely offers a similar award. To find out if your vocal talents or other musical accomplishments can reward you with a grant of $6,000 or more, contact your State Art Agency. Check your telephone directory or see the listings at the end of this chapter.

$37,000 FREE CASH TO PURSUE YOUR DREAM AS AN ENTERTAINER

It's never too late to be a star. As a matter of fact, if you're talented enough, government funded programs could provide you with up to $37,500 free cash to pursue your dream of being an entertainer. The National Endowment of the Arts provides funds to most State Art Agencies, which in turn award grants and fellowships to eligible "entertainers". Grants and fellowships are available to musicians, writers, actors, directors, playwrites, storytellers, mimes, dancers, and other artists.

To find out what grants and fellowships are available and eligibility requirements, contact your State Art Agency, or the

National Endowment for the Arts,
1100 Pennsylvania Avenue, NW,
Washington, DC 20506-0001; (202) 682-5441.

$20,000 FREE CASH TO WRITE THAT NOVEL, POEM OR PLAY YOU'VE ALWAYS WANTED TO WRITE

The bad news is that due to recent budget cuts, the National Endowment for the Arts (NEA) has had to eliminate most of its grants and fellowships to individual artists. The good news is that the NEA Literature Fellowship Program is still alive. That means you still may be able to get up to $20,000 to write that poem, novel or play you've always wanted to write.

The NEA offers Literature Fellowships to creative writers in the areas of prose and poetry (and the translation of both into English). The fellowships are non-matching grants of $20,000, which can be used to cover expenses while you write, conduct research or travel.

For more information about the Literature Fellowships Program, including eligibility requirements and how to apply, contact:

Director, Literature,
National Endowment for the Arts,
1100 Pennsylvania Avenue, NW,
Washington, DC 20506-0001; (202) 682-5428.

$45,000 TO PURSUE YOUR PASSION FOR DANCE

If dance is your passion, the National Endowment for the Arts offers a program that could provide you up to $45,000 to "dance the night away". Through the NEA's Promotion of the Arts: Partnership Agreements, most state art agencies receive funding to provide support for performing arts, including dance and dance choreography. If you're a professional choreographer, are a member of a performing dance company or an organization that services the art of dance, you may be eligible for this funding. Past awards have averaged as much as $45,000.

To find out about the Promotion of the Arts Program, contact your state art agency (see the listings at the end of this chapter), or contact:

Director, State and Regional,
National Endowment for the Arts,
1100 Pennsylvania Avenue, NW,
Washington, DC 20506- 682-5429.

Smaller grants to individual artists in the discipline of dance also are available in most states. For example, the Colorado Council on the Arts' Artist Fellowship Program provides awards of $4,000 to individual artists in dance choreography. To find out if your state offers similar awards, contact your State Art Agency.

$6,000 TO UNLEASH YOUR CREATIVE JUICES

The recent cuts in NEA funding has brought about the demise of the Visual Arts Program. However, there's still a chance you can receive funding to unleash your creative juices. Most state art agencies offer grants to individual painters, sculptors, photographers, illustrators, and other visual artists. For example, the Maryland State Arts Council's Individual Artist Awards Program provides grants of up to $6,000 to individual visual artists to support and encourage their pursuit of artistic excellence.

With more time to devote to your creative talents, you could use a little “support” money to help keep the creative juices flowing. Contact your State Art Agency to find out what financial support is available in your area.

$5,000 FREE CASH FOR YOUR ORIGINAL STORIES

Those stories you create and tell your grandkids may be part of a folk tradition passed down from one generation to the next. As such, they may bring you an award of $5,000 or more. The National Endowment for the Arts provides funding to most state Art Agencies to support traditional folk arts including storytellers.

For example, the Louisiana State Arts Council and Division of the Arts offers financial assistance for a wide range of community-oriented arts projects including folk arts. The program provides apprenticeship grants up to $5,000 to master folk artists and apprentices, including storytellers.

A similar program may be available in your state that can help you turn your original stories that your grandkids love into free cash. Contact your State Art Agency for information.

$7,500 FREE CASH FOR THE ART, MUSIC AND CRAFTS YOU DO IN YOUR SPARE TIME

Now that you've finally got the time, your spare-time hobby can become a full-time passion. And you may be able to get a government grant to help you perfect that passion. There are programs in every state that provide funding for individuals involved in art, music, and crafts. Whether you paint, sing, or create traditional or unique craft items, there's most likely some sort of financial support available. For example, the South Carolina Arts Commission offers grants of $7,500 to artists in all disciplines. The Alabama State Arts Council offers grants up to $10,000 for crafts including clay, fiber, metal, glass, wood, and similar crafts. In Maryland, you can get up to $6,000 for visual arts crafts, musical composition, or creative writing.

You can contact your State Art Agency to find out what programs and awards are offered in your state.

STATE AND REGIONAL ART AGENCIES

Here is a state-by-state list of arts agencies and regional arts organizations working with the National Endowment for the Arts. The agencies utilize funds mandated by Congress as well as funds received from state governments and other sources.

State Arts Agencies

Alabama State Council on the Arts, Montgomery, AL 36130; (334)-242-4076.

Alaska State Council on the Art,411 West 4th Avenue, Suite 1E, Anchorage, AK 99501-2343, (907) 269-6610; asc@alaska.net.

Arizona Commission on the Arts, 417 West Roosevelt, Phoenix, AZ 85003; (602) 255-5882.

Arkansas Arts Council, 1500 Tower Building, 323 Center Street, Little Rock, AR 72201; (501) 324-9766; info@dah.state.ar.us

California Arts Council, 1300 I Street, #930, Sacramento, CA 95814; (916) 322-6555; cac@artswire.org.

Colorado Council on the Arts, 750 Pennsylvania Street, Denver, CO 80203-3699; (303) 894-2617

Connecticut Commission on the Arts, 755 Main Street, Hartford, CT 06103; (203) 566-4770.

Delaware Division of the Arts, State Office Building, 820 North French Street, Wilmington, DE 19801; (302) 577-3540; delarts@tmn.com.

District of Columbia Commission on the Arts & Humanities, 410 8th Street, NW, Washington, DC 20004; (202) 724-5613; carrien@tmn.com.

Florida Division of Cultural Affairs, Florida Department of State, The Capitol, Tallahassee, FL 32399-0250; (904) 488-5799.

Georgia Council for the Arts, 530 Means Street, NW, Suite 115, Atlanta, GA 30318-5730; (404) 651-7920.

Hawaii State Foundation on Culture & the Arts, 44 Merchant Street, Honolulu, HI 96813; (808) 586-0300.

Idaho Commission on the Arts, P.O. Box 83720, Boise, ID 83720-0008; (208) 334-2119.

Illinois Arts Council, State of Illinois Center, 100 West Randolph, Suite 10-500, Chicago, IL 60601; (312) 814-4831; 1larts@artswire.org.

Indiana Arts Commission, 402 West Washington Street, Room 072, Indianapolis, IN 46204-2741; (317) 232-1268.

Iowa Arts Council, 600 East Locust, State Capitol Complex, Des Moines, IA 50319; (515) 281-4451.

Kansas Arts Commission, Jayhawk Tower, 700 Jackson, Suite 1004, Topeka, KS 66603; (913) 296-3335.

Kentucky Arts Council, 31 Fountain Place, Frankfort, KY 40601; (502) 564-3757.

Louisiana Division of the Arts, Louisiana Department of Culture, Recreation, & Tourism, 1051 North 3rd Street, P.O. Box 44247, Baton Rouge, LA 70804; (504) 342-8180; arts@crt.state.la.us.

Maine Arts Commission, 55 Capitol Street, State House Station 25, Augusta, ME 04333; (207) 287-2724.

Maryland State Arts Council, 601 North Howard Street, 1st Floor, Baltimore, MD 21201; (410) 333-8232; msac@digex.net.

Massachusetts Cultural Council, 120 Boylston Street, 2nd Floor, Boston, MA 02116-4600; (617) 727-3668.

Michigan Council for Arts and Cultural Affairs, 1200 6th Street, Executive Plaza, Detroit, MI 48226; (313) 256-3731.

Minnesota State Arts Board, 400 Sibley Street, Suite 200, St. Paul, MN 55101-1949; (612) 215-1600; (800) 8MN-ARTS.

Mississippi Arts Commission, 239 North Lamar Street, Second Floor, Jackson, MS 39201; (601) 359-6030.

Missouri State Council on the Arts, Wainwright Office Complex, 111 North Seventh Street, Suite 105, St. Louis, MO 63101; (314) 340-6845.

Montana Arts Council, 316 North Park Avenue, Room 252, Helena, MT 59620; (406) 444-6430.

Nebraska Arts Council, The Joslyn Castle Carriage House, 3838 Davenport Street, Omaha, NE 68131-2329; (402) 595-2122.

Nevada State Council on the Arts, Capitol Complex, 602 North Curry Street, Carson City, NV 89710; (702) 687-6680.

New Hampshire State Council on the Arts, Phenix Hall, 40 North Main Street, Concord, NH 03301; (603) 271-2789.

New Jersey State Council on the Arts, 20 West State Street, 3rd Floor, Trenton, NJ 08625-0306; (609) 292-6130.

New Mexico Arts Division, 228 East Palace Avenue, Santa Fe, NM 87501; (505) 827-6490.

New York State Council on the Arts, 915 Broadway, New York, NY 10010; (212) 387-7000; nysca@artswire.org.

North Carolina Arts Council, Department of Cultural Resources, Raleigh, NC 27601-2807; (919) 733-2821.

North Dakota Council on the Arts, 418 East Broadway Avenue, Suite 70, Bismarck, ND 58501-4086; (701) 328-3954; thompson@pioneer.state.nd.us.

Ohio Arts Council, 727 East Main Street, Columbus, OH 43205; (614) 466-4541; bfisher@mail.oac.ohio.gov.

Oklahoma Arts Council, P.O. Box 52001-2001, Oklahoma City, OK 73152-2001; (405) 521-2931; okarts@oklaosf.state.ok.us.

Oregon Arts Commission, 775 Summer Street, NE, Salem, OR 97310; (503) 986-0082; lisa.m.rindfleisch@state.or.us.

Pennsylvania Council on the Arts, Finance Building, Room 216A, Harrisburg, PA 17120; (717) 787-6883.

Rhode Island State Council on the Arts, 95 Cedar Street, Suite 103, Providence, RI 02903; (401) 277-3880.

South Carolina Arts Commission, 1800 Gervais Street, Columbia, SC 29201; (803) 734-8696; kenmay@scsn.net.

South Dakota Arts Council, Office of Arts, 800 Governors Drive, Pierre, SD 57501-2294; (605) 773-3131; dennish@atlib.state.sd.us.

Tennessee Arts Commission, Parkway Towers, Suite 160, 404 James Robertson Parkway, Nashville, TN 37243-0780; (615) 741-1701.

Texas Commission on the Arts, P.O. Box 13406, Capitol Station, Austin, TX 78711; (512) 463-5535.

Utah Arts Council, 617 East South Temple Street, Salt Lake City, UT 84102; (801) 533-5895; dadamson@email.st.ut.us.

Vermont Arts Council, 136 State Street, Montpelier, VT 05633-6001; (802) 828-3291; info@arts.vca.state.vt.us.

Virginia Commission for the Arts, 223 Governor Street, Richmond, VA 23219; (804) 2225-3132; pbaggett@state.va.us.

Washington State Arts Commission, 234 East 8th Avenue, P.O. Box 42625, Olympia, WA 98504-2675; (360) 753-3860.

West Virginia Division of Culture & History, 1900 Kanawha Blvd. East, Capitol Complex, Charleston, WV 25305-0300; (304) 558-0220.

Wisconsin Arts Board, 101 East Wilson Street, 1st Floor, Madison, WI 53702; (608) 266-0190.

Wyoming Arts Council, 2320 Capitol Avenue, Cheyenne, WY 82002; 307) 777-7742.

National Assembly of State Arts Agencies, 1010 Vermont Avenue, NW Suite 920, Washington, DC 20005; (202) 347-6352; nasaa@tmn.com.

Americans for the Arts, 927 15th Street, NW, 12th Floor, Washington, DC 20005; nalaamem@artswire.org.

Regional Arts Organization

Arts Midwest, Hennepin Center for the Arts, 528 Hennepin Avenue, Suite 310, Minneapolis, MN 55403; (612) 341-0755; webcom@artsmidwest.org.

Consortium for Pacific Arts & Cultures, 2141C Atherton Road, Honolulu, HI 96822; (808) 946-7381.

Mid-America Arts Alliance, 912 Baltimore Avenue, Suite 700, Kansas City, MO 64105; (816) 421-1388.

Mid Atlantic Arts Foundation, 11 East Chase Street, Suite 2-A, Baltimore, MD 21202; (410) 539-6659; midarts@charm.net.

New England Foundation of the Arts, 330 Congress Street 6th Floor, Boston, MA 02210-1216; (617) 951-0010; nroberts@nefa.org.

Southern Arts Foundation, 181 14th Street, NE, Suite 400, Atlanta, GA 30309; (404) 874-7244.

Western States Arts Federation, 236 Montezuma Avenue, Santa Fe, NM 87501; (505) 988-1166; staff@westaf.org.

Chapter 2

Free Help Getting A Job Or Going To College

Age is no handicap when it comes to getting a good paying job or getting a college education. There are a number of Federal and State programs that can help you do either, especially if you're 50 and over.

Perhaps you've retired and found that your Social Security and pension income isn't enough to meet your needs. Or maybe you just want a part-time job to help keep you busy and provide you with some extra cash. Whatever the reason you're interested in re-entering the work force, you'll be able to find free help through several government agencies. This help is available even if you're 65, or if your job skills are rusty or limited. There are a number of programs that offer free job training and placement especially for older persons.

If you never had a chance to go to college before you retired, now you can. And you don't have to spend a lot of time worrying about how you can afford to get a degree in Archaeology, or English Literature. Nearly 400 colleges and universities across the country offer special financial assistance to senior citizens. These colleges offer free or low-cost tuition, discounts on fees, books, and housing.

So whether you need help finding a part-time job, or paying for a college education, your age is no barrier. There are government programs that can provide free help. Read on...

FREE JOB TRAINING AND JOB PLACEMENT

If you're 55 or over and looking for a part-time job, The Senior Community Service Employment Program (SCSEP) may be able to help. Also known as the "Older Worker Program", the SCSEP offers free training and placement in part-time community service oriented jobs to unemployed low-income persons who are at least 55 years old. You may land a part-time job (usually 20 hours per week) in your local library, senior citizen center, social service agency, or other community service setting. A variety of part-time jobs, including teachers aide, librarian, nutritional aide, bookkeeper, custodian, salesperson, security guard, food service worker, and many others, are available through this program.

Besides job training and placement, the SCSEP provides people 55 and over with a part-time income and an opportunity to serve the community. The program also assists participants in making the transition to unsubsidized employment in the private sector. Program enrollees may receive training, counseling, and support in searching for unsubsidized employment.

For general information about the SCSEP, contact the:

Office of Special Targeted Programs,
Employment and Training Administration,
Department of Labor, Room N4641,
200 Constitution Avenue, NW,
Washington, DC 20210; (202)-219-5500.

You also can contact your state Agency on Aging (listed in the Appendix) for information about and referrals to SCSEP sites in your area. To find out about programs and services in your area for older workers contact the nearest public employment office, usually listed as "Employment Service", "Job Service", or "State Department of Labor" in your phone directory under state government.

You also could receive job training and placement through the Job Training Partnership Act (JTPA). This program offers job training and related services to, among others, older workers who are in need of special training in order to obtain "productive employment". As an incentive to hire older workers who have completed the JTPA program, businesses in the private sector receive grant money through a "partnership" with state and local governments.

As a participant in the JTPA program you'll be eligible for free training and placement in a full- or part-time job in the private sector. Besides training, seniors participating in this program may also benefit from other services including job counseling, resume writing assistance, and job searches. Completion of the JTPA program could lead to a skill-oriented, relatively high-paying job in the private sector.

For general information, including eligibility requirements, about the JTPA program, contact the:

Employment and Training Administration,
Department of Labor,
200 Constitution Ave., NW,
Washington, DC 20210;
(202) 219-5580.

For information about the JTPA programs for older workers in your area, contact the appropriate Regional Employment and Training Office listed below (Your State Agency on Aging, listed in the Appendix, also can refer you to JTPA programs in your area):

Employment And Training Administration Regional Offices

Region I (CT, ME, MA, NH, RI, VT): One Congress Street, 10th Floor, Boston, MA 02114—2021; (617) 565-3630; Fax: (617) 565-2229.

Region II (NJ, NY, Puerto Rico, Virgin Islands): 201 Varick Street, Room 755, New York, NY 10014; (212) 337-2139; Fax: (212) 337-2144.

Region III (DE, District of Columbia, PA, VA, WV): P.O. Box 8796, Philadelphia, PA 19104; (215) 596-6336; Fax: (215) 596-0329.

Region IV (AL, FL, GA, KY, MS, NC, SC, TN): 1371 Peachtree Street NE, Room 400, Atlanta, GA 30367; (404) 347-4411; Fax: (404) 347-3341.

Region V (IL, IN, MI, MN, OH, WI): 230 S. Dearborn Street, Room 628, Chicago, IL 60604; (312) 353-0313; Fax: (312) 353-4474.

Region VI (AR, LA, NM, OK, TX): 525 Griffin Street, Room 317, Dallas, TX 75202; (214) 767-8263; Fax: (214) 757-5113.

Region VII (IA, KS, MO, NB): Ste. 1050 City Center Sq., 1100 Main Street, Kansas City, MO 64105; (816) 426-3796; Fax:(816) 426-2729.

Region VIII (CO, MT, ND, SD, UT, WY): 1999 Broadway, Ste. 1780, Denver, CO 80202-5716; (303) 391-5740; Fax: (303) 391-5751.

Region IX (AZ, CA, HI, NV): 71 Stevenson Street, Room 830, P.O. Box 193767, San Francisco, CA 94119-3767; (415) 744-6650; Fax: (415) 744-6225.

Region X (AK, ID, OR, WA): 1111 Third Ave., Ste. 900, Seattle, WA 98101-3212; (206) 553-7700; Fax: (206) 553-0098.

GET A FULLY-TRAINED, FULLY-PAID POSITION WITH THE U.S. FOREST SERVICE

Here's one for nature lovers. If you're age 55 or older, you may qualify for a fully-paid position with the U.S. Forest Service.The job is available through the Senior Community Service Employment Program ("SCSEP"; "Older Worker Program), which is designed to "foster and promote part-time work opportunities" in community service activities, including park systems. If eligible, you'll be trained for a position such as receptionist, visitor information, researcher, carpenter, or other related job, at a U.S. Forest Service Office in your area. You'll be paid at least minimum wage for an average 20 hour work week, and be eligible for certain health benefits. These jobs are available only to seniors 55 or older.

To find out more about this and other job possibilities through the SCSEP, contact your local Forest Service office.

The U.S. Forest Service,
U.S. Department of Agriculture,
Human Resources Program,
Box 96090, Washington, DC 20090,
or the
Office of Special Targeted Programs,
Employment and Training Administration,
Department of Labor,
Room N4641, 200 Constitution Ave., NW,
Washington, DC 20210; (202) 219-5500
(Contact: Paul A. Maynard).

THIS GOVERNMENT AGENCY PAYS $15 AN HOUR ONLY TO THOSE 55 AND OVER

Here's your opportunity to help protect the environment and earn up to $15 an hour for your efforts. The Senior Environmental Employment Program (SEE) recruits people 55 and older to provide assistance to Federal, State, and local environmental agencies for projects of pollution prevention, abatement and control. These environmental projects, which are funded by the Environmental Protection Agency (EPA) may include conducting non-agricultural pesticide surveys; monitoring for asbestos compliance in schools; research, general administrative work, clerical tasks; and other projects for the EPA. Besides an hourly wage, ranging from $6 to $15, program participants also receive full benefits, including health care, Social Security and workmen's compensation.

As a participant in this program, your hourly wage depends on the type job you have. For example, you could earn up to $10 an hour performing general administrative or clerical tasks for the EPA. Professionals with "relevant degrees" can earn as much as $15 an hour. The bottom line is that if you're at least 55 years old, the SEE program will pay you to utilize your special talents to assist in EPA funded projects. For general information about this program, contact:

Patricia Powers,
National Center for Environmental Research
and Quality Assurance, (8701),
Environmental Protection Agency,
Washington, DC 20460; (202) 260-2574;
or
Environmental Protection Agency,
Office of Research and Development,
National Center for Environmental
Research and Quality Assurance,
Washington, DC 20460.

You also can contact the following organizations, which recruit older workers whenever notified by the EPA of openings in regional offices:

American Association of Retired Persons, 601 E Street, NW, Washington, DC 20049; (202) 434-6153.

National Council of Senior Citizens, 1331 F Street, NW, Washington, DC 20004; (202) 627-9500.

National Council on Aging, 409 Third Street, SW, Washington, DC 20024; (202) 627-1200.

National Caucus and Center on Black Aged, Suite 500, 1424 K Street, NW, Washington, DC 20005; (202) 637-8400.

National Association for Hispanic Elderly, 2727 West 6th Street, Los Angeles, CA 90057; (213) 487-1922.

FREE INFORMATION TO HELP YOU DECIDE WHEN IT'S TIME TO RETIRE

When should you retire? That's not an easy decision. In fact, the decisions you make about your retirement will be some of the most important decisions you'll ever make. You'll need to consider your monthly Social Security Benefits and pension income and how much retirement income you'll need to maintain a comfortable lifestyle. You'll also need to consider that when you retire, your lifestyle will probably change. You may be faced with decisions about such things as planning leisure time or moving to a new location, such as a retirement community. You'll need to make these and other decisions dealing with retirement based on current, reliable information. That information is available free of charge from a number of government sources.

The Social Security Administration can give you a free estimate of what your Social Security benefit will be. You can get this free estimate by asking for "Request for Earnings and Benefit Estimate Statement" (SSA-7004). Upon your completion of this form, the Social Security Administration will prepare a Personal Earnings and Benefit Estimate which reflects your Social Security earnings history and how much Social Security taxes you've paid to date. You'll also receive an estimate of your future benefits as well as information explaining how to qualify for those benefits.

There are several ways you can obtain the request form. You can call Social Security's toll-free number, 1-800-772-1213 or write to the Social Security Administration, 6401 Security Blvd., Baltimore, MD 21235. If you have access to the Internet, you can download the "Request for Earnings and Benefit Estimate Statement (and other Social Security publications) at http://www.ssa.gov.

Social Security also offers several publications dealing with retirement issues. All of the following publications are available free by contacting Social Security:

"How Your Retirement Benefit Is Figured" (SSA 05-10070)

"Social Security Retirement Benefits"

"Social Security: Understanding The Benefits" (SSA-05-10024)

The U.S. Department of Labor's Pension and Welfare Benefits Administration (PWBA) also offers a number of free publications dealing with retirement issues. Relevant publications include:

"Protect Your Pension: A Quick Reference Guide"

"Top Ten Ways To Beat The Clock And Prepare for Retirement"

"What You Should Know About Your Pension Rights"

"Women and Pensions: What Women Need To Know and Do"

"How To Obtain Employee Benefit Documents from the Labor Department"

"How To File A Claim For Your Benefits"

"Pension and Welfare Brief: Can the Retiree Health Benefits Provided by Your Employer Be Cut?"

For single copies of these publications, contact:

The Pension and Welfare Benefits
Administration, 200 Constitution Avenue,
NW-Room N5625,
Washington, DC 20210; 202-219-9247

(brochure request line), or contact the appropriate PWBA field office from the following list:

If you live in...
— TN, NC, SC, GA, AL, MS, FL
Contact:
PWBA Atlanta Regional Office
Room 205, 1371 Peachtree St
NE, Atlanta, GA 30367
Phone: (404) 347-4090

or
PWBA Miami District Office
Suite 504, 111 NW 183rd St.
Miami, FL 33169
Phone:(305) 651-6464

If you live in...
— RI, VT, ME, NH, most of CT,
Contact:
PWBA Boston Regional Office
MA, Central and Western NY
One Bowdoin Square, 7th Floor
Boston, MA 02114
Phone: (617) 424-4950

If you live in...

— Northern IL, Northern IN, WI

Contact:

PWBA Chicago Regional Office

Suite 1600, 200 W. Adams St.

Chicago, IL 60606

Phone: (312) 353-0900

If you live in...

— MI, KY, OH, Southern IN

Contact:

PWBA Cincinnati Regional Office,

Suite 210, 1885 Dixie Hwy

Ft. Wright, KY 41011-2664

Phone: (606) 578-4680

or

PWBA Detroit District Office

Suite 1310, 211 West Fort St.

Detroit, MI 48226

Phone: (313) 226-7450

If you live in...

— AR, LA, NM, OK, TX

Contact:

PWBA Dallas Regional Office

Room 707, 525 Griffin St.

Dallas, TX 75202

Phone: (214) 767-6831

If you live in...

— CO, Southern IL, IA, KS, MN,
MO, MT, NB, ND, SD, WY

Contact:

PWBA Kansas City Regional Office

City Center Square,
1100 Main, Suite 1200
Kansas City, MO 64105
Phone: (816) 426-5131

or

PWBA St. Louis District Office

Room 338, 815 Olive St.
St. Louis, MO 63101
Phone: (314) 539-2691

If you live in...

— AZ, HI, Southern CA

Contact:

PWBA Los Angeles Regional Office

Suite 514, 790 East Colorado Blvd.
Pasadena, CA 91101
Phone: (818) 583-7862

If you live in...

— Eastern NY,
Northern NJ
Southern CT,

Contact:

PWBA New York Regional Office
Room 226, 1633 Broadway
New York, NY 10019
Phone: (212) 399-5191

If you live in...

— DL, District of Columbia, MD,
So. NJ, PA, VA, WV

Contact:

PWBA Philadelphia Regional Office
Room M300, Gateway Building
3535 Market Street
Philadelphia, PA 19104
Phone: (215) 596-1134

or

PWBA Washington District Office
Suite 556, 1730 K St., NW
Washington, DC 20006
Phone: (202) 254-7013

If you live in...

— AK, Northern CA,ID,NV, OR, UT, WA

Contact:

PWBA San Francisco Regional Office
Suite 915, 71 Stevenson St
P.O. Box 190250
San Francisco, CA 94119
Phone: (415) 744-6700

or

PWBA Seattle District Office
Room 860, 111 Third Ave
Seattle, WA 98101
Phone: (206) 553-4244

FREE HELP FROM THE GOVERNMENT IF YOU THINK YOU'VE BEEN DISCRIMINATED AGAINST BECAUSE OF YOUR AGE

With many baby boomers hitting the half-century mark, the nation's work force is taking on a more "mature" look. Unfortunately, the increase in the number of workers 50 and older has also seen an increase in the number of age discrimination cases. By some estimates, nearly one third of all discrimination complaints filed with the Equal Employment Opportunity Commission (EEOC) are related to age discrimination.

The Age Discrimination in Employment Act (ADEA) prohibits such discrimination. In fact, the ADEA protects all workers 40 and over by prohibiting age discrimination in hiring, discharging, promoting, pay and other employment practices. The ADEA also is designed to help employers and employees find ways to manage problems arising from the impact of age on employment. The Equal Employment Opportunity Commission is the federal agency in charge of implementing the ADEA. If you wish to file a charge of age discrimination in employment, you should contact the nearest EEOC field office (listed in the Appendix). If there is no field office in your area, call (800) 669-EEOC for more information. The EEOC investigates each individual complaint of age discrimination in employment.

You also can get free information dealing with age discrimination in employment, EEOC procedures, how the agency investigates complaints, and other aspects of the impact of age on employment.The General Accounting Office (GAO), which evaluates government programs and activities, has published several in-depth reports dealing with employment issues. Reports dealing with age discrimination include:

"Employment Discrimination: Most Private-Sector Employers Use Alternative Dispute Resolution" (GAO/HEHS-95-150)

"Discrimination Complaints: Monetary Awards In Federal EEO Cases" (GAO/GGD-95-28FS)

"EEOC's Expanding Workload: Increase In Age Discrimination" (HEHS-94-32)

"EEOC: Burgeoning Workload Calls for New Approaches" (GAO/T-HEHS-95-170)

"EEOC: Federal Affirmative Planning Responsibilities" (GAO/T-GGD-94-20)

You can get copies of these reports free upon request from the:

U.S. General Accounting Office,
P.O. Box 6015,
Gaithersburg, MD 20884-6015; (202) 512-6000. You also may fax your request to the GAO Document Distribution Facility at (301) 258-4066.

THOUSANDS OF DOLLARS IN COLLEGE TUITION FREE

If you're like many senior citizens, you started working full-time or raising a family as soon as you finished high school. There was never any time or money for you to go to college. Now you have the time, but you still can't afford college, right? Not quite. If you want to go to college, you can. There are nearly 400 colleges and universities in the United States that offer special programs for "older students". These programs include full or partial waivers on tuition, discounts on textbooks and other college-related fees, and in some cases special deals on housing. While you'll still be responsible for lab and other material fees, you could go to college tuition-free.

The following list includes colleges and universities which offer tuition waivers (full and partial) to senior citizens, as well as other assistance. For more information, contact the school(s) you're interested in attending. Find out what special programs for seniors are available and how to apply for a tuition waiver or senior discount.

Alabama

Faulkner University: Director of Financial Aid, Faulkner University, Montgomery, AL 36109-3398; 334-260-6195.

Jackson State University: Director of Financial Aid, Jackson State University, Pelham Rd., Jacksonville, AL 36265-9982; 205-782-5006.

University of Montevalla: Director of Student Financial Services, University of Montevalla, Station 6050, Montevallo, AL 35115; 205-665-6050.

Alaska

Alaska Pacific University: Director of Admissions and Financial Aid, Alaska Pacific University, 4101 University Drive, Anchorage, AK 99508-4672; (907) 564-8248.

University of Alaska Anchorage: Directory of Student Financial Aid, University of Alaska Anchorage, 3211 Providence Dr., Anchorage, AK 99508-8050; 907-786-6176.

University of Alaska Fairbanks: Director of Financial Aid, University of Alaska Fairbanks, 101 Eielson Building, P.O. Box 75630, Fairbanks, AK 99775-6360; 907-474-7256.

University of Alaska Southeast: Financial Aid Officer, University of Alaska Southeast, 11120 Glacier Hwy., Juneau, AK 99801-8680; 907-465-6255.

Arizona

Central Arizona College: Director of Financial Aid, Central Arizona College, 8470 North Overfield Road, Coolidge, AZ 85228: 602-426-4444.

Arkansas

Arkansas State University: Director of Financial Aid, Arkansas State University, Jonesboro, Arkansas 72467; 501-972-2310.

Arkansas Tech University: Director of Student Aid, Arkansas Tech University, Russellville, AR; 72801-2222; (501) 968-0399.

Harding University: Director of Financial Aid, Harding University, Box 2282, Searcy, AR 72149-0001; 501-279-4257.

Henderson State University: Director of Financial Aid, Henderson State University, Box 7812, Arkadelphia, AR 71999-0001; 501-246-5511 Ext. 3264.

John Brown University: Director of Financial Aid, John Brown University, 200 West University, Siloam Springs, AR 72761-2121; 501-524-3131 Ext. 124.

University of Arkansas: Director of Student Aid, University of Arkansas, 114 Silas H. Hunt Hall, Fayetteville, AR 72701-1201; 501-575-3806.

California

California Polytechnic State University, San Luis Obispo: Director of Financial Aid, California Polytechnic State University, San Luis Obispo, One Grand Ave., San Luis Obispo, CA 93407; (805) 756-5893.

California Polytechnic State University, Pomona: Director of Financial Aid, California Polytechnic State University, Pomona, 3201 West Temple Ave., Pomona, CA 91768-2557; (909) 869-3700.

California State University, Bakersfield: Associate Dean and Director, Financial Aid Scholarships, California State University, Bakersfield, 9001 Stockdale Hwy., Bakersfield, CA 93311-1099; (805) 664-3016.

California State University, Fresno: Director of Financial Aid, California State University, Fresno, 5150 North Maple Ave., Fresno, CA 93740-0064; (209) 278-2182.

California State University, Sacramento: Director of Financial Aid, California State University, Sacramento, Sacramento, CA 95819-6048; (916) 278-6554.

Fresno Pacific College: Director of Financial Aid, Fresno Pacific College, 1717 South Chesnut Ave, Fresno, CA 93702-4709; 209-453-2041.

Humboldt State University: Director of Financial Aid, Humboldt State University, Arcata, CA 95521-8299; 707-826-4321.

San Diego State University: Director of Financial Aid, San Diego State University, 5500 Campanile Dr., SSW 3605, San Diego, CA 92182-7436; 619-594-6323.

Colorado

Mesa State College: Director of Financial Aid, Mesa State College, P.O. Box 2647, Grand Junction, CO 81502-2647; 970-248-1396.

Metropolitan State College of Denver: Director of Financial Aid, Metropolitan State College of Denver, Campus P.O. Box 173362, Denver, CO 80217-3362; 303-556-4027.

Regis University: Director of Financial Aid, Regis University, Denver, CO 80221-1099; 303-458-4066.

Connecticut

Albertus Magnus College: Director of Financial Aid, Albertus Magnus College, 700 Prospect Street, New Haven, CT 06511-1189; (203) 773-8508.

Central Connecticut State University: Director of Financial Aid, Central Connecticut State University, 1615 Stanley Street, New Britain, CT 06050-4010; (860) 832-2201.

East Connecticut State University: Director of Financial Aid, East Connecticut State University, 83 Windham St., Willimantic, CT 06226-2295; 860-465-5205.

Delaware

Delaware State University: Associate Director of Financial Aid, Delaware State University, Dover, DE 19901-2277; 302-739-4908.

District of Columbia

American University: Director of Financial Aid, American University, 4440 Massachusetts Ave., NW, Washington, DC 20016-8001; 202-885-6100.

University of the District of Columbia: Director of Financial Aid, University of the District of Columbia, Washington, DC 20008-1175; 202-274-5060.

Florida

Florida Agricultural And Mechanical University: Director of Financial Aid, Florida Agricultural And Mechanical University, FHAC Suite 101, Tallahassee, FL 32307; 904-561-2824.

Florida Institute of Technology: Acting Director of Financial Aid, Florida Institute of Technology, 150 West University Blvd., Melbourne, FL 32901-6975; 407-768-8000 Ext. 8070.

Florida International University: Director of Financial Aid, Florida International University, University Park, Miami, FL 33199; 305-348-2347.

Florida State University: Director of Financial Aid, Florida State University, 4441 University Center, Tallahassee, FL 32306-1023; 904-644-5716.

Trinity College of Florida: Director of Financial Aid, Trinity College of Florida, New Port Richey, FL 34655; 813-376-6911.

Palm Beach Atlantic College: Director of Financial Aid, P.O. Box 24708; West Palm Beach, FL 33416-4708; 407-835-4320.

Georgia

Albany State University: Director of Admissions and Financial Aid, Albany State University, 504 College Dr., Albany, GA 31705-2717; (912) 430-4650.

Atlanta Christian College: Director of Financial Aid, Atlanta Christian College, 2605 Ben Hull Road, East Point, GA 30344-1999; (404) 761-8861.

Armstrong State College: Director of Financial Aid, Armstrong State College, 11935 Abercorn Street, Savannah, GA 31419-1997; 912-927-5272.

Augusta State University: Director of Financial Aid, Augusta State University, 2500 Walton Way, Augusta, GA 30904-2200; (706) 737-1431.

Berry College: Director of Financial Aid, Berry College, 5007 Berry College, Mount Berry, GA 30149-0159: (706) 236-2244.

Clayton State College: Director of Financial Aid, Clayton State College, P.O. Box 285, Morrow, GA 30260-0285; (770) 961-3511.

Columbus State University, Division of Financial Aid, Columbus State University, 42225 University Ave., Columbus, GA 31907-5645; (706) 568-2036.

Emmanuel College: Director of Financial Aid, Emmanuel College, P.O. Box 129, Franklin Springs, GA 30369-0129; 706-245-7226 Ext. 133.

Georgia State University: Director of Student Financial Services, Georgia State University, P.O. Box 4040, Atlanta, GA 30302; 404-651-2227.

Hawaii

University of Hawaii at Manoa: Director of Admissions and Records, University of Hawaii at Manoa, Honolulu, HI 96822; 808-956-8975.

University of Hawaii at Hilo: Financial Aid Coordinator, University of Hawaii at Hilo, Hilo, HI 96720-4091; 808-933-3324.

Idaho

Albertson College Of Idaho: Director, Office of Student Financial Services, Albertson College of Idaho, 2112 Cleveland Blvd., Box 39, Caldwell, ID 83605-4494; (208) 459-5308.

Boise Bible College: Director of Financial Aid, Boise Bible College, Boise, ID 83714-12201; (208) 376-7731.

Boise State University: Director of Financial Aid, Boise State University, Boise, ID 83725-0399; (208) 385-1664.

Idaho State University: Director of Financial Aid, Campus Box 8077, Pocatello, ID 83209; 208-236-2981.

Illinois

University: Director of Financial Assistance, Bradley University, Peoria, IL 61625-0002; (309) 677-3089.

Chicago State University: Director of Student Financial Aid, Chicago State University, Chicago, IL 60628; (312) 995-2399.

Elmhurst College: Director of Financial Aid, Elmhurst College, Goebel Hall 106A, Elmhurst, IL 60126-3296; 708-617-3079.

Greenville College: Director of Financial Services, Greenville College, P.O. Box 159, Greenville, IL 62246-0159; 618-664-1840 Ext. 4420.

North Central College: Director of Financial Aid, 30 North Brainard St., P.O. Box 3063, Naperville, IL 60566-7063; 708-637-5600.

North Park College: Director of Financial Aid, North Park College, 3225 West Foster Ave., Chicago, IL 60625-4895; 312-244-5746.

Quincy University: Director of Financial Aid, Quincy University, 1800 College Ave., Quincy, IL 62301-2699; 217-228-5260.

Indiana

Anderson University: Director of Financial Aid, Anderson University, 1100 East Fifth St., Anderson, IN 46012-3462; (317) 641-4180.

Ball State University: Director of Financial Aid, Ball State University, Financial Aid Office, Muncie, IN 47306-1099; (317) 285-8924.

Bethel College: Director of Financial Aid, Bethel College, 1001 West McKinley Ave, Mishawaka, IN 46545-5591; (219) 259-8511.

Calumet College of Saint Joseph: Director of Financial Aid, Calumet College of Saint Joseph, 2400 New York Ave., Whiting, IN 46394-2195; (219) 473-4219.

Carson-Newman College: Director of Financial Aid, Carson-Newman College, Russell Ave., Jefferson City, IN 37760; (615) 475-9061.

Franklin College of Indiana: Director of Financial Aid, Franklin College of Indiana, 501 East Monroe Street, Franklin, IN 46131-2598; 317-738-8075.

Huntington College: Financial Aid Director, Huntington College, 2303 College Ave., Huntington, IN 46750-1299; 219-356-6000 Ext. 1014.

St. Mary's College: Director of Financial Aid, St. Mary's College, 150 Le Mans Hall, Notre Dame, IN 46556; 219-284-4557.

Iowa

Briar Cliff College: Director of Financial Aid, Briar Cliff College, 3303 Rebecca Street, P.O. Box 2100, Sioux City, IA 51104-2100; (712) 279-5440.

Clarke College: Director of Financial Aid, Clarke College, 1550 Clarke Drive, Dubuque, IA 52001-3198;

(319) 588-6327.

Dordt College: Director of Financial Aid, Dordt College, 498 4th Ave. NE, Sioux Center, IA 68333-2430; 402-826-8260.

Drake University: Assistant Vice President for Business and Finance, Drake University, Des Moines, IA 50311-4516; 515-271-2905.

Graceland College: Director of Financial Aid, Graceland College, 700 College Ave., Lamoni, IA 50140-1681; 515-784-5136.

Grand View College: Director of Financial Aid, Grand View College, 1200 Grand View Ave., Des Moines, IA 50316-1599; 515-263-2820.

Kansas

Baker University: Financial Aid Director, Baker University, P.O. Box 65, Baldwin City, KS 66006-0065; (913) 594-6451 Ext. 595.

Benedictine College: Director of Student Financial Aid, Benedictine College, North Campus, Atchison, KS 66002-1499; (913) 367-5340 Ext. 2484.

Emporia State University: Director of Financial Aid, Emporia State University, 1200 Commercial

Street, Campus Box 4038, Emporia, KS 66801-5087; 316-341-5457.

Kansas Newman College: Financial Aid Director, Kansas Newman College, 3100 McCormick Ave., Wichita, KS 67213-2084; 316-942-4291.

Kansas Wesleyan University: Director of Financial Assistance, Kansas Wesleyan University, 100 East Claflin, Salina, KS 67401-6196; 913-827-5541 Ext. 217.

Kentucky

Asbury College: Director of Financial Aid, Asbury College, 1 Macklem Drive, Wilmore, KY 40390; (606) 858-3511 Ext. 2195.

Bellarmine College: Associate Director of Financial Aid, Bellarmine College, 20001 Newburg Road, Louisville, KY 40205-0671; (502) 452-8131.

Brescia College: Director of Financial Aid, Brescia College, 717 Frederica Street, Owensboro, KY 42301-3023; (502) 686-4290.

Campbellsville University: Director of Financial Aid, Campbellsville University, Campbellsville, KY 42718-2799; (502) 465-8158 Ext. 5207.

Kentucky State University: Director of Financial Aid, Kentucky State University, East Main St., Frankfort, KY 40601; 502-227-5960.

Spalding University: Director of Financial Aid, Spalding University, 851 South 4th St., Louisville, KY 40203-2188; 502-585-9911.

Louisiana

Grambling State University: Director of Student Financial Aid, Grambling State University, P.O. Box 629, Grambling, LA 71245; 318-274-2342.

Louisiana State University And Agricultural And Mechanical College: Director of Financial Aid, Louisiana State University And Agricultural And Mechanical College, LSU 202 Himes Hall, Baton Rouge, LA 70803-3103; 504-388-3113.

Louisiana State University In Shreveport: Director Of Financial Aid, Louisiana State University in Shreveport, Shreveport, LA 71115-2399; 318-797-5363.

Louisiana Tech University: Director of Financial Aid, Louisiana Tech University, P.O. Box 7925, Tech Station, Ruston, LA 71272; 318-257-2641

McNeese State University: Director of Financial Aid, McNeese State University, P.O. Box 93260, Lake Charles, LA 70609-3260; 318-475-5065.

Maine

College of the Atlantic: Director of Financial Aid, College of the Atlantic, 105 Eden Street, Bar Harbor, ME 94609-1198; (207) 288-5015.

Husson College: Director of Financial Aid, Husson College, One College Circle, Bangor, ME 04401-2999; 207-941-7156

University of Maine: Director of Student Financial Aid, University of Maine, 5781 Wingate Hall, Orono, ME 04469-5713; 207-581-1324.

Maryland

Baltimore Hebrew University: Financial Aid Counselor, Baltimore Hebrew University, 5800 Park Heights Ave, Baltimore, MD 21215-3996; (410) 578-6913.

Bowie State University: Director of Financial Assistance, Bowie State University, 14000 Jericho Park, RD., Bowie, MD 20715-3318; (301) 464-6546.

Columbia Union College: Director of Financial Aid, Columbia Union College, 7600 Flower Ave., Takoma Park, MD 20912-7794; 301-891-4005.

Frostburg State University: Director of Financial Aid, Frostburg State University, Hitchins Building, Room 128, Frostburg, MD 21532-2302; 301-687-4301.

Hood College: Director of Financial Aid, Hood College, 401 Rosemont Ave., Frederick, MD 21701-8575; 301-696-3411.

Morgan State University: Director of Financial Aid, Morgan State University, Baltimore, MD 21239; 410-319-3178.

Massachusetts

American International College: Directory of Financial Aid, American International College, Springfield, MA 01109-3189; (413) 747-6259.

Anna Maria College: Director of Financial Aid, Anna Maria College, Sunset Lane, Paxton, MA 01612; (508) 849-3367.

Art Institute of Boston: Director of Financial Aid, Art Institute, 700 Beacon St., Boston, MA 02215-

2598; (617) 262-1223.

Atlantic Union College: Interim Vice President of Financial Affairs, Atlantic Union College, South Lancaster, MA 01561-1000; 508-368-2284.

Boston University: Director of Financial Assistance, Boston University, 881 Commonwealth Ave., 5th Floor, Boston, MA 02215: (617) 353-4176.

Curry College; Director of Financial Aid, Curry College, 1071 Blue Hill Ave., Milton, MA 02186-9984; 617-333-2146.

Farmington State College: Director of Financial Aid, Farmington State College, 100 State Street, Farmington, MA 01701-9101; 508-626-4534.

Massachusetts College of Art: Director of Financial Aid, Massachusetts College of Art, Boston, MA 02115-5882; 617-232-1555.

Fitchburg State College: Director of Financial Aid, Fitchburg State College, Fitchburg, MA 01420-2697; 508-665-3156.

Michigan

Andrews University: Director of Financial Aid, Andrews University, Berrien Springs, MI 49104; 616-471-3334.

Grace Bible College: Director of Financial Aid, Grace Bible College, 1011 Aldon St., SW, P.O. 910, Grand Rapids, MI 49509-1921; 616-538-2330.

Lake Superior State University: Director of Financial Aid, Lake Superior State University, 1000 College Dr., Sault Sainte Marie, MI 49783-1699; 906-635-2678.

Marygrove College: Director of Financial Aid, Marygrove College, Detroit, MI 48221-2599; 313-862-8000 Ext. 436.

University of Michigan: Director of Financial Aid, University of Michigan, 2011 Student Activities Building, Ann Arbor, MI 48109-1316; 313-763-4119.

Minnesota

Augsburg College: Director of Student Financial Services, Augsburg College, 2211 Riverside Ave., Minneapolis, MN 55454-1351; 612-330-1046.

Bemidji State University: Director of Financial Aid, Bemidji State University, Bemidji, MN 56601-2699; (218) 755-2000.

Bethel College: Director of College Financial Planning, Bethel College, 3900 Bethel Dr., Saint Paul,

MN 55112-6999; (612) 638-6241.

College of Saint Catherine: Director of Financial Aid, College of Saint Catherine, Mail #F-11, 2004 Randolph Ave., Saint Paul, MN 55105-1789; (612) 690-6540.

College of Saint Scholastica: Associate Dean of Student Financial Planning, College of Saint Scholastica, 1200 Kenwood Ave., Duluth, MI 55811-4199; (218) 723-6397.

Concordia College: Division of Financial Aid, Concordia College, 275 North Syndicate Street, St. Paul, MN 55104-5494; 612-641-8209.

Mississippi

Belhaven College: Director of Financial Aid, Belhaven College, 1500 Peachtree Street, Jackson, MS 39202-1789; (601) 968-5933.

Delta State University: Director of Financial Aid, Delta State University, P.O. Box 3154, Cleveland, MS 38733-0001; 601-846-4670.

Mississippi State University: Director of Financial Aid, Mississippi State University, P.O. Box 9501; Mississippi State, MS 39762; 601-325-2450.

Missouri

Avila College: Director of Financial Aid, Avila College, Kansas City, MO 64145-1698; (816) 942-8400 Ext. 3600.

Columbia College: Director of Financial Aid, Columbia College, 1001 Rogers, Columbia, MO 65215-0002; 314-875-7362.

Culver-Stockton College: Director of Financial Planning, Culver-Stockton College, 1 College Hill, Canton, MO 63435-1299; 217-231-6306.

Drury College: Director of Financial Aid, Drury College, 900 North Benton Ave., Springfield, MO 65802-3791; 417-873-7312.

Fontbonne College: Director of Financial Aid, Fontbonne College, St. Louis, MO 63105-3098; 314-889-1414.

Missouri Southern State College: Director of Financial Aid, Missouri Southern State College, 3950 East Newman Rd., Joplin, MO 64801-1595; 417-625-9325.

Montana

Carroll College: Director of Financial Aid, Carroll College, 1601 North Benton Ave, Helena, MT 59625-0002; (406) 447-5427.

Montana State University- Billings: Director of Financial Aid, Montana State University- Billings, 1500 North 30th Street, Billings, MT 59101; 406-657-2188.

Montana State University- Bozeman: Director of Financial Aid Services, Montana State University-Bozeman, #135 Strand Union Building, Bozeman, MT 59717; 406-994-2845.

Montana State University- Northern: Director of Financial Aid, Box 7751, Havre, MT 59501-7751; 406-265-3787.

Montana Tech of the University of Montana: Director of Student Financial Aid, Montana Tech of the University of Montana, West Park St., Butte, MT 59701-8997; 406-496-4212.

Nebraska

Chadron State College: Director of Financial Aid, Chadron State College, Chadron, NE 69337; (308) 432-6230.

College of Saint Mary: Director of Financial Aid, College of Saint Mary, 1901 South 72nd Street,

Omaha, NE 68124-2377; 402-399-2416.

Creighton University: Director of Financial Aid, Creighton University, 2500 California Plaza, Omaha, NE 68178-0062; 402-280-2731.

Doane College: Director of Financial Aid, Doane College, 1014 Boswell Ave., Crete, NE 68333-2430; 402-826-8260.

Grace University: Financial Aid Administrator, Grace University, Ninth and William Sts., Omaha, NE 68108; 402-449-2810.

Hastings College: Director of Financial Aid, Hastings College, Hastings, NE 68902-0269; 402-461-7391.

Nevada

University of Nevada, Las Vegas: Director of Student Financial Services, University of Nevada, Las Vegas, P.O. Box 452016, Las Vegas, NV 89154-2016; 702-895-3424.

University of Nevada, Reno: Director of Student Financial Services, 200 TSS, MS 076, Reno, NV 89557; 702-784-4666.

New Hampshire

Daniel Webster College: Director of Financial Assistance, Daniel Webster College, 20 University Drive, Nashua, NH 03063-1300; 603-577-6590.

Franklin Pierce College: Director of Financial Aid, Franklin Pierce College, College Rd., P.O. Box 60, Rindge, NH 03461-0060; 603-899-4180.

Keene State College: Director of Student Financial Management, Keene State College, 229 Main St., Keene, NH 03435-2608; 603-358-2280.

New Hampshire College: Financial Aid Administrator, New Hampshire College, 2500 North River Road, Manchester, NH 03106-1045; 603-645-9653.

Rivier College: Director of Financial Aid, Rivier College: 420 Main Street, Nashua, NH 03060-5086; 603-888-1311 Ext. 8534.

Saint Anselm College: Director of Financial Aid, Saint Anselm College, 100 St. Anselm Drive- 1735, Manchester, NH 03102-1310; 603-641-7110.

New Jersey

Bloomfield College: Director of Financial Aid, Bloomfield College, Bloomfield, NJ 07003-9981; (201) 748-9000 Ext. 212.

Caldwell College: Director of Financial Aid, Caldwell College, 9 Ryerson Ave., Caldwell, NJ 07706-6195; (201) 228-4424 Ext. 222.

Centenary College: Dean of Admissions, Centenary College, Hackettstown, NJ 07840-2100; (908) 852-4696; (800) 236-8679.

College of New Jersey: Acting Director of Financial Aid, CN4700, Trenton, NJ 08650-4700; (609) 771-2211.

Drew University: Director of Financial Assistance, Drew University, 36 Madison Ave, Madison, NJ 07940-1493; 201-408-3112.

Felican College: Financial Aid Director, Felican College, 262 South Main Street, Lodi, NJ 07644; 201-778-1190 Ext. 6040.

Richard Stockton College of New Jersey: Director of Financial Aid, Richard Stockton College of New Jersey, Jim Leeds Road, Pomona, NJ 08240-9988; 609-652-4201.

New Mexico

College of Santa Fe: Director of Student Financial Aid, College of Santa Fe , 1600 Saint Michael's Drive, Santa Fe, NM 87505; (505) 473-6454.

New Mexico Highlands University: Director of Student Recruitment, New Mexico Highlands University, Las Vegas, NM 87701; 505-454-3256; 800-338-6648 (in NM).

New Mexico State University: Director of Financial Aid, New Mexico State University, Box 30001, Dept. 5100, Las Cruces, NM 88003-8001; 505-646-4105.

New York

Baruch College of The City University of New York: Financial Aid Director, Baruch College of The City University of New York, 151 East 25th St., Room 820, New York, NY 10010-5585; (212) 802-2240.

Brooklyn College of the City University of New York; Director of Financial Aid, Brooklyn College of the City University of New York, 2900 Bedford Ave., Brooklyn, NY 11210; (718) 951-5045.

City College of the City University of New York: Director of Financial Aid, City College of the City University of New York, New York City, New York 10031-6977; (212) 650-5819.

Daeme College: Director of Financial Aid, Daeme College, 4380 Main Street, Amherst, NY 14226-3592; 716-839-8254 Ext. 254.

Dowling College: Director of Financial Aid, Dowling College, Oakdale, NY 11769-1999; 516-244-3385

Five Towns College: Financial Aid Administrator, Five Towns College, 305 North Service Rd., Dix Hills, NY 11746-6055; 516-424-7000.

Hilbert College: Director of Financial Aid, Hilbert College, Hamburg, NY 14075-1597; 716-649-7900 Ext. 208.

Hofstra University: Director of Financial Aid, Hofstra University, 126 Hofstra University, Hempstead, NY 11550-1090; 516-463-6680.

Iona College: Director of Financial Aid, Iona College, 715 North Ave., New Rochelle, NY 10801-1890; 914-633-2497.

North Carolina

Appalachian State University: Director of Financial Aid, Appalachian State University, Hagaman Hall, Boone, NC 28608; 704-262-2190.

Barton College: Director of Financial Aid, Barton College, West Lee Street, Wilson, NC 27893; (919) 399-6316.

Belmont University: Director of Financial Aid, Belmont University, 1900 Belmont Boulevard, Nashville, TN 37212-3757; (615) 385-6403

Brevard College: Director of Financial Aid, Brevard College, 400 North Broad Street, Brevard, NC 28712-3306: (704) 884-8287.

Chowan College: Director of Financial Aid, Chowan College, P.O. Box 1848, Murfreesboro, NC 27855-8848; (919) 398-1229.

East Carolina University: Director of Financial Aid, East Carolina University, Greenville, NC 27858-4353; 919-328-6610.

North Carolina State University: Director of Financial Aid, North Carolina State University, #2005 Harris Hall, Box 7302, Raleigh, NC 27695-7302; 919-515-2421.

North Dakota

Dickinson State University: Director of Financial Aid, Dickinson State University, Dickinson, ND 58601-4896; 701-227-2371.

Jamestown College: Financial Aid Officer, Jamestown College, 6085 College Lane, Jamestown, ND 58405; 701-252-3467.

University of North Dakota: Director of Student Financial Aid, University of North Dakota, Box 8371, Grand Forks, ND 58202; 701-777-3121.

Ohio

Bowling Green State University: Director of Financial Aid, Bowling Green State University, Bowling Green, OH 43403; (419) 372-2651.

Capital University: Director of Financial Aid, Capital University, 2199 East Main Street, Columbus, OH 43209-2394: (614) 236-6511.

Cedarville College: Director of Financial Aid, Cedarville College, Box 601, Cedarville, OH 45314-0601; (513) 766-7866.

Cleveland State University: Director of Financial Aid, Cleveland State University, 2344 Euclid Ave #201, Cleveland, OH 44115; (216) 687-2054.

Columbus College of Art & Design: Director of Financial Aid, Columbus College of Art & Design, 107 North Ninth Street, Columbus, OH 43215-1758; 614-224-9101.

Defiance College: Director of Financial Aid, Defiance College, 701 North Clinton Street, Defiance, OH 43512-1610; 419-784-4010 Ext. 376.

Lake Erie College: Director of Admissions, Lake Erie College, Painesville, OH 44077-3389; 216-639-7879; 800-533-4996.

Ohio State University: Director of Admissions and Financial Aid, Ohio State University, 1800 Cannon Dr., Lincoln Tower, Columbus, OH 43210-1230; 614-292-1134.

University of Toledo: Director of Financial Aid, University of Toledo, Toledo, OH 43606-3398; 419-530-2056.

Oklahoma

Bartlesville Wesleyan College: Financial Aid Director, Bartlesville Wesleyan College, 2201 Silver

Lake Road, Bartlesville, OK 74006-6299; (918) 335-6282.

East Central University: Director of Financial Aid, East Central University, 14th and Francis Sts., Ada, OK 74820-6899; 405-332-8000 Ext. 241.

Northwestern Oklahoma State University: Director of Financial Aid, Northwestern Oklahoma State University, 709 Oklahoma Blvd., Alva, OK 73717-2799; 405-327-1700 Ext. 8540.

Phillips University: Director of Student Financial Aid, Phillips University, 100 South University Ave., Enid, OK 73701-6439; 405-237-4433 Ext. 280

University of Oklahoma: Director of Financial Aid, University of Oklahoma, 731 Elm, Norman, OK 73019-0230; 405-325-4521.

Oregon

Concordia College: Director of Financial Aid, Concordia College, 2811 Northeast Hampton, Portland, OR 97211-6099; 503-280-8514.

Eugene Bible College: Director of Financial Aid, Eugene Bible College, 2155 Bailey Hill Road, Eugene, OR 97405-1194; 503-485-1780.

George Fox University: Director of Financial Aid, George Fox University, 414 North Meridian, Newberg, OR 97132-2697; (503) 538-8383.

Portland State University: Co-Director of Student Financial Aid, Oregon State University, P.O. Box 751, Portland, OR 97207-0751; 503-725-5448.

Pennsylvania

Academy of the New Church College: Director of Financial Aid, Academy of the New Church College, Box 711, Bryn Athyn, PA 19009-0717; (215) 947-4200.

Alvernia College: Director of Financial Aid, Alvernia College, 400 Saint Bernadine Street, Reading, PA 19607-1799; (610) 796-8215.

Cabrini College, Director of Financial Aid, Cabrini College, 610 King of Prussia Road, Radnor, PA 19087-3698; (610) 902-8420.

Chestnut Hill College: Director of Financial Aid, Chestnut Hill College, 9601 Germantown Ave., Philadelphia, PA 19118-2695; (215) 248-7101.

Drexel University: Director of Financial Aid, Drexel University, 32nd and Chestnut Sts., Philadelphia, PA 19104-2875; 215-895-2537.

Duquesne University: Director of Financial Aid, Duquesne University, 600 Forbes Ave., Pittsburgh, PA 15282-0299; 412-396-6607.

Gannon University: Director of Financial Aid, Gannon University, University Square, Erie, PA 16541; 814-871-7337.

Immaculata College: Director of Financial Aid, Immaculata College, 19345-0901; 610-647-4400 Ext. 3028.

Rhode Island

Bryant College: Director of Financial Aid, Bryant College, 1150 Douglas Pike, Smithfield, RI 02917-1284; (401) 232-6020.

Rhode Island College: Director of Student Financial Aid, Rhode Island College, 600 Mt. Pleasant Ave., Providence, RI 02908-1924; 401-456-8684.

University of Rhode Island: Assistant Dean of Financial Aid, University of Rhode Island, Kingston, RI 02881; 401-874-2314.

South Carolina

Anderson College: Associate Director of Financial Aid, Anderson College, 316 Boulevard, Anderson, SC 29621-4035; (864) 231-2070.

Benedict College: Director of Financial Aid, Benedict College, Columbia, SC 29204; (803) 253-5105.

Clemson University: Director of Financial Aid, Clemson University, G01 Sikes Hall, Clemson, SC 29634-5123; (803) 656-2280.

College of Charleston: Director of Student Financial Aid, College of Charleston, 66 George Street, Charleston, SC 29424-0001; (803) 953-5540.

Converse College: Director of Financial Assistance, Converse College, 580 East Main St, Spartanburg, SC 29302-0006; (803) 596-9019.

Lander University: Director of Financial Aid, Lander University, Greenwood, SC 29649-2099; 864-388-8340.

Dakota

Augustana College: Director of Financial Aid, Augustana College, 2001 South Summit Ave., Sioux Falls, SD 57197; 605-336-5216.

Black Hills State University: Director of Financial Aid, Black Hills State University, University Station, Box 9509, Spearfish, SD 57799-9509: (605) 642-6254.

Dakota State University: Financial Aid Director, Dakota State University, 103 Heston Hall, Madison, SD 57942-1799; 605-256-5132.

University of South Dakota: Director of Financial Aid, University of South Dakota, Vermillion, SD 57069-2390; 605-677-5446.

Tennessee

Crichton College: Financial Aid Administrator, Crichton College, P.O. Box 757830, Memphis, TN 38175-7830; 901-367-9800.

Cumberland University: Director of Financial Aid, Cumberland University, Lebanon, TN 37087-3554; 615-444-2562 Ext. 231.

Freed-Hardeman University: Director of Financial Aid, Freed-Hardeman University, 158 East Main Street, Henderson, TN 38340-2399; 901-989-6662.

Lambuth University: Director of Financial Aid, Lambuth University, Lambuth Blvd., Jackson, TN 38301; 901-425-3330.

Lee College: Director of Student Financial Aid, Lee College, 1120 North Ocoee Street, P.O. Box 3450, Cleveland, TN 37320-3450; 423-478-7330.

University of Tennessee at Chattanooga: Director of Financial Aid, University of Tennessee at Chattanooga, 615 McCallie Ave., Chattanooga, TN 37403-2598; 423-755-4677.

Texas

Lamar University: Director of Academic Services, Lamar University, P.O. Box 10042, Beaumont, TX 77710; 409-880-8450.

University of Texas at Dallas: Director of Financial Aid, Richardson, TX 75083-0688; 214-883-2941.

Utah

University of Utah: Director of Financial Aid, University of Utah, 105 SSB, Salt Lake City, UT 84112; 801-581-8788.

Utah State University: Director of Financial Aid, Utah State University, University Hill UMC 1800, Logan UT 84322-1800; 801-797-0177.

Vermont

Burlington College: Director of Admissions, Burlington College, 95 North Ave., Burlington, VT 05401-2998; (802) 862-9616 Ext. 32.

College of Saint Joseph: Director of Financial Aid, College of Saint Joseph, Clement Road, Rutland, VT 05701-3899; (802) 773-5900.

Lyndon State College: Director of Financial Aid, Lyndon State College, Vail Hill, Lyndonville, VT 05851; 802-626-6218.

Middlebury College: Director of Financial Aid, Middlebury College, The Emma Williard House, Middlebury, VT 05753-6002; 802-388-3711 Ext. 5158.

University of Vermont: Director of Financial Aid, University of Vermont, 330 Waterman, South Prospect St., Burlington, VT 05401-3596; 802-656-3156.

Virginia

Averett College: Director of Financial Aid, Averett College, Danville, VA 24541-3692; (804) 791-5890.

Bluefield College: Director of Enrollment Management, Bluefield College, 3000 College Drive, Bluefield, VA 24605-1799; (703) 326-4214.

Christopher Newport University: Director of Financial Aid, Christopher Newport University, 50 Shoe Lane, Newport News, VA 23606-2998; (804) 594-7170.

College of William And Mary: Director of Student Financial Aid, College of William and Mary, P.O. Box 8795, Williamsburg, VA 23187-8795; (804) 221-2420.

Ferrum College: Director of Financial Aid, Ferrum College, Ferrum, VA 24088-9001; 540-365-4282.

James Madison University: Director of Financial Aid, James Madison University, Harrisonburg, VA 22807; 540-568-6644.

Longwood College: Director of Financial Aid, Longwood College, 201 High Street, Farmville, VA 23909-1898; 804-395-2077.

Lynchburg College: Director of Financial Aid, Lynchburg College, 1501 Lakeside Drive, Lynchburg, VA 24501-3199; 804-544-8228.

University of Virginia: Director of Financial Air, University of Virginia, P.O. Box 9021, Charlottesville, VA 22906; 804-243-7600.

Washington

Central Washington University: Director of Financial Aid, Central Washington University, 400 East 8th Avenue, Ellensburg, WA 98296-7495; (509) 963-1611.

Gonzaga University: Director of Financial Aid, Gonzaga University, East 502 Boone Ave., Spokane, WA 99258; 509-328-4220 Ext. 3185.

Seattle Pacific University: Director of Financial Aid, Seattle Pacific University, 3307 Third Ave. West, Seattle, WA 98119-1997; 206-281-2046.

Washington State University: Director of Financial Aid, Washington State University, 139 French Administration Building, Pullman, WA 99164-1015; 509-335-9727.

West Virginia

Salem-Teikyo University: Director of Financial Aid, 223 West Main Street, Salem, WV 26426-0500; 304-782-5205.

University of Charleston: Director of Financial Aid, University of Charleston, 2300 McCorkle Ave., SE, Charleston, WV 25304-1099; 304-357-4760.

Wisconsin

Lakeland College: Director of Financial Aid, Lakeland College, P.O. Box 359, Sheboygan, WI 53082-0359; 414-565-1297.

Marian College of Fond Du Lac: Director of Financial Aid, Marian College of Fond Du Lac, 45 South National Ave., Fond Du Lac, WI 54935-4699; 414-923-7614.

Marquette University: Director of Financial Aid, Marquette University, 1212 W. Wisconsin Ave., P.O. Box 1881, Milwaukee, WI 53201-1881; 414-288-5266.

Silver Lake College: Director of Financial Aid, Silver Lake College, 2406 South Alverno Road, Manitowoc, WI 54220-9319; 414-684-6418.

Wyoming

University of Wyoming: Director of Financial Aid, University of Wyoming, Box 3335, University Station, Laramie, WY 82071-3335; 307-766-2116.

Chapter 3

Free Health Care And Health Information

Do you know what foods you should be eating to maintain a healthful, nutritious diet? What types of exercises should you be doing at your age? Have you heard about the latest research into the causes, treatments and cures of cancer, heart disease, diabetes and other diseases? Can you get prescription medicines absolutely free? How about affordable medical treatment and health care? All of these questions are important for anyone 50 and over interested in living longer, healthier lives. And Uncle Sam can provide the answers to these questions, as well as free information and advice dealing with other aging and health-related concerns.

The process of aging and aging-related concerns is the focus of many government agencies. The National Institutes of Health, the National Cancer Institute, the National Institute on Aging, and other agencies all offer a variety of free publications and other materials to provide you with the latest information and advice to help you live a longer happier life.

FREE HOSPITAL CARE BASED ON FINANCIAL NEED

Living on a fixed income means making certain sacrifices. Unfortunately, those sacrifices sometimes include foregoing needed hospital care because the money just isn't there. The Hill-Burton Act, administered by the U.S. Department of Health and Human Services agencies Health Resources And Services Administration, was designed to remedy that situation.

Under the Hill-Burton Act, certain medical facilities, including hospitals, nursing homes, clinics, etc., are obligated to provide free or reduced-cost medical care to patients who cannot afford to pay. Generally, eligibility is based on a person's family size and income. However, you may qualify even if your income is up to double (or triple for nursing home services) the poverty income guidelines. What's more, you can apply for Hill-Burton assistance at any time, before or after you receive care. You even may apply for and receive assistance after a hospital bill has been turned over to a collection agency.

For more information, contact the Hill-Burton Hotline, 1-800-638-0742 (1-800-492-0359 in Maryland). In response to your Hotline inquiry, you'll receive in the mail a free copy of the Hill-Burton Free Care Brochure. The brochure describes the free care program and how to apply for services. You'll also receive the Poverty Guidelines, which are used to determine financial eligibility, and a list of Hill-Burton facilities in your area. You also can get information about the program by contacting the:

Health Resources And Services
Administration,
5600 Fishers Lane, Room 11-19,
Rockville, MD 20857.

Once you locate a Hill-Burton obligated facility in your area, you can apply for free care by contacting the facilities Admissions, Business or Patient Accounts Office. The local facility can tell you if you qualify for assistance and whether or not the specific service(s) you desire are covered.

FREE COOKBOOK FOR DIABETICS

Looking for some new "tasty" diabetic recipes? The National Diabetes Information Clearinghouse (NDIC) can help you out. The NDIC, a service of the National Institute of Diabetes and Digestive Kidney Diseases, can provide you with a "cookbook" full of delicious, healthful recipes for diabetics. The Clearinghouse also can provide you with timely, general information about diabetes including topics, such as nutrition, insulin, blood glucose monitoring, foot care, and exercise. Free publications of interest to diabetics include "Non-insulin Dependent Diabetes" and "Foot Care For The Diabetic Patient". Other NDIC publications, including fact sheets, brochures, and pamphlets on the topic of diabetes also are available. A complete list of publications is available free upon request.

For recipes, more information and/or a list of free publications, contact the:

National Information Clearinghouse,
1 Information Way,
Bethesda, MD 20892-3560; (301) 654-3327;
Internet: http://www.niddk.nih.gov.

FREE INFORMATION ON THE LATEST TREATMENTS, CURES, AND PREVENTION OF HEART DISEASE

What are the major risk factors for heart disease? How does the food you eat affect your cardiovascular health? Can regular exercise help prevent heart disease? You can get the answers to these questions and other concerns dealing with heart disease by contacting the National Heart, Lung and Blood Institute's (NHLBI) Information Center. The NHLBI offers a number of free publications on heart disease and its major risk factors, including cholesterol, high blood pressure and smoking. You also can get information on the latest treatments, cures and preventions.

Some NHLBI publications dealing with heart disease include:

"Facts About Heart Disease and Women: Preventing and Controlling High Blood Pressure"

"Check Your Healthy Heart I.Q."

"Facts About Coronary Heart Disease"

"Facts About Heart Failure

"Step By Step: Eating to Lower High Blood Cholesterol"

"So You Have High Blood Cholesterol"

For free copies of these and other publications dealing with heart disease, contact the

National Heart, Lung and Blood
Information Center, P.O. Box 30105,
Bethesda, MD 20824-0105; (800) 575-WELL;
Internet: http://www.nhlbi.nih.gov.

FREE HEALTH AND NUTRITION GUIDES FOR SENIORS

Most research in the last few years has shown that the foods people eat have a lot to do with how healthy they are— and how healthy they stay. Research has shown that eating a healthful diet low in fat, high in fiber, with plenty of fruits and vegetables may help to lower the risk of many diseases, including cancer. And the benefits of proper nutrition do not diminish with age. Eating the right foods can help you stay fit and trim at any age.

The Food and Drug Administration (FDA) offers a great selection of free publications and health guides to help people 50 and over keep on the right track when it comes to nutrition. Publications of special interest include:

"Growing Older, Eating Better"

"Taking The Fat Out Of Food"

"Olestra And Other Food Substitutes"

"Planning A Diet For A Healthy Heart"

"More People Trying Vegetarian Diets"

"Consumer Guide To Fats"

"Dietary Guidelines For Americans"

"How The New Food Label Can Help You Plan A Healthy Diet"

"Using The New Food Label To Choose Healthier Foods"

Most of these and other related FDA publications are available free from the FDA's public affairs specialists in FDA offices throughout the United States (listed in the appendix). If there is no FDA office in your area, you can contact the:

Office of Consumer Inquiries,
FDA, HFE-88, 5600 Fishers Lane,
Rockville, MD 20857; (301) 443-9057.
If you have access to the Internet,
FDA publications can be found at
http://www.fda.gov/.

You also may contact the following sources for additional information on nutrition:

Center for Nutrition Policy and Promotion,
USDA, 1120 20th Street, NW, Suite 200
North Lobby, Washington, DC 20036.

Food and Nutrition Information Center,
USDA/National Agricultural Library, Room 304,
10301 Baltimore Blvd.,
Beltsville, MD 20705-2351.

Cancer Information Service,
Office of Cancer Communications,
National Cancer Institute, Building 31,
Room 10A16, 9000 Rockville Pike,
Bethesda, MD 20892.

Weight Control Information Network
(WIN) of the National Institute of Diabetes
and Digestive Kidney Diseases,
1 WIN WAY, Bethesda, MD 20892.

National Institute on Aging Information
Center, Building 31, Room 5C27,
National Institutes of Health,
Bethesda, MD 20892.

Office of Food Labeling,
FDA (HFS-150),
200 C Street, SW,
Washington, DC 20204.

FREE GOVERNMENT PUBLICATIONS TO HELP YOU PREVENT CANCER, HEART DISEASE AND DIABETES

There are a number of government agencies that offer accurate, up-to-date information on health-related topics. Most of this information is free upon request and deals with the latest research, causes, treatments and prevention of many diseases, such as cancer, heart disease and diabetes.

The Cancer Information Service (CIS), a network of nineteen regional field offices supported by the National Cancer Institute (NCI), provides information on the latest treatments and prevention of cancer. The CIS can provide specific information about particular types of cancer, as well as information on how to get second opinions and the availability of clinical trials through the distribution of NCI publications. Available NCI publications include:

"Clearing the Air: A Guide To Quitting Smoking"—this 24-page pamphlet offers a variety of approaches to stop smoking.

"5 A Day Brochures"— this is a series of brochures that encourage increased consumption of fruits and vegetables.

"Eat More Fruits and Vegetables"— this brochure provides information about fruits and vegetables that are good sources of vitamins A, C, and fiber.

"Cancer Tests You Should Know About: A Guide for People 65 And Over"— this 14-page pamphlet discusses the cancer tests recommended for people 65 and over. It also provides a checklist for men and women to keep a record of when the cancer tests occur, and it describes the steps to follow should cancer be found.

"A Mammogram: Once A Year For Lifetime"— this brochure is for all women age 40 or older. It describes the importance of regular mammograms in the early detection of breast cancer. It also explains NCI guidelines for mammography.

"Get A New Attitude About Cancer"— this 12-page pamphlet informs black adults of the specific cancers that are the leading causes of cancer death for black men and women.

"Testicular Self-Examination"— this pamphlet provides information about risks and symptoms of testicular cancer, and instructions on how to perform testicular self-examination.

"Understanding Breast Changes: A Health Guide For All Women"— this 56-page booklet explains how to evaluate breast lumps and other normal breast changes that often occur and are confused with breast cancer.

Other NCI publications include:

"A Mammogram Could Save Your Life"
"Anticancer Drug Information Sheets"

"Advanced Cancer: Living Each Day"
"Chemotherapy and You: A Guide to Self-Help During Treatment"
"Eating Hints: Recipes & Tips for Better Nutrition During Treatment".
"Facing Forward: A Guide For Cancer Survivors"
"Ten Important Facts To Know About Cancer"

To order these and other free cancer-related publications, contact the:

National Cancer Institute,
Information Specialist,
31 Center Drive, MSC-2580, Building 31,
Room 10A16, Bethesda, MD 20892-2580,
or call the Cancer Information Service at
1-800-4-CANCER (422-6237).

The National Heart, Lung, and Blood Institute (NHLBI) Education Programs Information Center provides free materials on treatment and prevention of cardiovascular diseases. Some of the publications available include:

"Facts About Coronary Heart Disease"
"Facts About Heart Disease And Women: Are You At Risk?"
"Facts About Heart Failure"
"Facts About Angina"

"Facts About Heart Disease and Women: Preventing And Controlling High Blood Pressure"

"Check Your Physical Activity and Heart Disease IQ"

"Step by Step: Eating To Lower High Blood Cholesterol"

To order these and/or a complete list of NHLBI publications dealing with heart disease, contact:

NHLBI, P.O. Box 30105, Bethesda, MD 20824; 301-251-1223; http://www.nhlbi.nih.gov/.

The National Diabetes Information Clearinghouse (NDIC), a service of the National Institute of Diabetes and Digestive and Kidney Diseases, offers free fact sheets, brochures and pamphlets on the topic of diabetes. Free publications include:

"Dependent Diabetes"

"Insulin-Dependent Diabetes"

"Foot Care For The Diabetic Patient"

"Kidney Disease of Diabetes"

"Diabetes Overview"

"Diabetic Eye Disease"

"Do Your Level Best" (basic information about type 1 or type 2 diabetes)

"Questions To Ask Your Doctor About Blood Sugar Control"

Copies of these publications and a complete list of materials are available upon request from the:

National Diabetes Information Clearinghouse, 1 Information Way, Bethesda, MD 20892-3560; 301-654-3327; Internet: http://www.niddk.nih.gov.

FREE MEDICAL AND NUTRITION ADVICE TO HELP YOU LIVE A LONGER, HAPPIER, AND SEXIER LIFE

Ponce De Leon never found the fountain of youth. His search for a legendary spring believed to have the power of rejuvenation was futile, and he died at the relatively young age of 61. Today, the quest to discover the fountain of youth has taken a more scientific approach. The National Institute on Aging (NIA), part of the National Institutes of Health, promotes healthy aging by conducting and supporting biomedical research and training relating to the aging process. The NIA's research also involves diseases and other special problems and needs of the aged.

While there may not be an age rejuvenating fountain of youth, the NIA's research into all facets of the aging process including nutrition, disease prevention, and sexuality, can provide you with valuable information to help you lead a longer, healthier, happier, and sexier life. Science-based educational materials on a wide range of topics related to health and aging available free upon request from the NIA include:

"The National Institute on Aging: Research For A New Age"- this 46-page booklet describes the NIA's research efforts into the aging process.

"With The Passage of Time: The Baltimore Longitudinal Study of Aging"— this 52-page booklet describes America's longest running scientific examination of human aging, conducted by the NIA Gerontology Research Center.

"Hearts and Arteries: What Scientists Are Learning About Age and the Cardiovascular System"— a 33-page booklet that describes what happens to the heart during the process of normal aging.

"In Search of the Secrets of Aging"— this 35-page booklet examines the current state of knowledge about longevity, theories of aging, and other aging-related topics.

Other NIA publications include:

"Can Hormones Reverse Aging?"
"Aging And Your Eyes"
"What's Your Aging IQ"
"Sexuality In Later Life"
"Life Extension: Science or Science Fiction"
"What To Do About The Flu"

"Arthritis Medicines"

"Finding Good Medical Care For Older Americans"

"Hints For Shopping, Cooking, And Enjoying Meals"

"Skin Care And Aging"

"Hearing And Older People"

"Don't Take It Easy— Exercise!"

"Considering Surgery"

"Talking With Your Doctor: A Guide For Older People"

"Nutrition: A Lifelong Concern"

For free copies of these and other aging-related publications, contact the:

Public Information Office,
National Institute on Aging, Building 31,
Room 5C27, 31 Center Drive,
MSC 2292, Bethesda, MD 20892-2292;
1-800-222-2225.

FREE EXERCISE PROGRAMS

Research has shown that regular exercise can help virtually anyone live a longer, healthier life. The problem for many people is finding the right exercise program to fit their individual needs and lifestyles. For many people 50 and over, strenuous exercising is not the ideal solution. These people need exercise programs designed for their own special needs and abilities.

The President's Council on Physical Fitness and Sports (PCPFS) encourages all Americans to raise their fitness levels. To that end, the Council distributes information to the public about the health-related benefits of regular exercise. You can send away for the following free publications, which provide easy exercises tailored to seniors:

"Pep Up Your Life"— this is a fitness book (produced in collaboration with the American Association of Retired Persons) for people 50 and over. The book offers a variety of exercises for all levels of ability.

"The Nolan Ryan Fitness Guide"— this fitness guide is designed for adults age 40 and over.

"Fitness Fundamentals"— provides guidelines for regular personal exercise.

"Walking For Exercise and Pleasure"

For copies of these and other related publications, contact the:

President's Council on Physical Fitness and Sports,
Suite 250, 701 Pennsylvania Ave.
NW, Washington, DC 20004;
(202) 272-3421; Fax: (202) 504-2064.

GET FAST RELIEF FROM CONSTIPATION WITH THESE FREE BOOKLETS

Constipation may not be a polite topic of conversation but it is an uncomfortable reality for many people, especially mature adults. In fact, older adults are five times more likely than younger adults to report problems with constipation. Poor diet, lack of exercise, insufficient intake of fluids, and some drugs used to treat other conditions all can result in constipation. That's the bad news, the good news is that fast relief may be just a free booklet away. The National Digestive Diseases Information Clearing House, the Food And Drug Administration, and the Aging Information Center, are a few of the agencies which can provide free publications on this delicate but serious topic. Here are some of the publications available:

"Constipation"— discusses the causes of and treatment for constipation in older adults. This booklet is available free upon request from the

National Digestive Diseases Information
Clearing House, 2 Information Way,
Bethesda, MD 20892-3570.

"Overuse Hazardous:Laxatives Rarely Needed"— discusses the dangers of the overuse of laxatives and suggests alternative methods for treating constipation. Reprinted from the "FDA Consumer", this article is available from the

Food and Drug Administration,
5600 Fishers Lane,
Rockville, MD 20857.

"Diet, Nutrition, & Cancer Prevention: The Good News" (NIH Publication No. 87-2878)— discusses high-fiber diet and fiber-rich foods. The booklet is available upon request from the:

Cancer Information Service,
Office of Cancer Communications,
National Cancer Institute, 9000 Rockville Pike,
Bethesda, MD 20892; 1-800-4-CANCER.

The National Institute on Aging Information Center also can provide you with free publications dealing with constipation and proper nutrition, including:

"Constipation"
"Digestive Do's and Don'ts"
"Nutrition: A Lifelong Concern"

For free copies of these and other related publications, contact the:

National Institute on Aging
Information Center, P.O. Box 8057,
Gaithersburg, MD 20898-8057;
1-800-222-2225.

FREE PRESCRIPTION MEDICINES

It's not a widely known fact, but most drug manufacturers offer "patient assistance" programs which provide certain people with free medicines. You won't find out about these programs through advertisements, because drug companies would rather be paid for their medicines than give them away free of charge. Nevertheless, the programs do exist, and if you qualify you could save a bundle on needed prescription medicines. Everything from Dilantin to Zantac is available absolutely free. Here's how it works:

Under many patient assistance or "indigent patient" programs, a doctor's request is all that's required to make a patient eligible. Your doctor must confirm that you need specific prescription medicines and that you cannot afford to pay for them. You cannot enroll in these programs on your own. Your doctor must contact the drug companies directly.

Most programs also require a minimal amount of paperwork. After your doctor submits a request, you'll be required to fill out application forms. You'll also need to confirm your income. Since these assistance programs are targeted for "medically indigent" patients, you'll need to meet specific income requirements. These requirements can vary considerably from company to company. Several companies provide free medicines to persons with annual incomes of $25,000 or more. Generally, however, indigent is defined as an "uninsured person with an annual income below $25,000.

Once the paperwork is completed, the medicines will be sent to your doctor's office where you can pick them up for free. Under most assistance programs, you'll be able to obtain a one-time supply (usually three to six months worth) of a medicine.

Most doctors are aware of patient assistance programs, but some are not. Both you and your doctor can find out more about these programs by contacting the:

Senate Committee On Aging,
Indigent Patient Programs,
Dirksen Senate Office Building, Room G-31,
Washington, DC 20510-6400; (202) 224-5364.

Ask for a report entitled, "Programs to Help Older Americans Obtain Their Medications". You'll also receive an explanation of the indigent patient programs available and a directory that lists most of the participating drug manufacturers.

You also can contact the Pharmaceutical Research and Manufacturers of America (PhRMA) for information about patient assistance programs. The PhRMA publishes pamphlets and booklets on a number of drug-related topics and also can provide with a list of participating pharmaceutical companies. Call or write the:

Director of Consumer Affairs,
1100 15th Street, NW, Suite 900,
Washington, DC 20005; (800) 862-4110.

The following directory lists several pharmaceutical manufacturers that offer free prescription medicines through patient assistance or indigent patient programs.

ADRIA LABORATORIES, INC.

Contact: Adria Laboratories, Patient Assistance Program, P.O. Box 9525, McClean, VA 22102; (800) 366-5570. Medicines available include: Adriamycin PFS, Adrucil, Folex, Idamycin, Neosar, Tarabine, and Vincasar.

ALLERGAN PRESCRIPTION PHARMACEUTICALS

Contact: Judy McGee, 1-800-347-4500, ext. 4280. Medicines available include Naphacon A, Propine, FML, HMS, and Pilogen.

AMGEN, INC

Contact: Amgen Safety Net Programs, Reimbursement Hotline, 1-800-272-9376. Medicines available include: Epogen and Neupogen. Enrollment in the Safety Net Program is based on a patient's insurance and financial status.

ASTRA PHARMACEUTICAL PRODUCTS, INC

Contact: FOSCAVIR Assistance And Information on Reimbursement (F.A.I.R.), 1-800-488-3247. Medicines available include: Foscavir (Foscarnet Sodium). Physician must sign and complete the application and return it within seven days to the address indicated on the form. The qualification form also must be accompanied by a signed prescription.

BOEHRINGER INGLEHEIM PHARMACEUTICALS, INC.

Contact: PARTNERS IN HEALTH, 1-800-556-8317. Medicines available include: Persantine, Atrovent, Alupent, Catapres. Controlled substances are not covered.

BRISTOL MYERS SQUIBB #1

Contact: Bristol-Myers Squibb, Indigent Patient Program, P.O. Box 9445, McLean, VA 22102-9998; 1-800-736-0003. Medicines available include: Duricef, Cefzil, BuSpar, Desyrel, Estrace, Ovcon-35, Ovcon-50, Natalins, Natalins RX, Vagistat-1, and Mycostatin.

BRISTOL MYERS SQUIBB #2

Contact: Cardiovascular Access Program, P.O. Box 9445, McLean, VA 22102-9998; 1-800-736-0003. Medicines available include: Capoten, Capozide, Corgard, Corzide, Klotrix, K-Lyte, Monopril, Naturetin, Pravochol, Saluron, Salutensin, and Vasodilan.

BRISTOL MYERS SQUIBB #3

Contact: Cancer Patient Access Program, 2400 West Lloynd Expressway, Evansville, IN 47721, Mail Code R-22; 1-800-437-0994. Medicines available include: BICNU, CEENU, Lysodren, Mutamycin, Mycostatin Pastilles, Paraplatin, Planitol, Planitol-AQ, VePesid, Blenoxance, Cytoxan, Lyophilized Cytoxan, Ifex, Mesnex, Megace.

BURROUGHS-WELLCOME

Contact: Jonas Dougherty, Patient Information Services, 1-800-722-9242. Medicines available include: Septra, Septra DS, Lanoxin, AZT, Zovirax, Zyloprim, Imuran, and Wellcovorin.

CIBA-GEIGY PHARMACEUTICALS

Contact: Jackie LaGuardia, Senior Information Assistant, Ciba-Geigy Corporation, 556 Morris Ave., D2O58, Summit, NJ 07091; 1-800-257-3273. Medicines available include: Lopressor, Lotensin, Lioresal, Slow K, Tegretol, Voltaren, Brethine, Estraderm, Transderm Nitro, Anturane, and Apresazide. Controlled substances are not covered under this program.

GENETECH

Contact: Indigent Patient Program, 1-800-879-4747. Medicines available include: Actimmune, Activase, Protropin, and Nutropin.

GLAXO, INC

Contact: Laura Newberry, Supervisor, Glaxo Indigent Patient Program, 1-800-452-9677. Medicines available include: Zantac, Ceftin, Ventolin, Beconase, Beconase AQ, and Trandate.

IMMUNEX CORPORATION

Contact: Professional Services Immunex Corporation, 1-800-466-8639. Medicines available include: Leukine, Novantrone, Thioplex, and all other prescription medications currently marketed by Immunex.

JANSEN

Contact: Patient Assistance Program, 1-800-544-2987. Medicines available include: Duragesic, Ergamisol, Imodium, Nizoral tablets, Sporanox (capsules), and Vermox.

KNOLL PHARMACEUTICAL COMPANY

Contact: Indigent Patient Program, 30 N. Jefferson RD., Whippany, NJ 07981; 1-800-524-2474. Medicines available include: Isoptin, Rythmol, and Santyl.

LEDERLE LABORATORIES

Contact: Jerry Johnson, Pharm. D., Director, Industry Affairs; 1-800-533-2273. Medicines available include: Diamox, Artane, Mincoin, Mitoxantrone, Leucovorin, Methotrexate, Thiotepa, Verelan. Controlled drugs are not covered.

ELI LILLY, INC.

Contact: Indigent Patient Program Administrator, Eli Lilly and Company, Patient

Assistance Program, P.O. Box 9105, McLean, VA 22102-0105; 1-800-545-6962. Medicines available include: Ceclor, Keflex, Prozac, Dymelor, and Axid. Controlled substances are not covered by this assistance program.

MARION-MERRELL DOW, INC

Contact: Indigent Patient Program, P.O. Box 8480, Kansas City, MO 64114; 1-800-362-7466. Medicines available include: Cardizem, Cardizem SR, Cardizem CD, Carafate, Pavabid, Seldane, Seldane-d, Nicorette, Rifidin, and Lorelco. Patient's physician determines whether or not he/she is eligible for this assistance program.

MILES PHARMACEUTICALS

Contact: Professional Services, Miles Indigent Patient Program, 400 Morgan Ave., West Haven, CT 06516; 1-800-682-6532. Medicines available include: Cipro, Nimotop, Tridesilon Cream.

ORTHO BIOTECH

Contact: Jacob Drapin, Director, Health Care Systems, Ortho Biotech Financial Assistance Program, 1800 Robert Fulton Drive, Reston, VA 22091; 1-800-553-3851. Medicines available include: Leustatin and Procrit.

PARKE-DAVIS

Contact: Indigent Patient Program, P.O. Box 9945, McLean, VA 22102; 1-800-755-0120. Medicines available include: Accupril, Cognex, Cilatin, Lopid, Neurotin, Nitrostar, Sublingual, Procan SR, and Zarotin.

PFIZER PHARMACEUTICALS, INC

Contact: Indigent Patient Program, P.O. Box 2547, Alexandria, VA 22314; 1-800-646-4455. Medicines available include: Diflucan, Antivert, Marax, Diabinese, Cardura, Minizide, Navane, Sinequan, Zithromax, and all other Pfizer products.

PROCTOR & GAMBLE PHARMACEUTICALS, INC.

Contact: Customer Service, 17 Eaton Avenue, Norwich, NY 13815; 1-800-448-4878. Medicines available include: Ascol, Dantrium, Didronel, Entex, and Macrodantin.

SANDOZ PHARMACEUTICALS, INC

Contact: Maria Hardin, Director, Sandoz Drug Cost Sharing Program, P.O. Box 8923, New Fairfield, CT; 1-800-447-6673. Medicines available include: Clorazil, DynaCirc, Eldepryl, Lescol, Sandimmune, Sandoglobulin, and Sandostatin.

SANOFI WINTHROP PHARMACEUTICALS

Contact: Product Information Department, 90 Park Avenue, New York, NY 10016; 1-800-446-6267.

Medicines available include: Intron-A, Eulexin, Aralen, Danocrine, and Winstrol.

SCHERING-PLOUGH

Contact: Drug Information Services Indigent Services, 1-800-526-4099. Medicines available include: Intron-A, Eulexin, Trinalin, Lotrimin, Lotrisone, Diprozone, and Optimine.

G.D. SEARLE & CO.

Contact: "Patients In Need" Foundation, Searle Co., P.O. Box 5110, Chicago, IL 60680; 1-800-542-2526. Medicines available include: Aldactone, Aldactazide, Calan, Calan SR, Cytotec, Kerlone, Norpace, Norpace CR, Nitrodisc, and Maxaquin.

SIGMA-TAU PHARMACEUTICALS, INC.

Contact: Michelle McCourt, Carnitor Drug Assistance Program, Administrator, National Organization for Rare Disease Disorders, P.O. Box 8923, New Fairfield, CT 06812-1783; 1-800-999-6673.Medicines available include: Carnitor (Levocarnitine). You must have no other means for obtaining the drug through insurance or state or federal assistance, and cannot afford to purchase the drug.

SMITHKLINE BEECHAM PHARMACEUTICALS

Contact: Access To Care Program, 1 Franklin Plaza FP 1320, P.O. Box 7929, Philadelphia, PA 19101-

7929; 1-800-546-0420. Medicines available include: Amoxil, Augmentin, Bactroban, Compazine, Dyazide, Famvir, Kytril, Relafen, Riduara, Tagamet, and other SmithKline Beecham prescription products.

SYNTEX LABORATORIES

Contact: Indigent Programs, 1-800-822-8255. Medicines available include: Naprosyn, Anaprox, Cardene, Synalar, Synemol, Ticlid, Toradol, Lidex, and all other Syntex products.

WYETH-AYERST LABORATORIES

Contact: Norplant Foundation, P.O. Box 25223, Alexandria, VA 22314; (703) 706-5933. Medicines available include: Norplant and other products.

ZENECA PHARMACEUTICALS

Contact: Yvonne A Graham, Manager, Professional Services, Zeneca Pharmaceuticals Group, P.O. Box 15197, Wilmington, DE 19850-5197; 1-800-424-3727. Medicines available include: Nolvadex, Zestoretic, Zoladex, Casodex, Arimidex, Zestril, and Tenormin.

PREVENT AND CURE DOZENS OF DISEASES WITH THIS FREE INFORMATION

The National Institute on Aging (NIA) conducts research on a variety of subjects relating to aging, including the causes, treatments and prevention of a number of diseases. The NIA publishes brochures and a series of fact sheets called "Age Pages", which cover a number of disease-related topics, including cancer, heart disease, diabetes, arthritis, osteoporosis, Alzheimer's disease, and other diseases and medical conditions. Some of the free Age Page publications available include:

"Cancer Facts For People Over 50"
"Dealing With Diabetes"
"Forgetfulness In Old Age: It's Not What You Think"
"High Blood Pressure: A Common But Controllable Disorder"
"Osteoporosis: The Bone Thinner"
"Pneumonia Prevention: It's Worth A Shot"
"Arthritis Advice"
"Depression: A Serious But Treatable Disease"
"HIV, AIDS and Older Adults"
"Prostate Problems"
"Stroke: Prevention and Treatment"
"A Good Night's Sleep"
"Constipation"

For free copies of these publications, and/or a complete list of Age Pages and other publications distributed by the National Institute on Aging, contact the:

NIA Information Center,
P.O. Box 8057, Gaithersburg, MD 20899-8057;
1-800-222-2225.

For Information on Alzheimer's disease and related disorders, contact:

National Institute on Aging Alzheimer's Disease Education and Referral Center,
P.O. Box 8250, Silver Spring, MD 20907;
1-800-438-4380.

FREE MEDICAL TREATMENT

Free medical treatment by the best doctors in the world is available through research studies conducted with volunteer patients. These studies, funded by the government, are called "clinical trials" and are designed to find ways to prevent, detect, diagnose, control, and treat a variety of diseases and medical conditions. There are clinical trials for every condition from cancer to cataracts. If your medical condition is being studied by medical researchers, you may qualify for free treatment as a participant in a clinical trial.

You can find out what clinical trials are being conducted across the country by contacting the National Institutes of Health Warren Grant Magnuson Clinical Center. The Clinical Center is the world's largest biomedical research hospital and offers some of the most advanced scientific and medical technology. Patients are admitted to the Clinical Center only on referral by a physician or dentist. Your doctor should submit your diagnosis and medical history to the:

Patient Referral Service,
Clinical Center, Building 10, Room 1C255,
10 Center Drive, Bethesda, MD 20892-1170,

or may call the Patient Referral Service at 301-496-4891. NIH physicians will review your medical history and decide whether or not you qualify to participate in an ongoing clinical trial at the Clinical Center.

The National Cancer Institute (NCI) offers a computer file about cancer and clinical trials. The file, called Physicians Data Query (PDQ), contains summaries of over 1,500 ongoing clinical trials that are available to patients. The information in PDQ is updated each month and can provide you or your doctor with the latest information on clinical trials being offered around the country. The file also can provide the names of physicians conducting the trials, as well as the names of hospitals treating patients on the trials. You can obtain PDQ information from your physician or by contacting the Cancer Information Service at 1-800-4-CANCER.

FREE AND LOW-COST DENTURES AND DENTAL CARE

If you think you can't afford a needed trip to the dentist, chew on this: every state offers numerous free and low-cost dental care programs. Many of these programs are designed specifically for people

50 and older who may not be able to afford regular dental care. In many cases, dental care services are offered with no income restrictions whatsoever. According to a survey conducted by the American Dental Association (ADA), nearly 60% of those dentists responding reported that their primary practice provided dental care services free of charge or at a reduced rate for low-income seniors. And nearly 35% of all dentists responding to the survey reported providing such services to seniors regardless of income.

Generally, dental care programs for seniors offer free or low-cost dentures and repairs, discounts of 70% and more, free dental implants, and all other dental services that will help you keep your smile for a long time. Many of these programs, including free dentures for seniors, are available through state and local health departments. Most dental schools also offer low-cost dental care, and dental societies in each state can provide information about and referrals to free and low-cost dental programs. You also can contact your local community health center or clinic for information on free or low cost dental care in your area.

You can use the following list of state health departments, dental societies, and dental schools to obtain information about dental programs available for seniors in your area. You also may obtain referrals to dentists who participate in these funded free and low-cost dental programs.

Alabama

Department of Public Health & Dental Health Program, 434 Monroe Street, Montgomery, AL 36130; (334) 242-5760.

Alabama Dental Society, 836 Washington Ave., Montgomery, AL 36104; (334) 265-1684; (800) 489-2532 (in Alabama).

School of Dentistry, University of Alabama, 1919 Seventh Ave, South, Birmingham, AL 35394; (304) 934-2700.

Alaska

Department of Public Health, P.O. Box 110610; Juneau, AK 99811-0610; (907) 561-4211.

Alaska Dental Society, 3305 Arctic Blvd., Suite 102, Anchorage, AK 99503; (907) 563-3003;
Fax: (907) 563-3009;
http://www.alaska.net/~akdental/tooth1.html.

Arizona

Department of Health Services, Office of Dental Health, 1740 West Adams St., Phoenix, AZ 85007; (602) 542-1866.

Arizona State Dental Association, 4131 N. 36th St., Phoenix, AZ 85018-4761; (602) 957-4777; (800) 866-2732; http://www.stat.com/asda.

Arkansas

Department of Health, Dental Division, 4815 West Markham, Little Rock, AR 72201; (501) 372-3368.

Arkansas State Dental Association, 2501 Crestwood Drive #205, North Little Rock, AR 72116; (501) 771-7650.

California

Health Services Department, Oral Health, 714 P. St., Sacramento, CA 95814; (916) 445-0714.

California Dental Association, P.O. Box 13749, Sacramento, CA 95853; (916) 443-0505; (800) 736-8702 (in California); http://www.cda.org.

Senior-Dent, California Dental Association (CDA); (800) 736-7071. The Senior-Dent program, sponsored by the CDA, offers dental work at a reduced fee to eligible seniors. To be eligible, you must be at least 60 years old; have an annual income of $20,000 or less; and not be receiving dental benefits from Denti-Cal or a dental insurance plan.

School of Dentistry, University of San Francisco, 707 Parnassus Ave., San Francisco, CA 94143; (415) 476-1891.

School of Dentistry, University of Los Angeles, 10833 LeConte Ave., Los Angeles, CA 90024-1668; (310) 206-3904.

School of Dentistry, University of Southern California, 325 W. 34th Street, Los Angeles, CA 90089; (213) 740-2800.

Colorado

Department of Health, Family and Community Health Services, Dentistry, 4300 Cherry Creek Dr., South, A4, Denver, CO 80222; (303) 692-2360.

Colorado Dental Association, 3690 South Yosemite, Ste. 100, Denver, CO 80237-1808; (303) 740-6900; (800) 343-3010; http://www.colodentist.com.

School of Dentistry, University of Colorado Medical Center, 4200 East Ninth Ave., Denver, CO 80262; (303) 270-8751.

Connecticut

Department of Health, Dental Health Division, 150 Washington St., Hartford, CT 06106; (203) 566-4800.

Connecticut State Dental Association, 62 Russ Street, Hartford, CT 06106-1589; (203) 278-5550; http://www.csda.com.

School of Dental Medicine, University of Connecticut, 263 Farmington Ave., Farmington, CT 06032; (203) 679-3400.

Delaware

Delaware Dental Society, 1925 Lovering Ave., Wilmington, DE 19806-2147; (302) 654-4335.

District of Columbia

Department of Health, Dental Health Division, 1660 L St., NW, Washington, DC 20036; (202) 673-6765.

District of Columbia Dental Society, 502 C. St., N.E., Washington, DC 20002-5810;
(202) 547-7613;
http://www.aimservices.com/dsds/index.htm.

College of Dentistry, Howard University, 600 W. St., NW, Washington, DC 20059; (202) 806-0100.

Florida

Department of Health and Rehabilitative Services, Public Health Dental Program, 1317 Winewood Blvd., Tallahassee, FL 32399-0700; (904) 487-1845.

Florida Dental Association, 1111 E. Tennessee St., Suite 102, Tallahassee, FL 32308-6914; (904) 681-3269; (800) 877-9922.

College of Dentistry, University of Florida, Gainesville, FL 32610; (904) 392-4261.

Georgia

Department of Human Services, Oral Health Section, Two Peachtree St., 6th Floor, Atlanta, GA 30303; (404) 657-2574.

Georgia Dental Association, 2801 Buford Highway Suite T60, Atlanta, GA 30329; (404) 636-7553; (800) 432-4357 (in Georgia); http://www.mind-spring.com/~gadental/.

School of Dentistry, Medical College of Georgia, 1459 Laney Walker Blvd., Augusta, GA 30912; (706) 721-2696.

Hawaii

Department of Health, Dental Health Division, 1700 Lanakila Ave., Room 203, Honolulu, HI 96817; (808) 832-5710.

Hawaii Dental Association, 1000 Bishop St., Suite 805, Honolulu, HI 96813; (808) 536-2135; (800) 359-6275 (in HI).

Idaho

Department of Health & Welfare, Dental Program, P.O. Box 83720, Boise, ID 83720-0036; (208) 334-5966.

Idaho State Dental Association, 1220 W. Hays St., Boise, ID 83702; (208) 343-7543; (800) 932-8153 (in Idaho).

Illinois

Department of Public Health, Dental Health Division, 535 West Jefferson St., Springfield, IL 62761-0001; (217) 785-4899.

Illinois State Dental Society, P.O. Box 376, Springfield, IL 62705; (217) 525-1406; (800) 475-4737 (in Illinois).

Denture Referral Service, Illinois Dental Society, (217) 523-8495. Sponsored by the Illinois Retired Teachers Foundation, this program provides dentures to eligible seniors. To qualify you must be a resident of Illinois, at least 65 years old, have no public assistance or private dental insurance, and meet the current income guidelines.

Dental School, Northwestern Unv, 240 E. Huron, 1st Flr, Chicago, IL 60611; (312) 908-5950.

School of Dental Medicine, Southern Illinois University, 2800 College Ave., Building 263, Alton, IL (618) 474-7000.

College of Dentistry, University of Illinois, 801 S. Paulina, Chicago, IL 60612; (312) 996-7558.

Indiana

Department of Public Health, Dental Health Division, P.O. Box 1964, Indianapolis, IN 46206; (317) 383-6417.

Indiana Dental Association, P.O. Box 2467, Indianapolis, IN 46206; (317) 634-2610; (800) 562-5646 (in Indiana).

School of Dentistry, Indiana University, 1121 West Michigan St., Indianapolis, IN 46202; (317) 274-7957.

Iowa

Department of Public Health, Dental Division, Lucas State Office Building, Des Moines, IA 50319-0075; (515) 281-5787 (in IA).

Iowa Dental Association, 505 5th Ave. #333, Des Moines, IA 50309; (515) 282-7250; (800) 828-2181.

College of Dentistry, University of Iowa, Dental Building, Iowa City, IA 52242-1001; (319) 335-7499.

Kansas

Department of Health & Environment, Dental Program, Landon State Office Building, 900 SW Jackson, Room 665, Topeka, KS 66612-1290; (913) 296-1500.

Kansas Dental Association, 5200 SW Huntoon St., Topeka, KS 66604; (913) 272-7360; http://www.tyrell.net/~kda.

Kentucky

Department of Health, Dental Health Division, 275 East Main St., Frankfort, KY 40621-0001; (502) 564-3246.

Kentucky Dental Association, 1940 Princeton Drive, Louisville, KY 40205; (502) 459-5373; (800) 292-1855 (in Kentucky).

College of Dentistry, University of Kentucky, 801 Rose St., Lexington, KY 40536; (606) 323-6525.

School of Dentistry, University of Louisville, Louisville, KY 40292; (502) 852-5096.

Louisiana

Department of Public Health, Dental Health Division, 1300 Perdido St. AE13, New Orleans, LA 70112; (504) 896-1337.

Louisiana Dental Association, 320 3rd St. #201, Baton Rouge, LA 70801; (504) 926-1986; (800) 388-6642 (in Louisiana).

School of Dentistry, Louisiana State University, 1100 Florida Ave., Building 101, New Orleans, LA 70119; (504) 947-9961.

Maine

Department of Human Services, Division of Dental Health, Bureau of Health, State House Station #11, Augusta, ME 04333; (207) 287-3121.

Maine Dental Association, P.O. Box 215, Manchester, ME 04351-0215; (207) 622-7900; (800) 369-8217 (in Maine).

Maryland

Maryland State Health Department, Dental Health Division- Baltimore, 201 West Preston St., Baltimore, MD 21201-2399; (800) 492-5231.

Maryland State Dental Association, 6450 Dobbin Road, Columbia, MD 21405; (410) 964-2880; (800) 766-2880 (in Maryland); http://www.msda.com.

Baltimore College of Dental Surgery, University of Maryland, 666 W. Baltimore St., Baltimore, MD 21201; (410) 706-5603.

Massachusetts

Department of Health and Hospitals, Community Dental Programs, 1010 Massachusetts Ave., Boston, MA 02118; (617) 534-4717.

Massachusetts Dental Society, 83 Speen Street, Natick, MA 01760; (508) 651-7511; (800) 943-9200; http://www.ultranet.com/~madental.

Harvard School of Dental Medicine, 188 Longwood Ave., Boston, MA 02115; (617) 432-1423.

School of Graduate Dentistry, Boston University, 100 E. Newton St., Boston, MA 02118; (617) 638-4671.

School of Dental Medicine, Tufts University, One Kneeland St., Boston, MA 02111; (617) 956-6547.

Michigan

Department of Public Health, Dental Health Division, 3423 Martin Luther King Jr., Blvd., P.O. Box 30195, Lansing, MI 48909; (517) 335-8898.

Michigan Dental Association, 230 North Washington Square, Suite 208, Lansing, MI 48933-1392; (800)589-2631; http://www.bizserve.com/mda/.

School of Dentistry, University of Detroit-Mercy, 2985 E. Jefferson Ave., Detroit, MI 48207; (313) 446-1800.

School of Dentistry, University of Michigan, 1011 North University, Ann Arbor, MI 48109-1078; (313) 763-6933.

Minnesota

State Health Department, Dental Division, 717 Delaware St. SE, Minneapolis, MN 55440; (612) 623-5441.

Minnesota Dental Association, 2236 Marshall Ave., St. Paul, MN 55104; (612) 646-7454; (800) 950-3368 (in Minnesota).

School of Dentistry, University of Minnesota, 2236 Marshall Ave., St. Paul, MN 55104-5792; (612) 625-8400.

Mississippi

Low-Cost Denture Referral Program, Mississippi Dental Association, 2360 Ridgewood Rd., Jackson, MS 39216-4920; (601) 982-0442.

Mississipi Dental Association, 2360 Ridgewood Rd., Jackson, MS 39216-4920; (601) 982-0442.

School of Dentistry, University of Mississippi, 2500 North State St., Jackson, MS 39216; (601) 984-6155.

Missouri

Department of Public Health, Dental Health Division, P.O. Box 570, Jefferson City, MO 65102; (314) 751-6247.

Missouri Dental Association, P.O. Box 1707, Jefferson City, MO 65102; (314) 634-3436; (800) 688-1907 (in Missouri).

School of Dentistry, University of Missouri, 650 E. 25th St., Kansas City, MO 64108-2795; (816) 235-2100.

Montana

Health Services Division, Dental Department, Health and Environment Sciences, P.O. Box 200901, Cogsweel Building, Helena, MT 59620-0901; (406) 444-0276 (in MT).

Montana Dental Association, P.O. Box 1154, Helena, MT 59624; (406) 443-2061; (800) 257-4988.

Nebraska

Health Department, Dental Health Division, 301 Centennial Mall South, P.O. Box 95007, Lincoln, NE 68509-5007; (402) 471-2822.

Nebraska Dental Association, 3120 O Street, Lincoln, NE 68510; (402) 476-2641; (800) 234-3120 (in Nebraska).

School of Dentistry, Creighton University, 2802 Webster Avenue, Omaha, NE 68178; (402) 280-2865.

College of Dentistry, University of Nebraska Medical Center, 40th and Holdrege Sts., Lincoln, NE 68583; (402) 472-1333.

Nevada

Nevada Health Department, Family Services, 505 East King St., Carson City, NV 89710; (702) 687-4740.

Nevada Dental Association, 6889 W. Charleston Blvd. #9, Las Vegas, NV 89117; (702) 255-4211; (800) 962-6710 (in Nevada).

New Hampshire

Department of Health, Dental Health Division, 6 Hazen Dr., Concord, NH 03301; (603) 271-4685.

New Hampshire Dental Society, P.O. Box 2229, Concord, NH 03302; (603) 225-5961; (800) 244-5961 (in New Hampshire). Sponsors the "Denture Program", which offers dentures to people of all ages at a reduced rate. Eligibility is based on financial circumstances.

New Jersey

Department of Health, Dental Health Division, CN 364, Trenton, NJ 08625-0364; (609) 292-1723.

New Jersey Dental Association, One Dental Plaza, P.O. Box 6020, North Brunswick, NJ 08902; (908) 821-9400; Fax: (908) 821-1082; http://www.njda.org/. Sponsors the "Senior Dent" program which offers seniors a discount on dental care. Contact the New Jersey State Division on Aging (800-792-8820) for more information.

New Jersey Dental School, University of Medicine and Dentistry, 110 Bergen St., Newark, NJ 07103; (201) 982-4300.

New Mexico

Department of Health, Dental Division, 1190 Saint Francis Drive, Santa Fe, NM 87502-6110; (505) 827-2389.

New Mexico Dental Association, 3736 Eubank Blvd., N.E. Suite C-1, Albuquerque, NM 87111; (505) 294-1368

New York

New York City Dept. of Health, Dental Health, 93 Worth Street, Room 1001, New York, NY 10013; (212) 566-8166.

Dental Society of The State of New York, 7 Elk St., Albany, NY 12207; (518) 465-0044; (800) 255-2100 (in New York). Sponsors the "Dental Access Program" which offers reduced-fee dental care to people 65 or older.

School of Dental and Oral Surgery, Columbia University, 630 W. 168th St., New York, NY 10032; (212) 305-5665.

College of Dentistry, New York University, 345 E. 24th Street, New York, NY 10010; (212) 998-9800.

School of Dental Medicine, State University of New York at Stony Brook, Rockland Hall, Health Science Center, Stony Brook, NY 11794; (516) 632-8974.

School of Dental Medicine, State University of New York at Buffalo, 325 Squire, 3435 Main St., Buffalo, NY 14214-3008; (716) 829-2720.

North Carolina

Health And Natural Resources Environment, Dental Department, 1815-8 Capital Blvd., Raleigh, NC 27604; (919) 733-3853.

North Carolina Dental Society, P.O. Box 12047, Raleigh, NC 27605; (919) 832-1222; (800) 662-8754 (in North Carolina).

School of Dentistry, University of North Carolina, 104 Brauer Hall, Chapel Hill, NC 27599.

North Dakota

Health Department, 600 E. Blvd. Ave, Bismarck, ND 58505-0200; (701) 224-2372.

North Dakota Dental Association, Box 1332, Bismarck, ND 58502; (701) 223-8870; (800) 795-8870 (in North Dakota). Sponsors the "Senior Dent" program which offers reduced-fee dental care services to eligible North Dakotans. Must be at least 55 years old.

Ohio

State Health Department, Dental Health Division, 246 North High Street, Columbus, OH 43215; (614) 466-4180.

Ohio Dental Association, 1370 Dublin Road, Columbus, OH 43215; (614) 486-2700; (800) 282-1526 (in Ohio); http://www.oda.org. Sponsors the 'Dentistry For All" program, which matches participating dentists with qualifying low-income patients who pay a discounted fee for dental services. To be eligible, patients must not qualify for Medicaid or other federally-funded dental care programs and must not have dental insurance.

College of Dentistry, Ohio State Univ., 305 W. 12th Ave., Columbus, OH 43210; (614) 292-2751.

School of Dentistry, Case Western Reserve University, 2123 Abington Rd., Cleveland, OH 44106; (216) 368-3200.

Oklahoma

State Department of Health, Dental Health Services, 1000 Northeast Tenth St., Oklahoma City, OK 73117-1299; (405) 271-5502.

Oklahoma Dental Association, 629 W. Interstate 44 Service Road, Oklahoma City, OK 73118; (405) 848-8873; (800) 876-8890. Sponsors the "Senior Dent Program", which offers reduced-fee dental care services to Oklahoma seniors age 65 and older.

College of Dentistry, University of Oklahoma, Health Sciences Center, P.O. Box 26901, Oklahoma City, OK 73190-3044; (405) 271-6056

Oregon

Department of Health, Dental Health Division, 800 NE Oregon St., Portland, OR 97232; (503) 731-4098.

Oregon Dental Association, 17898 S.W. McEwan Rd., Portland, OR 97224; (503) 620-3230; (800) 452-5628 (in Oregon).

School of Dentistry, Sam Jackson Park, Oregon Health Sciences University, 611 SW Campus Drive, Portland, OR 97201; (503) 494-8867.

Pennsylvania

Department of Public Health, Dental Health Division, 500 South Broad St., Philadelphia, PA 19146; (215) 875-5666.

Pennsylvania Dental Association, P.O. Box 3341, Harrisburg, PA 17105; (717) 234-5941; (800) 692-7256 (in Pennsylvania); http://www.padental.org.

School of Dentistry, Temple University, 3223 N. Broad St., Philadelphia, PA 19140; (215) 707-2900.

School of Dental Medicine, University of Pennsylvania, 4001 W. Spruce St., Philadelphia, PA 19104; (215) 898-8961.

School of Dental Medicine, University of Pittsbrugh, 3501 Terrace St., Salk Hall, Pittsburgh, PA 15261; (412) 648-8760.

Rhode Island

Department of Public Health, Oral Health Division, 3 Capital Hill, Providence, RI 02908-5097; (401) 277-2588.

Rhode Island Dental Association, 200 Centerville Road, Warwick, RI 02886-4339; (401) 732-6833.

South Carolina

Department of Health and Environmental Control, 2600 Bull St., Columbia, SC 29260; (803) 734-4972.

South Carolina Dental Association, 120 Stonemark Lane, Columbia, SC 29210; (803) 750-2277; (800) 327-2598 (in South Carolina). Sponsors the "Senior Care Program", which provides dental care to senior citizens at a reduced fee.

College of Dental Medicine, Medical University of South Carolina, 171 Ashley Ave., Charleston, SC 29425; (803) 792-2611..

South Dakota

Department of Health, Dental Division, Anderson Building, 445 E. Capitol Ave., Pierre, SD 57501; (605) 773-3361.

South Dakota Dental Association, P.O. Box 1194, Pierre, SD 57501-1194; (605) 224-9133.

Tennessee

Department of Health, Oral Health Services, Tennessee Tower, 11th Floor, 3128 Ave. North, Nashville, TN 37247-5410; (615) 741-7213.

Tennessee Dental Association, P.O. Box 120188, Nashville, TN 37212-0188; (615) 383-8962.

School of Dentistry, Meharry Medical College, 1005 D.B. Todd Blvd., Nashville, TN 37208; (615) 327-6669.

College of Dentistry, University of Tennessee, 875 Union Ave., Memphis, TN 38163; (901) 448-6257.

Texas

Texas Public Health Office. Contact a regional office of the Texas Public Health Office for information about reduced-fee dental care in your area. Check your phone directory for the number and address of the office nearest you.

Senior Dent, Texas Dental Association, P.O. Drawer 3358, Austin, TX 78764; (512) 443-3675; (800) 460-8700 (in Texas); http://www.tda.org. The Senior Dent program offers reduced-fee dental care services to Texas residents who are at least 65 years of age. Call for more information and other eligibility requirements.

Baylor College of Dentistry, 3302 Gaston Ave., Dallas, TX 75246; (214) 828-8100.

Health Science Center, Dental Branch, University of Texas, 6516 John Freeman Ave., Houston, TX 77030; (713) 792-4056.

Health Science Center, Dental School, University of Texas, 7703 Floyd Curl Dr., San Antonio, TX 78284; (210) 567-3222.

Utah

Department of Health, Dental Health Division, 288 North 1460 West, Salt Lake City, UT 84116; (801) 538-6179.

Utah Dental Association, 1151 E. 3900 S., #B-160, Salt Lake City, UT 84124; (801) 261-5315; (800) 662-6500 (in Utah).

Vermont

Island Pond Health Center, P.O. Box 425, Island Pond, VT 05846; (802) 723-4300.

Vermont State Dental Society, 132 Church Street, Burlington, VT 05401; (802) 864-0115; (800) 640-5099 (in Vermont).

Virginia

Health Department, Dental Division, 1500 E. Main, Room 239, Richmond, VA 23219; (804) 786-3556.

Virginia Dental Association, P.O. Box 6906, Richmond, VA 23230; (804) 358-4927; (800) 552-3886 (in Virginia); http://www.vadental.org.

School of Dentistry, Virginia Commonwealth University, Box 980566, Richmond, VA 23298; (804) 828-9095.

Washington

State Health Department, Dental Division, P.O. Box 47867, Olympia, WA 98504-7867; (206) 664-3427.

Washington State Dental Association, 2033 6th Avenue, #333, Seattle, WA 98121; (206) 448-1914; (800) 448-3368 (in Washington).

Seattle-King County Dental Society, 2201 Sixth Ave., Suite 1306, Seattle, WA 98121-1832; (206) 443-7607. This organization can provide referrals to clinics and programs that offer free or low-cost dental care.

School of Dentistry, University of Washington, Health Science Building, Northeast Pacific St., Seattle, WA 98195; (206) 543-5830.

West Virginia

Department of Health and Human Resources, Dental Information, State Capital Complex, Building 6, Charleston, WV 25305; (304) 926-1700.

West Virginia Dental Association, 1002 Kanawha Valley Building, 300 Capitol St., Charleston, WV 25301-1794; (304) 344-5246.

School of Dentistry, West Virginia University, The Medical Center, Morgantown, WV 26505; (304) 598-4810.

Wisconsin

Division of Health, 1 West Wilson, Madison, WI 53701; (608) 266-5152.

Wisconsin Dental Association, 111 E. Wisconsin Ave., Suite 1300, Milwaukee, WI 53202-4811; (414) 276-4520; (800) 364-7646.

School of Dentistry, Marquette University, 604 N. 16th St., Milwaukee, WI 53233; (414) 288-6500.

Wyoming

State Health Department, Dental Division, Hathaway Building, 4th Floor, Cheyenne, WY 82002; (307) 777-7945.

Wyoming Dental Association, P.O. Box 1123, Cheyenne, WY 82003; (307) 634-5878; (800) 244-0779 (in Wyoming).

FREE CASH & BENEFITS FOR 50 OR OVER

Chapter 4
Free And Low Cost Travel

You've earned the right to take some time and see the world. But before you contact your travel agent, check out the travel deals Uncle Sam has to offer. Free and discount travel programs are available for older persons who want to travel to the far corners of the world or those who just want to explore America. Everything from free passports to free airfare, to free travel information is available.

Here are some of the travel deals available from Uncle Sam:

SEE THE COUNTRY AND SAVE HUNDREDS OF DOLLARS WHEN YOU TRAVEL (LIFE TIME PASSPORT TO TRAVEL SAVINGS)

If you are 62 years or older, the Golden Age Passport will help you see the country and save hundreds of dollars on your travel expenses. With the money you save, you'll be able to travel more, and even visit the grandkids along the way!

The Golden Age Passport is a lifetime entrance pass to those national parks, monuments, historic sites, recreation areas, and national wildlife refuges that charge entrance fees. There's a one-time-only processing fee of $10 for the Golden Age Passport, which also provides a 50% discount on federal use fees charged for facilities and services, such as swimming, camping, parking, boat launching, or cave tours. You must purchase your Golden Age Passport in person (it's not available by mail or telephone) at any National Parks Service (NPS) entrance fee area. The only qualification is that you must be at least 62 years old.

Once you have your money-saving Golden Age Passport, you'll need to plan your travel itinerary. The National Parks Service offers several free or moderately-priced publications, such as "National Parks Index and Lesser-Known Areas" booklets, "National Park Handbooks", and informative colorful brochures, posters and charts, and other materials.

For more information about NPS publications, write:

Nancy McLoughlin, Division of Publications,
National Parks Service,
Harpers Ferry, WV
25425-0050; 304-535-6018;
Fax: 304-535-6176.

SAVE UP TO $75 WITH A FREE PASSPORT

Passports can be expensive, especially if you're planning an overseas trip on a limited budget or a fixed income. However, you might be able to save the cost of a passport (up to $75, in some cases) if you are a family member of a deceased veteran. Free passports are available for family members who are visiting overseas gravesites and memorial sites of World War I and World War II veterans. Those eligible for free passports include widows, parents, children, sisters, brothers, and guardians of the deceased who are buried or commemorated in permanent American military cemeteries on foreign soil.

For more information about "no-fee" passports, write to the:

American Battle Monuments Commission,
Room 5127, Pulaski Building,
20 Massachusetts Avenue NW,
Washington, DC 20314-0001.

The Commission is responsible for commemorating the U.S. Armed Forces by designing, constructing, operating, and maintaining burial grounds on foreign soil. The Commission operates and maintains 24 military burial grounds for War Dead and 73 memorial structures worldwide.

You also can get general passport information from any of the following passport agencies.

Boston Passport Agency, Thomas P. O'Neill Federal Building, Room 10, Causeway Street, Boston, MA 02222-1094; 617-565-6990 (public inquiries); 617-565-6998 (recording).

Chicago Passport Agency, Kluczynski Federal Office Building, Suite 380, 230 South Dearborn Street, Chicago, IL 60604-1564; 312-353-7155 or 7163 (public inquiries); 312-353-5426 (recording).

Honolulu Passport Agency, New Federal Building, First Hawaii Tower, 1132 Bishop Street, Suite 500, Honolulu, HI 96813-2809; 808-541-1918 (public inquiry); 808-541-1919 (recording).

Houston Passport Agency, Mickey Leland Federal Building, Suite 1100, 1919 Smith Street, Houston, TX 77002-8049; 713-653-3153 (public inquiries); 713-653-3159 (recording).

Los Angeles Passport Agency, Federal Building, 11000 Wilshire Boulevard, Room 13100, Los Angeles, CA 90024-3615; 213-209-7075 (public inquiries); 213-209-7070 (recording).

Miami Passport Agency, Claude Pepper Federal Office Building, 51 Southwest First Avenue, 3rd Floor, Miami, FL 33130-1680; 305-536-4681 (public inquiries); 305-536-5395 (recording).

New Orleans Passport Agency, Postal Services Building, Room T- 12005, 701 Loyola Avenue, New Orleans, LA 70113-1931; 504-589-6161 (public inquiries); 504-589-6728 (recording).

New York Passport Agency, Rockefeller Center, Room 270, 630 Fifth Avenue, New York, NY 10111-0031; 212-541-7710 (public inquiries); 212-541-7700 (recording).

Philadelphia Passport Agency, U.S. Customs House, 200 Chestnut Street, Room 103, Philadelphia, PA 19106-2970; 215-597-7480 (public inquiries); 215-597-7482 (recording).

San Francisco Passport Agency, 95 Hawthorne Street, 5th Floor, San Francisco, CA 94105-3901; 415-974-9941 (public inquiries); 415-974-7972 (recording).

Seattle Passport Agency, Federal Office Building, Room 992, 915 Second Avenue, Seattle, WA 98174-1091; 206-442-7945 (public inquiries); 206-442-7941 (recording).

Stamford Passport Agency, One Landmark Square, Broad and Atlantic Streets, Stamford, CT 06901-2767; 203-325-3535 or 3530 (public inquiry); 203-325-4401 (recording).

Washington Passport Agency, 1111 19th Street, N.W., Washington, DC 20524-0002; 202-647-0518 (public inquiries).

Information about and applications for No-Fee passports also is available by contacting:

Special Issuance Agency, 1111 19th Street, N.W., Washington, DC 20522-1705.

LET THE GOVERNMENT PAY YOU TO TAKE A TRIP

Here's an opportunity to let your age, experience and expertise help you see the world. The U.S. Information Agency offers a program that will actually pay you to take a trip. The U.S. Speakers Program utilizes individuals, including older Americans who have particular areas of expertise as speakers on a variety of topics in foreign countries.

If you qualify for this program, you could travel to virtually any country in the world. What's more, the government will pay for your airfare and provide up to $100 a day in expense money. You'll be required to present a series of speaking programs providing information about your special area of expertise and the U.S. to foreign government officials, journalists, students, business people, and others interested about in life in the United States. The programs typically include informal lectures and/or discussions.

If you have a special area of expertise, the ability to communicate information and ideas, and a yen for world travel, contact the:

U.S. Information Agency,
301 4th Street SW, Room 567,
Washington, DC 20547; (202) 619-4779,

for more information about the U.S. Speakers Program.

FREE WORLD TRAVEL

If you meet the governments qualifications you may be able to travel almost anywhere in the world for free. Besides the U.S. Speakers Program, the U.S. Information Agency also offers the opportunity for world travel through its Office of Arts America's American Cultural Specialist Program (ACULSPECs). This program recruits and sends out American experts in various artistic fields to oversee projects at cultural institutions in foreign countries. Projects could involve theater arts, academies, museums, orchestras, universities, or dance companies, for residency periods of from two to six weeks.

American Cultural Specialist Grantees in 1995 included artists, playwrights, craft curators, photographers, sculptors, fundraising specialists, arts management, theatre directors, graphic artists, arts administrators, arts consultants, document conservationists, print artists, printmakers, music instructors, curators, and arts management consultants. If you are a professional in any of these or other related areas, you may qualify for the American Cultural Specialist Program.

If you're interested in this program, send a cover letter describing your professional experience and background plus a Curriculum Vita to:

Cultural Specialist Program, Arts America,
U.S. Information Agency,301 4th Street SW,
Room 567, Washington, DC 20547;
(202) 619-4779; Fax: (202) 619-6315.

You also can write this address for general information about the cultural specialist program.

FREE TRAVEL INFORMATION

Alabama Bureau of Tourism & Travel, 401 Adams Ave., P.O. Box 4927, Montgomery, AL 36103-4927; (334) 242-4169; (800) ALA-BAMA. Provides lodging information, calendars, maps, tourist attractions, and statewide vacation guides.

Alaska Division of Tourism, P.O. Box 110801, Juneau, AK 99811-0801; (907) 465-2010; (907) 465-2012. Provides lodging information, calendars, maps, and a list of tourist attractions.

Arizona Office of Tourism, 100 W. Washington, Phoenix, AZ 85007; (602) 542-8687; (800) 842-8257.

Arkansas Department of Parks & Tourism, One Capitol Mall, Little Rock, AR 72201; (501) 371-7777; (800) NATURAL.

California State Board of Tourism, 801 K Street, #1600, Sacramento, CA 95814; (916) 322-2881; (800) 862-2543.

Colorado Travel & Tourism Authority, P.O. Box 3524, Englewood, CO 80155; (800) COLORAD(0).

Connecticut State Board of Tourism, 865 Brook Street, Rocky Hill, CT 06067-3405; (203) 258-4355.

Delaware Tourism Office, 99 Kings Hwy., P.O. Box 1401, Dover, DE 19903; (302) 739-4271; (800) 441-8846.

Washington DC Convention & Visitors Association, 1212 New York Avenue, N.W., #600, Washington, DC 20005; (202) 789-7000. Provides lodging information, calendars, maps, and a list of tourist attractions.

Florida State Board of Tourism, Collins Bldg., 107 W. Gaines Street, Tallahassee, FL 32399-2000; (904) 487-1462.

Georgia State Board of Tourism, P.O. Box 1776, Atlanta, GA 30301; (404) 656-3590; (800) 847-4842.

Hawaii State Board of Tourism, 2270 Kalakaua Avenue, #801, Honolulu, HI 96815; (808) 923-1811.

Idaho Division of Travel Promotion, 700 W. State Street, Boise, ID 83720-2700; (208) 334-2470; (800) 635-7820.

Illinois State Board of Tourism, 100 W. Randolph, Room 3-300, Chicago, IL 60604; (312) 280-5740; (800) 223-0121.

Indiana State Board of Tourism, One North Capitol, #700, Indianapolis, IN 46204; (317) 232-8860; (800) 289-6646.

Iowa St.Dep. of Tourism, 200 East Grand Ave, Des Moines, IA 50309; (515)281-3100; (800) 345-IOWA.

Kansas State Board of Tourism, 400 S.W. Harrison, #1300, Topeka, KS 66603-3712; (913) 296-2009; (800) 2KANSAS.

Kentucky Department of Travel, Capital Plaza Tower, 22nd Floor, 500 Mero St., Frankfort, KY 40601; (502) 564-4930; (800) 225-TRIP.

Louisiana State Board of Tourism, P.O. Box 94291, Baton Rouge, LA 70804; (504) 342-8119; (800) 33GUMBO.

Maine Publicity Bureau, P.O. Box 2300, Hallowell, ME 04347; (207) 623-0363. Provides lodging information, calendars of events, maps, a list of tourist attractions.

Maryland State Board of Tourism, 217 E. Redwood Street, Baltimore, MD 21201; (410) 333-6611; (800) 543-1036.

Massachusetts Office of Travel & Tourism, 100 Cambridge Street, 13th Floor, Boston, MA 02201; (617) 727-3201; (800) 447-6277.

Michigan State Board of Tourism, P.O. Box 30226, Lansing, MI 48909; (800) 543-2937. Provides lodging information, calendars of events, maps, tourist attractions, and other tourist information.

Minnesota Office of Tourism, 100 Metro Square, Saint Paul, MN 55101; (612) 206-5029; (800) 657-3700. Provides lodging information, calendars, maps, attractions, and personal itinerary planning.

Mississippi Department of Tourism Development, 550 High Street, P.O. Box 849, Jackson, MS 39205; (601) 359-3297; (800) 927-6378.

Missouri Board of Tourism, P.O. Box 1055, Truman State Office Building, Jefferson City, MO 65102; (314) 751-4133; (800) 877-1234.

Travel Montana, 1424 9th Avenue, Helena, MT 59620; (406) 444-2654; (800) 548-3390.

Nebraska Tourism, P.O. Box 94666, Lincoln, NE 68509; (402) 471-3798; (800) 228-4307.

Nevada State Board of Tourism, Capitol Complex, Carson City, NV 89710; (800) NEVADA-8.

New Hampshire Tourism, 172 Pembroke Road, P.O. Box 1856, Concord, NH 03302-1856; (603) 271-2343; (800) 386-4664. Provides travel kits, lodging, calendars and maps.

State of New Jersey Division of Travel & Tourism, 20 W. State Street, CN 826, Trenton, NJ 08625; (609) 292-2470; (800) JERSEY 7.

New Mexico State Board of Tourism, 491 Old Santa Fe Trail, Santa Fe, NM 87503; (505) 827-0291; (800) 545-2040.

Empire State Development, Division of Tourism, One Commerce Plaza, Albany, NY 12245; (518) 474-4116; (800) 225-5697.

North Carolina State Board of Tourism, 430 N. Salisbury Street, Raleigh, NC 27611; (919) 733-4171; (800) VISIT-NC.

North Dakota Tourism Department, 604 East Blvd., Bismarck, ND 58505; (701)328-2525; (800) 435-5663. Provides lodging information, calendars, maps, and a list of tourist attractions.

Ohio Division of Travel & Tourism, 77 S. High Street, P.O. Box 0001, Columbus, OH 43266; (614) 466-8844; (800) BUCKEYE.

Oklahoma Tourism & Recreation Department, 505 Will Rogers Building, 2401 N. Lincoln, Oklahoma City, OK 73105; (405) 521-2406; (405) 522-3935. Provides lodging information, calendars, maps, tourist attractions, and vacation guides.

Oregon Tourism Division, 775 Summer Street N.E., Salem, OR 97310; (503) 373-1200; (800) 547-7842.

Pennsylvania Office of Travel Marketing, 433 Forum Building, Harrisburg, PA 17120; (717) 787-5433; (800) VISIT PA.

Rhode Island Board of Tourism, 7 Jackson Walkway, Providence, RI 02903; (401) 277-2601; (800) 556-2484.

South Carolina Division of Tourism, 1205 Pendleton Street, #106, Columbia, SC 29201; (803) 734-0122; (803) 734-0135; (800) 872-3505.

South Dakota State Board of Tourism, 711 E Wells Avenue, Capital Lake Plaza, Pierre, SD 57501; (605) 773-3301. Provides lodging information, calendars, maps and tourist attractions.

Tennessee Department of Tourist Development, 320 6th Avenue North, Nashville, TN 37202; (615) 741-2158; (800) 836-6200; Provides calendars, maps, tourist attractions, state-wide information and specific contacts.

Texas Department of Commerce— Tourism Division, Box 12728, Capitol Station, Austin, TX 78711; (512) 462-9191; (800) 8888-TEX.

Utah State Board of Tourism, Council Hall, Capitol Hill, Salt Lake City, UT 84114; (801) 538-1030.

Vermont Department of Travel & Tourism, 134 State Street, Montpelier, VT 05602; (802) 828-3236.

Virginia Division of Tourism, 901 East Byrd Street, Richmond, VA 23919; (804) 786-4484. Provides lodging information, calendars, maps and tourist attractions.

Washington State Board of Tourism, Olympia, WA 98504; (206) 753-5600; (800) 544-1800.

West Virginia State Board of Tourism, 2101 Washington Street East, Charleston, WV 25305; (304) 558-2286; (800) 225-5982.

Wisconsin Tourism Development, P.O. Box 7970, Madison, WI 53702; (608) 266-7621; (800) 432-TRIP.

Wyoming State Board of Tourism, I-25 at College Drive, Cheyenne, WY 82002; (307) 777-7777; (800) CALL-WYO.

NOTES

Chapter 5

Free Cash And Information For Your Home

Your home may not be a castle but it's probably your biggest asset. Uncle Sam knows that and offers a number of programs that will enable you to "cash in" on your primary asset. As an older American, you can get thousands of dollars in free cash to fix up your home, winterize your home, slash your home-heating bill, or turn the equity in your home into a ready line of cash to use as you please. Depending on where you live, the government even may pick up the tab for your property taxes.

Renters also are taken care of. There are government programs that will allow you to live practically rent-free, any where you like. You could save hundreds of dollars every year by letting Uncle Sam pay most of your rent. There's also an abundance of information available about housing opportunities for the elderly, and it's all free from Uncle Sam.

$15,000 FREE CASH TO FIX UP YOUR HOME

Got a leaky roof? Need a new furnace? Rural Housing Preservation Grants (RHPG) are available to take care of those and other needed home improvements. If you qualify for a HPG, you could get free money to repair or "rehabilitate" your home. While the average HPG is $7,500, you could get as much as $15,000. And that's money you can use to fix up your home without worrying about paying it back.

To qualify for a RHPG, you must meet certain low-income requirements and own or rent a home in a rural area— generally in a community with a population of up to 10,000. The money must be used to fix up your home in order to bring it up to code standards. You can rehabilitate your home's plumbing system, repair your roof, install a new heating/cooling system, or make other needed home repairs or improvements.

Rural Housing Preservation Grants are available through local groups and organizations, which receive money from the federal government for rural housing preservation. You can find out more about the program, including eligibility requirements and which local group is administering the grant money by contacting your local or regional office of the Rural Housing and Development Service (see appendix).

For general information about the RHPG program, you also may contact:

Multiple Family Housing
Processing Division,Rural Housing Service,
Department of Agriculture,
Washington, DC 20250; (202) 720-1660.

LIVE PRACTICALLY RENT-FREE THROUGH THIS LITTLE-KNOWN GOVERNMENT PROGRAM

Could you use some help paying the rent? If so, the Rural Housing Service (RHS) has a program that may help you save thousands of dollars in rent money. Under the program, Rental Assistance payments are available to certain low-income seniors who live in rural areas.

To qualify for rural rental assistance payments, you must occupy eligible Rural Rental Housing (RRH), Rural Cooperative Housing (RCH), and Farm Labor Housing projects financed by the Rural Housing Service. Generally, this rental assistance may be used by low-income seniors (or families) whose rents exceed 30% of their adjusted annual incomes.

To find out about the Rural Rental Assistance Payments program in your area, consult your local phone directory for the Rural Development district office number. If there is no listing, contact the appropriate Rural Development State Office (see the Appendix). For general information about this program, you also may contact:

Multi-Family Housing Servicing and Property Management Division,
Rural Housing Community Development Service, Department of Agriculture, Washington, DC 20250; 202-760-1600.

LIVE WHEREVER YOU LIKE AND LET UNCLE SAM PAY THE RENT

The U.S. Department of Housing and Urban Development (HUD) sponsors a program that could help you pay your rent. The program, known as the Section 8 Rental Voucher Program, is available to most "low-income" renters. If you qualify for the program, you'll receive special vouchers to cover part of your rent. Generally, the vouchers cover the difference between the "local payment standard" and 30% of your adjusted income. That means the most you'll have to pay for rent is 30% of your adjusted income. You may only have to pay as little as 10% of your gross monthly income for rent, and still live anywhere you like. And while this program is designed for "low-income" renters, you may qualify if your income is nearly $25,000 a year.

To learn more about the Rental Voucher Program, and/or to apply for this type of rental assistance, contact the HUD office nearest you (see appendix). You also may contact the:

Office of Rental Assistance,
Department of Housing
and Urban Development,
Washington, DC, 20410; 202-708-0477.

THIS SPECIAL PROGRAM GIVES SENIORS THE EQUITY IN THEIR HOMES BEFORE THEY SELL THEIR HOMES

Wouldn't it be nice to turn the equity in your home into cash on hand? And wouldn't it be nice to use that cash anyway you like? Imagine having money to fix up your home, pay medical expenses, take a long overdue vacation, or anything else you desire.

If you're at least 62 years old, you may qualify for a "reverse mortgage" through the U.S. Department of Housing and Urban Development's (HUD) Home Equity Conversion Mortgage (HECM) program. This program allows homeowners, 62 years of age or older, to convert equity in their homes to monthly streams of income or lines of credit. If you qualify, you can borrow thousands of dollars against the equity in your home. You'll have the money in hand, to spend anyway you want, and you won't have to pay it back until you move, sell your home, or die.

You can get more information on the HECM—eligibility requirements, how to apply, etc., by calling 1-800-217-6970 or by contacting the nearest local or regional HUD office (see appendix). You also may contact:

Director, Insured Family Development
Division, Office of Single Family Housing,
Department of Housing and Urban
Development, Washington, DC 20410;
(202) 708-2700.

LIVE LIKE A KING, WITH MEALS, VALET SERVICE, HOUSEKEEPING AND OTHER SERVICES PROVIDED FREE BY UNCLE SAM

You don't have to be in a castle to live like a king. There's a government housing program that offers everything from free meals to valet service. The Congregate Housing Services Program (CHSP) provides older persons the opportunity to live in approved rental housing with free meals and other support services available.

As a CHSP participant, you'll most likely have your own apartment, which includes a kitchen where you can prepare light meals. Depending on your health and physical condition, you may be expected to take care of your personal needs, such as laundry. The Congregate Housing program is designed to offer independent living in separate apartments, and opportunities to share activities of daily living with other residents.

Besides meals, many congregate housing arrangements also provide a number of other services, such as housekeeping, transportation, recreational and social activities, and religious services. Some homes also may provide personal care, health screening, and/or other types of assistance for "frail elderly" or non-elderly disabled or temporarily disabled individuals.

The CHSP is funded by HUD, which provides money to cover up to 40 percent of the cost of supportive services. Housing owners who participate in the program, pay at least 50 percent of the costs. Individual renters are required to pay fees that total at least 10% of program costs. Total fees can be no more than 20% of your adjusted gross income.

To be eligible for the Congregate Housing Services Program, you must reside in an approved housing project and meet other eligibility requirements. To find out more about the program, and whether or not you qualify, contact the Director of Housing or Director of Multifamily Housing in the appropriate HUD state/area office (see the Appendix), or the:

Program Management Division,
Office of Multi-family Asset
Management and Disposition,
Department of Housing
and Urban Development,
Washington, DC 20410; 202-708-3291.

You also may find congregate housing facilities in your area in the Yellow pages under:

Retirement Communities and Homes

Life Care Communities and Homes

Nursing Homes

Residential Care Facilities

GET A VIRTUALLY INTEREST-FREE HOME LOAN FROM THE GOVERNMENT

Here's your chance to escape from the rat race of the city to a slower more peaceful rural setting. With a Section 502 Rural Housing Loan, you can leave the congestion of the city behind and enjoy a new life in the wide open spaces.

The Section 502 Loan program offers low-interest loans to qualified applicants to obtain new or existing housing in rural areas. Loans range from $1,000 to $105,000, with the average loan for new construction $59,000, and $56,000 for existing cost. The interest rate may be as low as 1% for a term up to 38 years. To qualify for this type of Rural Housing Loan, you must meet certain income requirements and be unable to obtain the necessary credit from other sources at prevailing terms and conditions.

For more information about Section 502 Rural Housing Loans, contact your local or state Rural Development office (see appendix). You also may contact:

Director, Single Family Housing,
Processing Division,
Rural Housing Service,
Department of Agriculture,
Washington, DC 20250;
202-720-1474.

ADD HUNDREDS OF DOLLARS TO YOUR MONTHLY INCOME AND LET THE GOVERNMENT PAY YOUR PROPERTY TAXES FOR YOU

It's tough enough making ends meet on a limited budget, without having to worry about paying property taxes. Just think how much money you could save if you didn't have to pay property taxes. For some people, that savings could amount to hundreds of dollars added to their monthly incomes. You may be in line for just such a savings through a state-sponsored senior property tax deferral program.

Under a senior property tax deferral program, state government pays the homeowners' taxes to the local government. The state maintains the account as a loan to the homeowner, secured by equity in the home. Interest, which accrues on the loan, also is deferred. The loan is repaid to the state only upon the sale of the property or death of the homeowner. In other words, if you qualify for such a program, you won't have to pay property taxes as long as you live in and retain ownership of your home.

Eligibility requirements to take advantage of a Senior Property Tax Deferral Program vary from state to state, but are generally similar. For example, to qualify for the senior tax deferral program in Oregon, homeowners must be at least 62 years old, have an adjusted gross income of $29,000 or less, live on the property, and have a deed or recorded sales contract. In Washington, the age requirement for the

Senior Tax Deferral Program is 60 or older, and a participant's household income may not exceed $34,000.

Your county assessor's office should be able to provide you with information, including eligibility requirements, about a senior property tax deferral program in your state. You also may contact your State Department of Taxation or Department of Revenue for information.

$1,700 TO WARM YOU UP

You may be able to take the chill out of winter with up to $1,700 in free "weatherization" assistance from Uncle Sam. Under the Department of Energy's Weatherization Assistance Program, funds are allocated to winterize the homes of low-income persons, particularly the elderly and the handicapped. The average grant is around $1,700 and may be used to warm you up through the installation of attic insulation, caulking, weatherstripping and storm windows, a new energy-efficient furnace, or efficiency modifications to existing heating and cooling systems in your home or apartment.

You must meet certain income requirements in order to qualify for free home weatherization assistance. For more information and to find out if you qualify for the Weatherization Assistance Program in your area, contact your State Department of Energy or:

ector, Weatherization
istance Programs Division,
Stop EE-532, Office of Energy Efficiency
Renewable Energy, Department of Energy,
Forrestal Building,
Washington, DC 20585;
202-426-1698.

GET FREE CASH EVERY MONTH TO SLASH YOUR HEATING BILL

Monthly energy bills can put a serious strain on the family budget, especially if you're living on a fixed income. Sometimes, this strain may be so severe, you're forced to decide what bills to pay. Fortunately, Uncle Sam has a program specifically designed to ease this financial strain. The Low Income Home Energy Assistance Program (LIHEAP) assists low-income homeowners or renters with the payment of their winter energy bills. If you qualify for this program you may get free cash every month to slash your heating bill all winter long. You can pocket the savings to spend any way you like.

LIHEAP eligibility requirements vary from state to state, but generally household income is the determining factor. For example, in Ohio, households may be eligible for help on their heating bills if the household's income falls within the income range of up to $11,610 for a one person household to up to $31,260 for a six person household.

LIHEAP payments may be made directly to eligible households or to home energy suppliers. The assistance may be cash, vouchers, or payments to third parties, such as utility companies or fuel dealers. Owners and renters both are eligible for this assistance.

To find out more about this program, you can contact the appropriate State HEAP coordinator from the following list, or:

Director, Division of Energy Assistance, Office of Community Services, Administration for children and families, Department of Health and Human Services, 370 L'Enfant Promenade, SW, Washington, DC 20447; (202) 401-9351.

ALABAMA: LIHEAP Coordinator, Department of Economic and Community Affairs, 401 Adams Ave., P.O. Box 5690, Montgomery, AL 36103-5690; (334) 242-5351.

ALASKA: Energy Assistance Coordinator, Department of Health and Social Services, Division of Public Assistance, 400 W. Willoughby Ave, #301, Juneau, AK 99801-1731; (907) 465-3058.

ARIZONA: Program Manager, Arizona Department of Economic Security, Community Services Administration, 086Z-A, P.O. Box 6123-010A, Phoenix, AZ 85005; 602-542-6611.

ARKANSAS: LIHEAP Unit, OCS/Division of Economic and Medical Services, Department of Human Services, P.O. Box 1437/Slot 1330, Little Rock, AR 72203-1437; 501-682-8726.

CALIFORNIA: Deputy Director of Programs, California Department of Economic Opportunity, 700 N. 10th Street, Room 272, Sacramento, CA 95814; 916-323-8694.

COLORADO: LIHEAP Administrator, Division of Self Sufficiency, Department of Social Services, 1575 Sherman Street, 3rd Floor, Denver, CO 80203; (303) 866-5972.

CONNECTICUT: Program Supervisor, Energy Services Unit, Department of Social Services, 25 Sigourney St., 6th Floor, Hartford, CT 06106; 203-424-5891.

DELAWARE: Program Manager, Department of Health and Human Services, Division of State Service Centers, Carvel State Office Building, 4th Floor, P.O. Box 8911, Wilmington, DE 19801; 302-577-3491.

DISTRICT OF COLUMBIA: Citizen Energy Resources Division, DC Energy Office, 613 G St., NW, Suite 500, Washington, DC 20001; 202-727-9700.

FLORIDA: Program Coordinator, Bureau of Community Assistance, Department of Community Affairs, 2740 Centerview Drive, Tallahassee, FL 32399-2100; (904) 488-7541.

GEORGIA: Director, Office of Community Services, Division of Family and Children Services, Two Peachtree Street, NW, Atlanta, GA 30334-5600; 404-656-6697.

HAWAII: LIHEAP Coordinator, Hawaii Department of Human Services, 810 Richards Street, Honolulu, HI 96809; 808-586-5744.

IDAHO: LIHEAP Program Specialist, EOO, Division of Welfare, Dept. of Health and Welfare, 450 W. State Street, Statehouse, Boise, ID 83720; 208-334-5732.

ILLINOIS: Office of Human Services, Department of Commerce and Community Affairs, 620 E. Adams St., B-4, Bressmer Building, Springfield, IL 62701; 217-785-6135.

INDIANA: LIHEAP Coordinator, Family and Social Services Administration, Division of Family and Children, P.O. Box 7083, Indianapolis, IN 46207-7083; 317-232-7015.

IOWA: Bureau of Energy Assistance, Division of Community Action Agencies, Department of Human Rights, Lucas State Office Building, Des Moines, IA 50319; 515-281-3838.

KANSAS: Energy Program Administrator, Division of Income, Maintenance, DSRS, Docking State Office Building, 6th Floor, 915 SW Harrison Street, Topeka, KS 66612-1570; 913-296-1158.

KENTUCKY: Energy Assistance Branch, DMD, Department of Social Insurance, Cabinet for Human Resources, 275 E. Main Street, 2nd Floor, Frankfort, KY 40621; 502-564-4847.

LOUISIANA: Program Manager, Department of Social Services, Office of Community Services, P.O. Box 3318, Baton Rouge, LA 70821; 504-342-2274.

MAINE: LIHEAP Coordinator, Maine State Housing Authority, 353 Water Street, P.O. Box 2669, Augusta, ME 04338-2669; 207-626-4678.

MARYLAND: Energy Assistance Program, Community Services Administration, Department of Human Resources, 311 W. Saratoga Street, Baltimore, MD 21201; 410-767-7218.

MASSACHUSETTS: Director, EOCD/BEP, Saltonstall Building, Room 1803, 100 Cambridge Street, Boston, MA 02202; 617-727-7004 Ext. 533.

MICHIGAN: Director, Energy Services, Department of Social Services, 325 Grand Ave., P.O. Box 30037, Lansing, MI 48909; 517-373-8023.

MINNESOTA: Mr. Mark D. Kaszynski, Coordinator, Energy Assistance Program, Division of Community Based Services, EPU, 390 N. Robert Street, Room 125, St. Paul, MN 55101; 612-297-2590.

MISSISSIPPI: LIHEAP Branch Director, Division of Community Services, Mississippi Department of Human Services, 750 N. State Street, Jackson, MS 39202-3524; 601-359-4769.

MISSOURI: Administrator, Division of Family Services, P.O. Box 88, Jefferson City, MO 65103; 314-751-0472.

MONTANA: Division of Family Assistance, Department of Social and Rehabilitation Services, P.O. Box 4210, Helena, MT 59604-4210; 406-444-4546.

NEBRASKA: Public Assistance Unit, Program and Planning Specialist, Department of Social Services, 310 Centennial Mall South, 5th Floor, P.O. Box 95026, Lincoln, NE 65809; 402-471-9172.

NEVADA: LIHEAP Program Manager, Nevada Department of Human Services, Welfare Division, 2527 N. Carson Street, Carson City, NV 89710; 702-687-6919.

NEW HAMPSHIRE: Fuel Assistance Program Manager, Governor's Office of Energy and Community Services, 57 Regional Drive, Concord, NH 03301-8506; 603-271-2611.

NEW JERSEY: Coordinator, Home Energy Assistance Unit, DHS, Division of Economic Assistance, CN 716, Trenton, NJ 08625; 609-588-2488.

NEW MEXICO: Planner Director, Division of Income Support, Department of Human Services, P.O. Box 234B, Pollen Plaza, Santa Fe, NM 87504-2348.

NEW YORK: Director, Bureau of Energy Programs, NY State Dept. of Social Services, 40 N. Pearl Street, Albany, NY 12243-0001; 518-474-9321.

NORTH CAROLINA: Public Assistance Section, Division of Social Services, Department of Human Resources, 325 N. Salisbury Street, Raleigh, NC

27603; 919-733-7831.

NORTH DAKOTA: LIHEAP Coordinator, Energy Assistance and Emergency Services, Department of Human Services, State Capitol Building, 3rd Floor, Bismarck, ND 58505; 701-224-2359.

OHIO: Program Administrator, Home Energy Assistance Program, Ohio Department of Development, P.O. Box 1240,Columbus, OH 43216; 614-644-6858; 800-282-0880 (in Ohio)

OKLAHOMA: Program Supervisor, Division of Family Support Services, Department of Human Services, P.O. Box 25352, Oklahoma City, OK 73125; 405-521-4089.

OREGON: LIHEAP Coordinator, Community Services, Oregon Housing and Community Services, 1600 State Street, Salem, OR 97310-0161; 503-986-2094.

PENNSYLVANIA: LIHEAP Director, Division of Cash Assistance, DPW, Complex 2, Room 224, Willow Oak Building, P.O. Box 2675, Harrisburg, PA 17105; 717-772-6451.

RHODE ISLAND: Manager, Energy Assistance Program, Governor's Office of Housing, Energy and Intergovernmental Relations, 275 Westminster Mall, Providence, RI 02903; 401-277-6920.

SOUTH CAROLINA; Deputy Director for Energy Programs, Division of Economic Opportunity, 1205 Pendleton Street, Columbia, SC 29201; 803-734-0672.

SOUTH DAKOTA: Program Administrator, Office of Energy Assistance, Department of Social Services, 206 West Missouri Avenue, Pierre, SD 57501-4517; 605-773-4131.

TENNESSEE: LIHEAP Coordinator, Department of Human Services, Citizens Plaza Building, 400 Deaderick Street, Nashville, TN 37219; 615-741-6640.

TEXAS: Director, Energy Assistance, Texas Department of Housing and Community Affairs, P.O. Box 13941, Austin, TX 78711-3941; 512-475-3935.

UTAH: Home Energy Assistance Target Program, Office of Family Support Administration, 120 N. 200 West, 3rd Floor, P.O. Box 45000, Salt Lake City, ut 84145-0500; 801-538-4212.

VERMONT: LIHEAP Block Grant Manager, Department of Social Welfare, 103 S. Main Street, Waterbury, VT 05676; 802-241-2994.

VIRGINIA: Energy and Emergency Assistance Unit, Virginia Department of Social Services, Theater Row Building, 730 E. Broad Street, 7th Floor, Richmond, VA 23219-1849; 804-692-1704.

WASHINGTON: EAP/ECIP Coordinator, Department of Community Development, Division of Community Services, 9th and Columbia Building-N/X GH51, Olympia, WA 98504; 206-753-3403.

WEST VIRGINIA: Income Maintenance Bureau, Department of Health and Human Resources, Building 6, Room B-617, State Capitol Complex, Charleston, WV 25305; 304-558-8290.

WISCONSIN: Supervisor, Energy Assistance Program, Division of Economic Support, Department of Health and Social Services, P.O. Box 7935, Madison, WI 53707-7935; 608-266-7601.

WYOMING: Consultant, LIHEAP Program, Department of Family Services, Room #343 Hathaway Building, Cheyenne, WY 82002-0490; 307-777-7747.

Chapter 6

Free Legal Services And Tax Advice

Who needs a lawyer? Federal and state government resources are available to provide expert legal advice and other legal services to older persons free of charge. You can find experts to help you write your will, legal hotlines staffed by attorneys who can offer free advice and referrals to competent attorneys you can afford, tax attorneys to answer the most complex tax questions, and even free help preparing your income tax returns. There's no need to spend your life savings on a legal "dream team" when the government may be able to take care of most of your legal concerns for free.

FREE LEGAL SERVICES

There are more lawyers per person in the United States than in any other country. So finding an attorney is not too difficult. The problem is finding a competent attorney at a price you can afford. To help solve this problem, Uncle Sam created the

Legal Services Corporation (LSC). The LSC funds legal aid offices in all 50 states, Puerto Rico, the Virgin Islands, Guam, and Micronesia. The legal aid programs funded by the LSC provide free legal services to persons with low incomes, including many older persons.

The LSC handles civil (not criminal) cases, such as landlord-tenant issues, credit and utilities disputes, and family issues such as divorce, adoption, and guardianship cases. Generally, there are income and asset guidelines you must meet to qualify for LSC-funded legal services. However, some LSC programs also receive funding through the Older Americans Act (see below) and provide free legal services to people 60 years of age or older, regardless of income or assets.

To locate a LSC-funded office in your area, look in your telephone book under "legal aid" or "legal services", or call the Federal Information Center (see the appendix). For general information and a directory of all LSC programs, you also may contact:

Public Affairs, Legal Services Corporation,
750 First Street NE, 11th Floor,
Washington, DC 20002-4250;
(202) 336-8800.

You also may qualify for free legal services from one of more than 1,000 Legal Aid offices around the country. Legal Aid offices help individuals who cannot afford to hire private attorneys. These offices are staffed by lawyers, paralegals,and law students. All offer free legal services to those who qualify. Funding is provided by a variety of sources, including Federal, state and local governments and private donations. Many law schools across the country conduct clinics in which law students, as part of their training, assist practicing attorneys with these cases.

Generally, Legal Aid offices offer free legal assistance with such problems as landlord-tenant disputes, credit, utilities, family matters (divorce, adoption, etc.), foreclosure, home equity fraud, social security, welfare, unemployment and workers' compensation. Each office determines the kinds of cases to be handled. If the Legal Aid office in your area does not handle your type of case, it should be able to refer you to other local, state or national organizations that can provide advice or help. Check the phone directory to find the Legal Aid office nearest you. You also can get a directory of Legal Aid offices around the country by contacting the

National Legal Aid and Defender Assoc,
1625 K Street, N.W., 8th Floor,
Washington, DC 20006;
202-452-0620.

Free legal services also are available to many older people through the Older Americans Act (OAA). Under Title III of the OAA, each state is required to fund a local Area Agency on Aging (AAA) program that provides free legal help on noncriminal matters to people 60 and over. There are no income guidelines to meet in order to qualify for OAA-funded free legal services, however, priority is generally given to low-income people over 60.

You can locate programs or offices providing free legal help to older persons, by contacting your local or state Agency on Aging (see the appendix). A national directory of OAA legal service providers is available from the American Bar Associations Commission on the Legal Problems of the Elderly. The directory, titled "The Law and Aging Resource Guide", provides a state-by state breakdown of the addresses and phone numbers of each OAA legal service provider. Printed single state profiles are free. The complete guide is available for $20.00 (plus $3.95 shipping and handling). Contact the:

American Bar Association Commission
on the Legal Problems of the Elderly,
740 15th Street NW,
Washington, DC 20005-1009;
(202) 662-8690.

Some states also offer "pro bono" or free legal services to people who are unable to pay for them. State level pro bono services are made possible through the volunteer efforts of lawyers, paralegals, and others associated with the legal profession. Contact your local bar association to find out about pro bono services in your area.

Another potential source of free legal service is Legal Hotlines, available in many states. The hotlines are staffed by attorneys who give advice, send pamphlets, or make referrals. Most hotlines provide legal advice to callers 60 or older free of charge. The following list provides contact information for many of these Legal Hotlines, as well as several state level pro bono services. If your state is not among those listed, contact your State Agency on Aging (see the appendix).

Alaska: Legal Services Corporation, 1016 West Sixth Ave., Suite 200, Anchorage, AK 99501; (907) 272-9431; (800) 478-9431. This is a private, non-profit corporation that provides free civil legal assistance to low-income Alaskans. The program is funded through grants and contracts from federal, state, and local sources.

Arizona: Legal Hotline For The Elderly, Southern Arizona Legal Aid, 160 Alemeda Street, Tucson, AZ 65701; (800) 231-5441; (602) 623-5137. Provides advice and referrals.

Arkansas: UALR School of Law, Little Rock, AR; (501) 376-9263. This pro bono program serves 67 counties .

California: Senior Legal Hotline, Legal Services of Northern California, 1004 18th Street, Sacramento, CA 95814; (800) 222-1753; (916) 442-1212.

District of Columbia: Legal Council For The Elderly, 601 E. Street NW, Building A, Fourth Floor, Washington, DC 20049; (202) 434-2120. Provides advice and referrals. Services are offered on a reduced-fee scale based on age and income. Also provides publications, including "Finding Legal Help:

An Older Person's Guide"; and "Effective Counseling of Older Clients".

Florida: Legal Hotline For Older Floridians, 3000 Biscayne Blvd., 4th Floor, P.O. Box 370705, Miami, FL 33137; (800) 262-5997; (306) 576-5997.

Kansas: Elder Law Hotline, 1-888-353-5337. In operation since July of 1996, this hotline provides Kansans age 60 or older toll-free access to a lawyer to answer their legal questions. Private volunteer lawyers, recruited through the Kansas Bar Association, provide free advice and referrals to callers on a full range of civil legal issues.

Maine: Legal Services For The Elderly, P.O. Box 2723, 712 Winthrop Street, Augusta, ME 04338; (800) 750-5353; (602) 623-1797 (in Augusta). LSE provides legal services statewide to people aged 60 and over free of charge.

Michigan: Senior Alliance Inc., 3850 Second Street, Suite 160, Wayne, MI 46184; (800) 347-LAWS (in MI); (517) 372-5959. Provides advice and referrals over the phone. Will also provide a list of attorneys that will work pro bono for people 60 or older.

New Mexico: Lawyer Referral Services For The Elderly, P.O. Box 25883, Albuquerque, NM 87125; (800) 876-6657; (505) 842-6252. Provides advice and referrals.

Ohio: ProSeniors Inc., 105 E. Fourth Street, Suite 1715, Cincinnati, OH 45202-4008; (800) 488-6070; (513) 621-8721. Provides advice and referrals over the telephone.

Pennsylvania: Legal Hotline For Older Americans, P.O. Box 2318, Pittsburgh, PA 15222; (800) 262-5297; (412) 261-5297. A phone service providing legal information, advice and referral for persons 60 and over.

Neighborhood Legal Services Association, Elderly Law Project, 9278 Penn Avenue, Pittsburgh, PA 15222; (412) 255-6700. A private, non-profit program that provides free legal services focusing on people 60 and over.

Rhode Island: Legal Information and Referral Service for the Elderly, 115 Cedar Street, Providence, RI 02903; (401) 521-5040. This is a public service program of the Rhode Island Bar Association designed to help persons 60 and older obtain legal information and advice. Persons 60 and older may qualify for a free 30 minute consultation with a private attorney.

Tennessee: Legal Aid Society and Nashville Bar Pro Bono Service, 800 Stahlman Building, Nashville, TN 37201; (615) 244-6601. This charitable, non-profit organization provides legal services to income-eligible clients and elderly people. The organization deals with civil cases that are non-fee generating only.

Texas: Legal Hotline For Older Texans, State Bar of Texas, P.O. Box 12487, Austin, TX 78711-2487; (800) 622-2520; (512)463-1463. Provides legal advice and referrals.

FREE TAX ADVICE

Why pay an accountant hundreds of dollars to deal with your taxes when the IRS will provide all the tax information and advice you need for free? Often, your tax questions can be answered by reading tax forms and related publications, which are available for free from the IRS. For example, IRS Publication 554, "Tax Information For Older Americans" provides information about filing requirements, taxable and nontaxable income, retirement plans and pensions, social security benefits, credit for the elderly, earned income credit, and more. Publication 554 and many others are available free upon request by calling the IRS at 1-800-829-3676.

If you can't find answers to your tax questions by reading the tax form instructions or one of the IRS publications, you can call the IRS at 1-800-829-1040 for assistance. You also can visit your local IRS office with questions about your tax account, tax rules, or for general information about IRS procedures and services. IRS representatives can provide you with accurate and complete answers to all your tax questions. They also can refer you to government tax attorneys who can provide advice and answer specific questions about complicated tax matters. For example, government tax attorneys are available to answer your questions regarding retirement and pension plan matters. These tax specialists are available Monday through Thursday from 1:30 to 4 p.m. at the:

> **Employee Plans Technical**
> and Actuarial Div, Internal Revenue Service,
> U.S. Department of the Treasury,
> Room 6550, 1111 Constitution Avenue, NW,
> Washington, DC 20224;
> (202) 622-6074 or 6075.

Before you hand over your wallet to an accountant, it might be a good idea to contact the IRS and find out what free help is available.

SAVE $50 OFF YOUR TAXES EVERY YEAR

If you've been paying $50 or more every year for tax preparation services, consider this: your friends at the IRS will help you prepare your tax return for free! That's right, many IRS programs offer free assistance with tax return preparation or tax counseling using volunteers trained by the IRS.

Tax Counseling for the Elderly (TCE) is designed primarily for persons 60 years of age or older. IRS-trained volunteers from non-profit organizations provide free tax counseling and basic income tax return preparation. Typically, these volunteers are retired individuals who will travel to taxpayers' homes, if they are unable to come to a local TCE site. Call your local IRS office, listed in your local telephone directory, for more information on the TCE program and to find locations of TCE assistance in your area. You also may call the IRS Information Line at 1-800-829-1040 for information on the TCE program.

Another program, Volunteer Income Tax Assistance Program (VITA), provides free tax help to people with low and fixed income who can't afford paid professional assistance. IRS-trained VITA volunteers provide free tax assistance such as basic tax return preparation, including Forms 1040, 1040A, 1040EZ, and some basic schedules. VITA sites are generally located at community locations, such as libraries, schools, shopping malls, houses of worship, community centers, and other convenient locations.

The Community Outreach Tax Education Program offers free tax assistance to groups of people with common tax concerns, such as retirees, farmers and small business owners. The program offers two kinds of assistance. One provides line-by-line self-help tax return preparation for people who want to prepare their own returns. The other provides free tax seminars on various tax topics. Outreach sessions may be co-sponsored by community organizations and other government agencies.

For additional information about IRS tax return assistance programs, contact your local IRS office. Look in the phone book under "United States Government, Internal Revenue Service" or contact the office nearest you from the following list. If your local calling area is not listed, phone the IRS Information Line at (800) 829-1040.

California: Oakland— 510-839-1040

Colorado: Denver— 303-825-7041

Florida: Jacksonville— 904-354-1760

Georgia: Atlanta— 404-522-0050

Maryland: Baltimore— 410-962-2590

Massachusetts: Boston— 617-536-1040

Missouri: St. Louis— 314-342-1040

New York: Buffalo— 716-685-5432

Ohio: Cincinnati— 513-621-6281;
Cleveland— 216-522-3000

Oregon: Portland— 503-221-3960

Pennsylvania:
Philadelphia— 215-574-9900;
Pittsburgh— 412-281-0112

Tennessee: Nashville—615-834-9005

Texas: Dallas— 214-742-2440;
Houston—713-541-0440

Virginia: Richmond— 804-698-5000

Washington: Seattle— 206-442-1040.

THIS LITTLE-KNOWN BRANCH OF GOVERNMENT WILL HELP YOU WRITE YOUR WILL FREE OF CHARGE

The best way to ensure that your assets will be distributed after your death according to your wishes is to prepare a will. But even though wills are generally simple to create, nearly half of all Americans die without one. In that event, the state will take over and dispose of your estate. In many cases, people simply don't want to think about the eventuality of death. For others, the expense involved in hiring an attorney to help draw up a will, or purchasing "how to" books or software is prohibitive. Whatever the reason, no adult should put off writing a will.

If you need help writing your will, you may be able to enlist the services of your county Cooperative Extension office. Many local Extension services offer free will-writing assistance in the form of instructional pamphlets and other printed material. Some offices even offer classes and general forms you need to create a will. These services generally are available free of charge, allowing you to save your money for your grandkids.

Contact your local Cooperative Extension office (listed in your phone book) to find out what services are available locally, or contact your State Cooperative Extension Office, listed below.

State Cooperative Extension Offices

ALABAMA: Stephen B. Jones, Director,

Alabama Cooperative Extension System, 109 A Duncan Hall, Auburn University, Auburn, AL 36849-5612; (334) 844-4444

Administrator, Alabama Cooperative Extension Service, P.O. Box 222, Normal, AL 35762; (205) 851-5710.

Director, Cooperative Extension Program, Department of Agriculture, Tuskegee University, 207 N. Main Street, Suite 400, Tuskegee, AL 36083-1731; (205) 727-8806.

ALASKA: Hollis D. Hall, Director, Alaska Cooperative Extension, University of Alaska Fairbanks, P.O. Box 756180, Fairbanks, AK 99775-1680; (907) 474-7246.

ARIZONA: Director, Cooperative Extension Office, University of Arizona, Forbes 301, Tucson, AZ 85721; (602) 621-7205.

ARKANSAS: Director Cooperative Extension Service, P.O. Box 391, Little Rock, AR 72203; (501) 671-2000.

CALIFORNIA: University of California, Division of Agriculture And Natural Resources, 300 Lakeside Drive, 6th Floor, Oakland, CA 94612-3560; (510) 987-0060.

COLORADO: Director, Colorado State University, Cooperative Extension, 1 Administrative Building, Fort Collins, CO 80503; (303) 491-6281.

CONNECTICUT: Director, Cooperative Extension System, University of Connecticut, 1376 Storrs Road, Storrs, CT 06269-4036; (203) 486-4125.

DELAWARE: Director, Cooperative Extension, 131 Townsend Hall, University of Delaware, Newark, DE 19717-1303; (302) 831-2504

Delaware State College, Cooperative Extension Service, 1200 N. DuPont Hwy., Dover, DE 19901; (302) 739-5157.

DISTRICT OF COLUMBIA: Cooperative Extension Service, University of the District of Columbia, 901 Newton Street, NE, Washington, DC 20001; (202) 576-6993.

FLORIDA: Director, Florida Cooperative Extension Service, P.O. Box 110210, University of Florida, Gainesville, FL 32611-0210.

Director, Cooperative Extension Service, 215 Perry Paige Building, Florida A&M University, Tallahassee, FL 32307; (904) 599-3546.

GEORGIA: Director, Cooperative Extension Service, University of Georgia, 1111 Conner Hall, Athens, GA 30602; (706) 542-3824.

Director, Cooperative Extension Service, P.O. Box 4061, Fort Valley State College, Fort Valley, GA 31030; (912) 825-6269.

HAWAII: Director, Cooperative Extension Service, 3050 Maile Way, Honolulu, HI 96822; (808) 956-8397.

IDAHO: Dr. Leroy D. Luft, Director Cooperative Extension System, AG Sciences Building, Room 51, College of Agriculture, University of Idaho, Moscow, ID 83844-2338; (208) 885-6639.

ILLINOIS: Director, University of Illinois Cooperative Extension Service, 122 Mumford Hall, 1301 W. Gregory Drive, Urbana, IL 61801; (217) 333-2660.

INDIANA: Director, 1140 AGAD, Cooperative Extension Service Administration, Purdue University, West Lafayette, IN 47907-1140; (317) 494-8489.

IOWA: Director, Cooperative Extension Service, 315 Boardshear, Iowa State University, Ames, IA 50011; (515) 294-9434.

KANSAS: Richard D. Wooten, Associate Director, Cooperative Extension Service, Kansas State University, 123 Umberger Hall, Manhattan, KS 66506-3401; (913) 532-5820.

KENTUCKY: Director, Cooperative Extension Service, 310 W.P. Garrigus Building, University of Kentucky, Lexington, KY 40546; (606) 257-1846. Director, Kentucky State University Cooperative Extension Program, Frankfort, KY 40601; (502) 227-5905.

LOUISIANA: Director Cooperative Extension Service, Louisiana State University, P.O. Box 25100, Baton Rouge, LA 70894-5100; (504) 388-4141.

Cooperative Extension Program, Southern University and A&M College, P.O. Box 10010, Baton Rouge, LA 70813; (504) 771-2242.

MAINE: Director, Cooperative Extension Service, University of Maine, 5741 Libby Hall, Room 102, Orono, ME 04469-5741; (207) 581-3188.

MARYLAND: Regional Directors Office, Cooperative Extension Service, Room 2120, Simons Hall, University of Maryland, College Park, MD 20742; (301) 405-2907.

Cooperative Extension Service, UMES, Princess Anne, MD 21853; (410) 651-6206.

MASSACHUSETTS: Director, 210C Stockbridge Hall, University of Massachusetts, Amherst, MA 01003; (413)545-4800.

MICHIGAN: Director, Michigan State University Extension, Room 108, Agriculture Hall, Michigan State University, East Lansing, MI 48824; (517) 355-2308.

MINNESOTA: Director, Minnesota Extension Service, University of Minnesota, 240 Coffey Hall, 1420 Eckles Avenue, St. Paul, MN 55108; (612) 625-3797.

MISSISSIPPI: Director, Cooperative Extension Service, Mississippi State University, P.O. Box 9601, Mississippi State, MS 39762; (601) 325-3034.

Dean, P.O. Box 690, Alcorn Cooperative Extension Program, Lorman, MS 39096; (601) 877-6128.

MISSOURI: Director, Cooperative Extension Service, University of Missouri, 309 University Hall, Columbia, MO 65211; (314) 882-7754..

Director, Cooperative Extension Service, Lincoln University, 110A Allen Hall, P.O. Box 29, Jefferson City, MO 65102-0029; (314) 681-5550.

MONTANA: Andrea Pagenkopf, Vice Provost for Outreach and Director of Extension, 212 Montana Hall, Montana State University, Bozeman, MT 59717; (406) 994-4371.

NEBRASKA: Kenneth R. Bolen, Director, Cooperative Extension Division, 211 Agricultural Hall, University of Nebraska-Lincoln, Lincoln, NE 68583-0703; (402) 472-2966.

NEVADA: Director, Nevada Cooperative Extension, University of Nevada, Reno, Mail Stop 189, Reno, NV 89557-0106; (702) 784-1614.

NEW HAMPSHIRE: Director, University of New Hampshire Cooperative Extension, 59 College Road, Taylor Hall, Durham, NH 03824; (603) 862-1520.

NEW JERSEY: Director, Rutgers Cooperative Extension, P.O. Box 231, New Brunswick, NJ 08903; (908) 932-9306.

NEW MEXICO: Cooperative Extension, New Mexico State University, Box 3AE, Las Cruces, NM 88003; (505) 646-3016.

NEW YORK: Director, Cornell Cooperative Extension, 276 Roberts Hall, Ithaca, NY 14853; (607) 255-2237.

NORTH CAROLINA: Director, Cooperative Extension Service, North Carolina State University, Box 7602, Raleigh, NC 27695; (919) 515-2811.

Director, Cooperative Extension Program, North Carolina A & T State University, P.O. Box 21928, Greensboro, NC 27420-1928; (910) 334-7956.

NORTH DAKOTA: Dr. Sharon Anderson, Director, North Dakota State University Extension Service, Morrill 315, NDSU, Fargo, ND 58105; (701) 231-8944.

OHIO: Director, Ohio State University Extension, 2120 Fife Road, Agriculture Administration Building, Columbus, OH 43210; (614) 292-6181.

OKLAHOMA :Director,Oklahoma Cooperative Ext. Service, Oklahoma St.Univ., 139 Agriculture Hall, Stillwater, OK 74078; (405) 744-5398.

Director, Cooperative Research and Extension, P.O. Box 730, Langston University, Langston, OK 73050; (405) 466-3836.

OREGON: Director, Oregon State Extension Service Administration, Oregon State University, Ballard Extension Hall #101, Corvallis, OR 97331-3606; (503) 737-2711.

PENNSYLVANIA: Director, Pennsylvania State University, Room 217, A.G. Administration, University Park, PA 16802; (814) 863-0331.

RHODE ISLAND: Director, Cooperative Extension Education Center, University of Rhode Island, East Alumni Avenue, Kingston, RI 02881-0804; (401) 792-2900.

SOUTH CAROLINA: Director, Clemson University Cooperative Extension Service, P.O. Box 995, Pickens, SC 29671; (803) 868-2810.

Director, Cooperative Extension Service, P.O. Box 7265, South Carolina State University, Orangeburg, SC 29117; (803) 536-8928.

SOUTH DAKOTA: Director, South Dakota State University Cooperative Extension, Box 2270D, AG Hall 154, Brookings, SD 57007; (605) 688-4792.

TENNESSEE: Agricultural Extension Service, University of Tennessee, P.O. Box 1071, Knoxville, TN 37901-1071; (615) 974-7114.

Extension Leader, Davidson County Agricultural Service, Tennessee State University, 800 Second Ave. N., Suite 3, Nashville, TN 37201-1084; (615) 254-8734.

TEXAS: Director, Texas Agricultural Extension Service, Texas A&M University, College Station, TX 77843; (409) 845-7967.

Director, Cooperative Extension Program, P.O. Box Drawer-B, Prairie View, TX 77446-2867; (409) 857-2023.

UTAH: Vice President for Extension and Continuing Education, Utah State University, Logan, UT 84322-4900; (801) 750-2200.

VERMONT: Dean, Division of Agriculture, Natural Resources and Extension, University of Vermont, 601 Main, Burlington, VT 05401-3439; (802) 656-2990.

VIRGINIA: Director, Virginia Cooperative Extension, Virginia Tech, Blacksburg, VA 24061-0402; (703) 231-5299.

Director, Cooperative Extension, Virginia State Univ., Petersburg, VA 23806; (804) 524-5961.

WASHINGTON: WSU Cooperative Extension, College of Agriculture and Home Economics, 411 Hulbert, Washington State University, Pullman, WA 99164-6230; (509) 335-2811.

WEST VIRGINIA: Robert H. Maxwell, Director, Cooperative Extension Service, Room 817 Knapp Hall, P.O. Box 6031, West Virginia University, Morgantown, WV 26506-6031; (304) 293-5691.

WISCONSIN: Carl O'Conner, Director, University of Wisconsin Cooperative Extension, 432 N. Lake Street, Room 601 Extension Building, Madison, WI 53706; (608) 263-5110.

WYOMING: Director, University of Wyoming Cooperative Extension Service, P.O. Box 3354, Laramie, WY 82071-3354; (307) 766-5124.

NOTES

Chapter 7

Miscellaneous Free Cash And Benefits

This Chapter of "Free Cash & Benefits For 50 Or Over" features a variety of government resources which provide everything from free cash to free cooking classes. There's something for everyone!

KNOCK $84 OFF YOUR PHONE BILL EVERY YEAR

You may be able to knock off up to $7 a month of your phone bill courtesy of the Federal Communications Commission'S (FCC) Lifeline Program. Under the federal Lifeline program, subscribers who satisfy a state-determined income requirement can reduce their monthly phone bills by waiving or reducing the line charge. And, those savings are available with no reduction in current equipment or service.

Income requirements vary from state to state, with some states imposing an age requirement as well. For example, to be eligible for the Lifeline program in Colorado (also known as the Colorado Low-Income Telephone Assistance Fund), a subscriber must receive Old Age Pension, Aid to the Blind, Aid to the Needy Disabled, or Supplemental Security Income. The Colorado Department of Social Services determines eligibility in that state. Participants are eligible to receive a 25% discount on basic local telephone service. In California, Lifeline telephone service is intended to ensure that every household that wishes to can have basic telephone services. Subscribers pay no FCC access charge, which amounts to a savings of $3.50 per month. Eligibility for the California program is based on household size and income.

Currently, most states and the District of Columbia have federally approved Lifeline programs. For more information about the program and/or to find out if Lifeline assistance is available in your area, contact your local telephone company. For general information about the program, you also can contact:

Common Carrier, Federal Communications
Commission, 1919 M Street, NW,
Washington, DC 20554; (202) 418-0940.

The following state agencies oversee state-level Lifeline and Link-Up programs. To contact the agency in your state, look in your telephone directory under "state government". If your state is not among those listed, contact th above address.

Alabama: Public Service Commission, P.O. Box 991, Montgomery, AL 36101-0991; (800) 392-8050. To be eligible, participants must be recipients of Supplemental Security Income (SSI), Aid For Dependent Children (AFDC), or Food Stamps.

Arizona: Corporation Commission, 1200 West Washington Street, Phoenix, AZ 85007; (800) 222-7000. To be eligible for Lifeline assistance, income must be below 150% of the poverty level; Link Up assistance eligibility requirements include an income at or below poverty level and a participant in the Senior Telephone Discount Program.

Arkansas: Public Service Commission, P.O. Box 400, Little Rock, AR 72203-0400; (501) 682-1453. Participants must be recipients of SSI, AFDC, HEAP, Food Stamps, Medicaid, or Subsidized housing. The Arkansas Department of Human Services determines eligibility.

California: Public Utilities Commission, 505 Van Ness Avenue, Room 5218, San Francisco 94102; (415) 703-3703. Eligibility for this program is based on household size and income.

Colorado: Public Utilities Commission, 1580 Logan Street, Office Level 2, Denver, CO 80203; (800) 888-0170. To be eligible for the Colorado Low-Income Telephone Assistance Fund, a person must receive Old Age Pension, SSI, Aid to the Blind, or Aid to the Needy Disabled. The Colorado Department of Social Services determines eligibility.

Connecticut: Department of Utility Control, 10 Franklin Square, New Britain, CT 06051; (800) 382-4586. Participants must be eligible for any low-income assistance administered by the Connecticut Department of Human Resources or Connecticut Department of Income Maintenance or SSI.

District of Columbia: Public Service Commission, 450 Fifth Street, N.W., Suite 800, Washington, DC 20001; (202) 626-5120. Eligibility is determined by the District of Columbia Energy Office.

Florida: Public Service Commission, 2540 Shumard Oak Boulevard, Tallahassee, FL 32399-0850; (800) 342-3552. To receive this assistance, you must be a recipient of Food Stamps or Medicaid. Eligibility is determined by the Florida Department of Health and Rehabilitative Services.

Georgia: Public Service Commission, 244 Washington Street, SW, Atlanta, GA 30334; (800) 282-5813, Must be a recipient of SSI, AFDC, and/or Food Stamps. Eligibility is determined by the Georgia Department of Human Services.

Hawaii: Public Utilities Commission, 465 South King Street, Room 103, Honolulu, HI 96813; (808) 586-2020. Participants must be at least 60 years old or handicapped with an income below poverty. Eligibility is determined by the Hawaiian Telephone Company.

Idaho: Public Utilities Commission, P.O. Box 83720, Boise, ID 83720-0074; (800) 377-3529. Participants must receive AFDC, Food Stamps, Aid to the Aged, Blind and Disabled, or Medical Assistance.

Illinois: Commerce Commission, 527 East Capitol Avenue, P.O. Box 19280, Springfield, IL 62794-9280; (217) 782-7907. Participants must receive public assistance in programs administered by the Illinois Department of Public Aid. Eligibility is determined by the Illinois Department of Public Aid.

Indiana: Utility Regulatory Commission, 302 West Washington Street, Indianapolis, IN 46204; (800) 851-4268. Participants must receive SSI, AFDC, HEAP, Medicaid, or Food Stamps. Eligibility is determined by local exchange companies.

Iowa: State Utilities Board, Lucas State Office Building, 5th Floor, Des Moines, IA 50319; (515) 281-5979. Eligible participants must receive SSI, AFDC, LIHEAP, or Food Stamps. Eligibility is determined by local exchange companies.

Kansas: Corporation Commission, 1500 SW Arrowhead Road, Topeka, KS 66604-4027; (800) 662-0027. Participants must be recipients of SSI, AFDC, Food Stamps, Medicaid, or General Assistance. Eligibility is determined by local exchange companies.

Kentucky: Public Service Commission, 730 Schenkel Lane, P.O. Box 615, Frankfort, KY 40602; (502) 564-3940. Participants must receive SSI, AFDC,

Food Stamps, or Medical Assistance. Eligibility is determined by the Cabinet for Human Services.

Louisiana: Public Service Commission, P.O. Box 91154, Baton Rouge, LA 79821-9154; (800) 256-2413. Participants must receive SSI, AFDC, or Food Stamps.

Maine: Public Utilities Commission, 242 State Street, Augusta, ME 04333; (800) 452-4699. Participants must receive SSI, AFDC, HEAP, Medicaid, or Food Stamps. Eligibility is determined by the Maine Department of Human Services.

Maryland: Public Service Commission, 6 St. Paul Street, 16th Floor, Baltimore, MD 21202; (800) 492-0474.Participants must receive General Assistance. Eligibility is determined by the Maryland Department of Human Resources.

Massachusetts: Department of Public Utilities, 100 Cambridge Street, Boston, MA 02202; (617) 727-3500. Must be a recipient of SSI, AFDC, General Public Welfare, Food Stamps, Medicaid, and Fuel Assistance. Eligibility is determined by the Department of Public Welfare and/or Office of Fuel Assistance.

Michigan: Public Service Commission, 6545 Mercantile Way, P.O. Box 30221, Lansing, MI; (800) 292-9555. Participants' income must be at or below 130% of the poverty level. Eligibility is determined by the Michigan Department of Social Services to the Aging.

Minnesota: Public Utilities Commission, 121 Seventh Place East, St. Paul, MN 55101-2147; (800) 657-3782. Participants must be at least 65 years old or have an income level which meets state poverty levels. Eligibility is determined by the Minnesota Department of Human Services.

Missouri: Public Service Commission, P.O. Box 360, Jefferson City, MO 65102; (800) 392-4211. Participants must receive Medicaid. Eligibility is determined by the Missouri Department of Social Services.

Montana: Public Service Commission, 1701 Prospect Avenue, P.O. Box 202601, Helena, MT 59620-2601; (800) 646-6150. Participants must receive SSI, AFDC, or Medicaid.

Nebraska: Public Service Commission, 300 The Atrium, 1200 "N" Street, Lincoln, NE 68509; (800) 526-0017. Participants must receive SSI, AFDC, Energy Assistance, Food Stamps, Medicaid, or Aid to the Aged, Blind or Disabled. Eligibility is determined by the Nebraska Department of Social Services or Food Stamp program.

Nevada: Public Service Commission, 555 East Washington Avenue, Las Vegas, NV 89101; (800) 992-0900. Participants must receive SSI, AFDC, Energy Assistance, Food Stamps, Indian General Assistance, Commodity Foods, or VA Improved Pension. Eligibility is determined by proof of enrollment in the listed assistance programs.

New Hampshire: Public Utilities Commission, 8 Old Suncock Road, Concord, NH 03301; (800) 852-3793. Participants must receive SSI, AFDC, Food Stamps, Fuel Assistance, Old Age Assistance, Aid To Permanently/Totally Disabled, Women, Infants and Children Feeding Program, Welfare, Title XX, or Subsidized Housing.

New Jersey: Public Service Commission, Two Gateway Center, Newark, NJ 07102; (800) 621-0241. To be eligible, participants must receive SSI, AFDC, HEAP, Pharmaceutical Assistance to the Aged, or Welfare. Eligibility is determined by local exchange companies.

New York: Public Service Commission, 3 Empire State Plaza, Albany, NY 12223; (518) 474-2530. Must receive SSI, AFDC, Food Stamps, Medicaid, or Home Relief. Eligibility is determined by the Administering Agency.

North Carolina: Utilities Commission, P.O. Box 29510, Raleigh, NC 27626-0510; (919) 733-4249. Must receive SSI or AFDC. Eligibility is determined by the North Carolina Department of Human Resources.

North Dakota: Public Service Commission, State Capitol, 12th Floor, Bismarck, ND 58505-0480; (701) 328-2400. Participants must receive Food Stamps, Fuel Assistance, AFDC, or Medical Assistance. Eligibility is determined by County Social Service Boards.

Ohio: Public Utilities Commission, 180 East Broad Street, Columbus, OH 43215-3793; (614) 466-3292. Participants must receive HEAP, Ohio Energy Credits Program, SSI, AFDC, and Medicaid. Eligibility is determined by local exchange companies.

Oklahoma: Corporate Commission, Jim Thorpe Office Commission, 2101 North Lincoln Boulevard, Oklahoma City, OK 73105; (800) 522-8154. To be eligible, persons must receive aid from state low income programs. Eligibility is determined by the Oklahoma Department of Human Services.

Oregon: Public Utilities Commission, 550 Capitol St. NE, Salem, OR 97310-1380; (800) 848-4442. Participants must be receiving Food Stamps, Medicaid or SSI. Eligibility is determined by the Oregon Department of Human Resources.

Pennsylvania: Public Utilities Commission, P.O. Box 3265, Harrisburg, PA 17105; (800) 782-1110. Must receive SSI, AFDC, Food Stamps, or General Assistance. Eligibility is determined by the Pennsylvania Department of Public Welfare.

Rhode Island: Public Utilities Commission, 100 Orange Street, Providence, RI 02903; (800) 341-1000. Participants must receive SSI, AFDC, General Assistance, or Medical Assistance. Eligibility is determined by the Rhode Island Department of Human Services.

South Carolina: Public Utilities Commission, P.O. Box Drawer 11649, Columbia, SC 29211; (800)

922-1531. Must receive AFDC, Food Stamps, Medicaid, or Temporary Emergency Food Assistance. Eligibility is determined by local exchange companies.

Tennessee: Public Service Commission, 460 James Robertson Parkway, Nashville, TN 37243-0505; (800) 342-8359. Participants must receive SSI, AFDC, Medicaid, or Food Stamps.

Texas: Public Utilities Commission, 7800 Shoal Creek Boulevard, Austin, TX 78757; (512) 458-0100. Must be eligible for SSI, AFDC, LIHEAP, Food Stamps, Medicaid, Medical Assistance, or Maternal Health Program. Eligibility is determined by local exchange companies.

Utah: Public Service Commission, 160 East 300 South Street, Salt Lake City, UT 84111; (801) 530-6716. Participants must self-certify that they are currently eligible for public assistance under AFDC, Emergency Work Programs, Food Stamps, General Assistance, Home Energy Assistance Target Programs, Medical Assistance, Refugee Assistance, or SSI.

Vermont: Public Service Board, 112 State Street, Montpelier, VT 05620-2701; (802) 828-2358. Must receive SSI, AFDC, Food Stamps, Medicaid, or Fuel Assistance. Eligibility is determined by the Vermont Department of Social Welfare.

Virginia: Corporation Commission, P.O. Box 1197, Richmond, VA 23209; (800) 552-7945.

Participants must be recipients of Virginia Universal Service Plan. Eligibility is determined by the Virginia Department of Medical Assistance Services.

Washington: Utilities and Transportation Commission, P.O. Box 47250, Olympia, WA 98504-7250; (800) 562-6150. Must receive SSI, AFDC, Food Stamps, Refugee Assistance, Chore Services, or Community Options Program Entry System. Eligibility is determined by the Washington Department of Social and Health Services.

West Virginia: Public Service Commission, P.O. Box 812, Charleston, WV 25323; (800) 344-5113. Must be disabled or at least 60 years old and receive SSI, AFDC, or Food Stamps or is eligible for SSI. Eligibility is determined by the West Virginia Department of Human Services.

Wyoming: Public Services Commission, 700 West 21st Street, Cheyenne, WY 82002; (800) 877-9965. Must receive SSI, AFDC, LIHEAP, or Food Stamps. Eligibility is determined by the Wyoming Department of Health and Social Services.

FREE COOKING CLASSES FOR SENIORS

You don't have to be a master chef to prepare a good meal. You don't even have to enjoy cooking. The most important thing is cooking nutritious, healthful meals. Whether you like to cook for fun or for survival, your local Cooperative Extension Office can help you get the most of every meal. Most county Cooperative Extension offices offer free cooking classes, informational pamphlets and other material dealing with good nutrition and meal preparation. Your local office may even have "how to" videos on cooking.

To find out what your local Cooperative Extension Office has to offer, look in the phone book under "local government" for the office nearest you, or contact the main state office (see state listings in chapter 6 "Free Legal Services and Tax Advice"). For general information about the Cooperative Extension Service and its programs, contact:

Cooperative State Research Education and Extension Service, U.S. Department of Agriculture, Washington, DC 20250-0900; (202) 720-3029; Fax: (202)690-0289; Internet: http://www.reeusda.gov/new/csrees.htm.

SAVE HUNDREDS OF DOLLARS EACH YEAR ON THEATRE AND SYMPHONY TICKETS

You don't have to spend another weekend in front of the TV just because you're low on cash. Your senior status can get you discounts on admission to a variety of cultural events. Would you like to take in a performance by a symphony orchestra? How about tickets to the theatre? Most performing arts organizations, including symphony orchestras, theatres, and ballets offer discounted tickets for senior citizens. You could end up paying half price admission to a number of cultural events.

The following list is an example of nonprofit cultural groups and other organizations across the country that provide senior discounts on admission. The organizations are typical of those that receive funding from the National Endowment For the Arts or state arts agencies.

Appalshop, Inc., 306 Madison Street, Whitesburg, KY 41858; (606) 633-0108. Provides programs that promote indigenous traditional Appalachian culture. Many of Appalshop's programs are oriented toward older persons.

Arkansas Symphony Orchestra, P.O. Box 7328, Little Rock, AR 72217; (501) 666-1761; Fax: (501) 666-3193. Provides discounted tickets to senior citizens 62 and over.

Boston-Fenway, Inc., Elder Arts Project, 590 Huntington Ave., Boston, MA 02115; (617) 445-0047. This program provides older adults with complimentary tickets and transportation to selected performances of the Boston Symphony Orchestra, Huntington Theatre, and other cultural events in Massachusetts.

The Cornerstone Theatre Company, 1653 18th Street, #6, Santa Monica, CA 90404.

Detroit Symphony Orchestra, 3711 Woodward Ave., Detroit, MI 48201; (313) 833-3700. Senior citizens, 60 and over, may purchase unsold "rush" tickets for a same day performance at 50% off the regular full price.

Greensboro Symphony Society, P.O. Box 20303, Greensboro, NC 27420; (910) 333-7490. Provides discounted tickets to senior citizens.

Performance Space 122, 150 1st Avenue, New York, NY 10036; (212) 477-5288. Provides senior citizen discounts on dance tickets for selected events.

Robert W. Woodruff Arts Center, Inc., 1280 Peachtree Street, NE, Atlanta, GA 30309; (404) 733-4200. Provides discounted theatre tickets for persons 65 and older.

Theatre Development Fund, 1501 Broadway Avenue, New York, NY 10036; (212) 221-0013. Provides discounted theatre and dance tickets for senior citizens, and nonprofit community and senior citizen centers.

Besides discounted tickets, some symphony orchestras offer other special programs to senior citizens, including complimentary tickets to symphonies. The following orchesteral groups offer such programs:

Augusta Symphony, Augusta, GA

Boston Symphony Orchestra, Boston, MA

Eastern Connecticut Symphony, New London, CT

Fort Wayne Philharmonic Orchestra, Fort Wayne, IN

Greensboro Symphony Society,
Greensboro, NC

Jacksonville Symphony Association,
Jacksonville, FL

Kansas City Symphony, Kansas City, MO

Louisville Orchestra, Louisville, KY

Memphis Orchestral Society, Memphis, TN

Missouri Symphony Society, Columbia, MO

Mississippi Orchestra Association in
Jackson, MS

Modesto Symphony Orchestra,
Modesto, CA

Philharmonic Symphony Society,
New York City, NY

Santa Barbara Symphony Orchestra
Association, Santa Barbara, CA

Stamford Symphony Orchestra,
Stamford CT

Tucson Symphony Society, Tucson, AZ

To find out what senior discount programs are available in your area, contact your state arts agency (see chapter 1, "Free Cash From The Government") or your state Department of Aging (see the Appendix).

GET UP TO $3,000 FOR HELPING CHILDREN

Now that you're retired, you may have more free time on your hands than you know what to do with. You also may be short of spending cash. If that's the case, there's a government program that will keep you busy and provide a modest income, as well. The National Senior Service Corps' Foster Grandparents Program (FGP) can be the answer to both your problems.

The Foster Grandparent Program provides part-time volunteer service opportunities for low-income persons, age 60 and over. As a Foster Grandparent, you'll be involved in the challenging and rewarding work of helping special and exceptional needs children on a one-to-one basis. Foster Grandparents also work with youth needing literacy assistance and with teen parents and their children. Other volunteer Foster Grandparents serve as mentors to youth.

Examples of the activities Foster Grandparents undertake include: working in hospitals for the mentally retarded, emotionally disturbed or physically handicapped, or in homes for abused, disturbed, or physically handicapped, or in homes for abused children.

To qualify for the Foster Grandparent Program, you must be at least 60 years old, and willing to work 20 hours a week. You also must meet income eligibility guidelines established for your state. If accepted into the Foster Grandparent Program, you'll receive 40 hours of pre-service orientation and training, plus 4 hours of in-service training monthly from your sponsoring agency. You'll also receive a modest tax-free allowance (on average, around $3,000), reimbursement for transportation, accident and liability insurance while on duty, and an annual physical exam.

If you have the time, and are capable and willing to help needy children, you can contact the:

Foster Grandparent Program,
Corporation For National Service,
1201 New York Avenue, NW,
Washington, DC 20525;
(202) 606-5000; (800) 424-8867.

EASE THE BURDEN OF CARING FOR ELDERLY PARENTS WITH THIS FREE KIT

Caring for elderly parents or a seriously ill spouse can place a great demand on your time and finances. Few people are fully prepared for all the aspects such caregiving entails. Meal preparation, personal care, paying bills, and transportation are some of the things involved with caregiving for elderly dependents.

Besides those concerns, many caregivers also must work full-time jobs. Often the time and stress involved with eldercare can lead to problems at work. The Family and Medical Leave Act provides some relief, allowing employees to take uo to 12 weeks of unpaid leave each year to care for a spouse or parent. To take advantage of this legislation, an employee must have been on the job for one year, and employers must have at least 50 employees.

To make things easier, the Work And Family Clearinghouse offers a free "Work and Family Resources Kit". The Kit provides information about caregiving and options available. The Kit also provides information about family and medical leave questions. To get a free Work and Family Resource Kit and more information, contact the:

Work and Family Clearinghouse,
U.S. Department of Labor, Women's Bureau,
200 Constitution Avenue, NW,
Washington, DC 20210; (800) 827-5335.

FREE FOOD!

If you're at least 60 years old, you may be able to take a bite out of the millions of dollars in free food the government gives away every year. The Commodity Supplemental Food Program, administered by the Food and Consumer Service (FCS), is a direct food distribution program, which targets, among others, the elderly. The program, one of 15 federal food assistance programs administered by the FCS, is designed to improve the health and nutritional status of low-income elderly persons who may be at nutritional risk. The supplemental foods may include iron-fortified adult cereal, fruit, eggs, milk, cheese, dried beans, peas, peanut butter, vegetable juice, and other nutrient-rich foods.

To be eligible for the Commodity Supplemental Food Program, you must be 60 years of age or older, meet state-designated low-income guidelines and be at nutritional risk as determined by a competent health professional.

In most states, the health department oversees the supplemental food program. You can contact your local health department to find out about participation, eligibility and other matters regarding the Commodity Supplemental Food Program in your area. You also can obtain general information about any of the federal food assistance programs by contacting any of the following Food and Consumer Service Regional Public Information Offices:

Darlene Barnes, Director, Public Information, Food and Consumer Service, 3101 Park Center Drive, Room 819, Alexandria, VA 22302-1594; (703) 305-2286; Fax: (703) 305-1117.

Or for the:

Northeast Region (Connecticut, Maine, Massachusetts, New Hampshire, New York, Rhode Island, Vermont)

Charles DeJulius, Public Affairs Director, 10 Causeway Street, Boston, MA 02222-1069; (617) 565-6418; Fax: (617) 565-6472.

Mid-Atlantic Region (Delaware, District of Columbia, Maryland, New Jersey, Pennsylvania, Virginia, West Virginia)

Walt Haake, Public Affairs Director, Mercer Corporate Park, 300 Corporate Boulevard, Robbinsville, NJ 08691-1518; (609) 259-5091; Fax: (609) 259-5147.

Southeast Region (Alabama, Florida, Georgia, Kentucky, Mississippi, North Carolina, South Carolina, Tennessee)

Sara Harding, Public Affairs Director, 77 Forsyth Street, SW, Suite 112, Atlanta, GA 30303-3427; (404) 730-2588; Fax: (404) 730-9155.

Midwest Region (Illinois, Indiana, Michigan, Minnesota, Ohio, Wisconsin)

Lawrence Rudmann,Public Affairs Director, 77 W. Jackson Boulevard, 20th Floor, Chicago, IL 60604-3507; (312) 353-1044; Fax: (312) 353-0171.

Mountain Plains Region (Colorado, Iowa, Kansas, Missouri, Montana, Nebraska, North Dakota, South Dakota, Utah, Wyoming)

Craig Forman, Public Affairs Director, 1244 Speer Boulevard, Suite 903, Denver, CO 80204-3581; (303) 844-0312; Fax: (303) 844-6203.

Southwest Region (Arkansas, Louisiana, New Mexico, Oklahoma, Texas)

Barron, Public Affairs Director, 1100 Commerce Street, Room 5-C-30, Dallas, TX 75242-0222; (214) 290-9802; Fax: (214) 767-6249.

Western Region (Alaska, Arizona, California, Hawaii, Idaho, Nevada, Oregon, Washington)

Cordelia Morris, Public Affairs Director, 550 Kearney Street, Room 400, San Francisco, CA 94108-2518; (415) 705-1311; Fax: (415) 705-1364.

TURN YOUR HOME INTO A CASH MACHINE WITH FREE ASSISTANCE FROM YOUR UNCLE SAM

Your home is one of your greatest assets. In fact, your home can be a veritable "cash machine", providing you with enough money to make needed home repairs, buy gifts for the grandkids, or pay bills. So, how can you turn your home into a money-maker? One way is to convert the value of your home into ready cash with a home equity loan or reverse mortgage. The Federal Trade Commission (FTC) can provide you with free information on those and other home mortgage options, with a number of publications, including:

"Getting A Loan: Your Home As Security"
"Home Equity Credit Lines"
"Home Financing Primer"
"Mortgage Discrimination"
"Mortgage Servicing"
"Reverse Mortgages"
"Refinancing Your Home"

For copies of these and other free FTC publications, contact:

Federal Trade Commission,
Public Reference, Room 130,
Washington, DC 20589; (202) 326-2222;
or any of the following FTC Regional Offices:

Atlanta Regional Office (Alabama, Florida, Georgia, Mississippi, North Carolina, South Carolina, Tennessee, and Virginia), Federal Trade Commission, 1718 Peachtree Street, NW, Atlanta, GA 30367; (404) 656-1390; Fax: (404) 656-1379.

Boston Regional Office (Connecticut, Maine, Massachusetts, New Hampshire, Rhode Island, and Vermont), Federal Trade Commission, 101 Merrimac Street, Suite 810, Boston, MA 02114-4719; (617) 424-5960; Fax: (617) 424-5998.

Cleveland Regional Office (Delaware, District of Columbia, Maryland, Michigan, Ohio, Pennsylvania, and West Virginia), Federal Trade Commission, 668 Euclid Avenue, Suite 520-A, Cleveland, OH 44114-3006; (216) 522-4207; Fax: (216) 522-7239.

Chicago Regional Office (Illinois, Indiana, Iowa, Minnesota, Missouri, Wisconsin, and Kentucky), Federal Trade Commission, 55 East Monroe Street, Suite 1860, Chicago, IL 60604-1073. (312) 353-8156; Fax: (312) 353-4438.

Dallas Regional Office (Arkansas, Louisiana, New Mexico, Oklahoma, and Texas), Federal Trade Commission, 1999 Bryan Street, Suite 2150, Dallas, TX 75201-6808; (214) 979-0213.

Denver Regional Office (Colorado, Kansas, Montana, Nebraska, North Dakota, South Dakota, Utah, and Wyoming), Federal Trade Commission, 1961 Stout Street, Suite 1523, Denver, CO 80294-0101; (303) 844-2271.

Los Angeles Regional Office (Arizona and Southern California), Federal Trade Commission, 11000 Wilshire Boulevard, Suite 13209, Los Angeles, CA 90024; (310) 235-4000.

New York Regional Office (New Jersey and New York), Federal Trade Commission, 150 William Street, Suite 1300, New York, NY 10038; (212) 264-1207; Fax: (212) 264-0459.

San Francisco Regional Office (North California, Hawaii, and Nevada), Federal Trade Commission, 901 Market Street, Suite 570, San Francisco, CA 94103; (415) 356-5270; Fax: (415) 356-5284.

Seattle Regional Office (Alaska, Idaho, Oregon, and Washington), Federal Trade Commission, 2806 Federal Building, 915 Second Avenue, Seattle, WA 98174; (206) 220-6350; Fax: (206) 220-6366.

Another way to turn your home into a cash machine is by starting a small home business. If you're retired, with plenty of free time on your hands, a part-time home business can keep you occupied while generating a nice income. If you've got a home business in mind, the Small Business Administration (SBA) can provide you with loads of free assistance. The SBA offers a number of publications dealing with starting and operating a home business. Some of the publications available include:

"How To Start A Small Business"
"How To Start A Home-Based Business"
"Information: The Key To Success"
"How To Raise Money For A Small Business"
"Computerizing Your Business"
"Pricing Your Products and Services"
"Advertising Your Business"
"The Importance of Good Record Keeping"

To order these and other SBA publications, contact the SBA office nearest you. Look under "U.S. Government" in your telephone directory or call the SBA Answer Desk at (800) 8-ASK-SBA. You also can fax your request to (202) 205-7064, or access the SBA Internet site at http://www.sba.gov.

Chapter 8

Special Bargains On Government Property

Among the many benefits offered by Uncle Sam is the opportunity to buy surplus government property at bargain prices. While you don't have to be a senior citizen to take advantage of government property sales, the 50 or over crowd does have a distinctive advantage when it comes to tracking down super deals on everything from computers to vans. That advantage is time. The key to getting government property bargains is having the time to do the research and legwork involved in locating property sales which offer the kind of items you want.

Now that the demands of family and career have eased somewhat, and you have more time, you may want to investigate these surplus property sales conducted by a number of federal and state government agencies. While stories about the $100 yacht or Mercedes car aren't true, you can find some great bargains on a number of items if you know where to look.

Surplus government property includes cars, trucks, vans, computers, office equipment, recreational and athletic equipment, tools, cameras, clothing, jewelry, homes, antiques, furniture, china, public land, and hundreds of other items of real and personal property no longer needed by the government. The property is generally sold by sealed bid, auction, spot bid, or fixed priced sales. In most cases you'll have an opportunity to inspect sale property before making an offer. You'll be wise to do so, because most of the property sold by Uncle Sam is used and as such, may have flaws or deficiencies. The property is usually sold "as is", with the government agency conducting the sale making a reasonable effort to point out deficiencies to potential buyers. "Let the buyer beware" is a good motto to remember when buying surplus property from the government.

In this chapter of "Free Cash & Benefits For 50 Or Over", we've done a lot of the legwork for you. The following pages feature a number of government agencies which offer real and personal property for sale. You'll find scores of names, addresses and phone numbers that will help you track down the information you need to find government property bargains that could mean a savings of 50 percent and more. Now that you have the time, you can enjoy tracking down these bargains and saving a bundle of money, courtesy of Uncle Sam.

GENERAL SERVICES ADMINISTRATION (GSA)

The General Services Administration (GSA) sells a wide variety of personal property procured from nonmilitary federal agencies. Personal property sold includes cars, trucks, vans, boats, hardware, plumbing and heating equipment, computers, printers, copiers, typewriters and other office machines, furniture, medical items, textiles, industrial equipment, and thousands of other items. The property is sold at fair market value. And while it's not likely you'll find a $100 yacht or Mercedes car, you can find some special bargains.

For example, most of the vehicles sold by the GSA are purchased new and driven by government employees for official purposes. These vehicles are sold when they reach replacement age and/or mileage. Regular maintenance, relatively low age and mileage, and desired features like automatic transmission, air conditioning, power steering, and power brakes, make these vehicles some of the best buys in the marketplace. They're generally sold for approximately wholesale value.

The condition of the property sold by the GSA ranges from excellent to poor. And while the GSA attempts to point out deficiencies, when known, an item may still have flaws and come without a guarantee. That's why prospective bidders are urged to inspect sale property before making an offer.

Items are sold by one of four sales methods: sealed bid, auction, spot bid, and fixed price sales. Surplus personal property is sold by sealed bid whenever the sales items are in scattered locations. An "Invitation for Bid" (IFB) is mailed to prospective buyers on GSA's mailing lists. The IFB features descriptions of sale items, sale terms and conditions, locations and item inspection times, and a bid form.

GSA auctions are held to dispose of a large number of items in one location. Traditional auction methods are used, and prospective bidders receive descriptions, bidding instructions, and an opportunity to inspect sale items prior to or on the day of the sale.

Spot bid sales are similar to traditional auctions except that bids are in writing rather than voiced. Merchandise is offered "item by item' and awarded to the highest bidders. Prospective bidders receive sale property descriptions and instructions for bidders prior to each auction.

There is no bidding— either written or oral— at fixed-price-sales. Selling prices are posted on each item, and sales are made on a "first-come" basis.

You can find out about GSA personal property sales and auctions several ways. Sales information is advertised in local newspapers, on radio and TV, and posted in public buildings, such as town halls, post offices, and federal government buildings. Sales that might be of nationwide interest also may be advertised in national newspapers, trade journals, and periodicals.

Sales of national interest also are advertised in the "Commerce Business Daily", a publication of the U.S. Department of Commerce. Your local library or Chamber of Commerce may have a copy of the Commerce Business Daily. For subscription information call the U.S. Government Printing Office order line at (202) 512-1800, or write to the:

Superintendent of Documents,
U.S Government Printing Office,
Washington, DC 20402.

The GSA also maintains mailing lists for "frequent purchasers" of government property. To be placed on a mailing list, or to get more information about GSA personal property sales, contact the GSA regional sales office nearest you (see listing at the end of this chapter).

Besides surplus government personal property, the GSA also sells surplus real property. Sale properties may be in any of the 50 states or U.S. territories or possessions and include residences, building lots, warehouses and office buildings, land for commercial development, farms, and rural underdeveloped acreage. These properties are usually sold by sealed bid and by auction. Bidders must place a bid deposit and a sale is made to the highest bidder.

Public sales of real property are advertised in local and national newspapers, in trade publications, on radio, and in the GSA's booklet,"U.S. Real Property Sales List". The sales list is divided into the following four regional sections:

Boston Real Estate Office
(CT, IL, IN, ME, MA, MI, MN, NH, NJ, NY, OH, RI, VT, WI):
U.S. General Services Administration, 10 Causeway Street, Boston, MA 02222;
(800) 755-1946; Fax: (617) 565-5720.

Atlanta Real Estate Office
(AL, DE, District of Columbia, FL, GA, KY, MD, MS, NC, PA, SC, TN, VA, WV):
U.S. General Services Administration,
401 West Peachtree Street, Atlanta, GA 30365-2550; (800) 473-7836; Fax: (404) 331-2727.

Fort Worth Real Estate Sales Office
CO, IA, KS, LA, MO, MT, NE, NM, ND, OK, SD, TX, UT, WY): U.S. General Services Administration,

819 Taylor Street, Fort Worth, TX 76102;
(800) 833-4317; Fax: (817) 978-7063.

San Francisco Real Estate Sales Office
(AK, AZ, CA, HI, ID, OR, WA):
U.S. General Services Administration,
450 Golden Gate Ave.,
4th Floor East, San Francisco, CA 94102;
(415) 522-3429; Fax: (415) 522-3213.

Contact the regional office nearest you, and request a copy of the latest "U.S. Property Sales List", or write to the:

Office of Property Disposal,
U.S. General Services Administration,
18th and F Streets, NW, Room 4244,
Washington, DC 20405;
(202) 501-0084; Fax: (202) 208-1714.

If you have a computer equipped with a modem, and you have access to the internet, you also can get real property information through the World Wide Web at:
http://www.gas.gov:80/regions.htm.

DEPARTMENT OF DEFENSE (DoD)

Military surplus personal property, excluding weapons and items of an offensive or defensive nature, is available to the general public through both local and national sales for the Department of Defense (DoD). The Defense Reutilization and Marketing Service (DRMS) manages the DoD sales program for the Defense Logistics Agency. What all this means is that you can find some great bargains on surplus military property no longer needed by the components of the DoD including the Army, Navy, Air Force, Coast Guard, and many other agencies.

The property sold by the DRMS varies in type and value. Past sales have featured computers, typewriters, clothing, office furniture and equipment, aircraft and components, vehicles, household paints and thinners, recyclable materials such as iron, aluminum, copper, plastics, paper, textiles, rubber, used oil and lubricants, and much more. Sales are conducted on a nation and local level by various sales methods through the National Sales Office (NSO), and more than 200 Defense Reutilization and Marketing Offices (DRMOs) located on or near major military bases worldwide.

National sales are conducted by the NSO, which prepares sales catalogs that describe the property, sale location, property location, inspection and sale dates, and contacts for further information. Sales catalogs are mailed well in advance of the sale date to allow prospective bidders enough time for inspection. The NSO maintains a single National Bidders List for automatic mailing of sales catalogs to those individuals interested in national sales. To have your name placed on this national list, you need to complete an application which provides the NSO with the geographical area and type of property you're interested in. The application and a free booklet, "How To Buy Surplus Property from the U.S. Department of Defense" is available upon request from:

Defense Reutilization and Marketing
Service, National Sales Office,
Box 5275 DDRC, 2163 Airways
Boulevard, Memphis, TN 38114-5201;
(800) 222-DRMS [3767].

Local sales of surplus military property are conducted by the DRMOs throughout the country. Each DRMO maintains the bidders list for their local sales. To be placed on a local bidders list and to receive information on upcoming sales, contact your nearest DRMO. These offices are listed in the free booklet, "How To Buy Surplus Property from the U.S. Department of Defense", which is available from the DRMS at the above address. You also can locate your nearest DRMO by calling: 1-800-GOVT-BUY (800) 468-8289.

Local sales also are advertised locally in newspapers, on radio and television, and occasionally via flyers.

If you're not interested in bidding, you still can find some bargains on surplus military property at the DRMS Retail Sales Outlet Stores where property is offered at a fixed price. You can buy clothing, office and household furnishings, hand tools, and consumer electronics without having to outbid other prospective buyers. There are DRMS retail stores worldwide, and all offer thousands of surplus items at reasonable prices. Call the above toll-free number to find the location of your nearest DRMS sales office (or see the listings of DRMS retail outlets at the end of this chapter). If you have access to the Internet, you also can reach the DRMS through the World Wide Web at http://www.drms.dia.mil.

U.S. CUSTOMS SERVICE

As the agency that manages our nation's borders, the U.S. Customs Service seizes a wide variety of property when customs laws have been violated. Most of this property ends up for sale to the public at U.S. Customs Service Auctions.

Property seized and then auctioned can be any type of material including all types of cars, boats, real estate, jewelry, artwork, industrial equipment, clothing, household items, and antiques. For example, a recent U.S. Customs Service auction in Edison, New Jersey featured fabrics and notions, industrial goods (aluminum castings, aircraft parts, plasticware, bearing plates); electronics (cameras, car stereos, tape players, CD players, televisions, VCRs, computers, cellular phones); jewelry; household items (chairs, dining room furniture, glassware, linens, wallpaper); vehicles; boats; clothing; and sporting goods.

The sale of seized property is conducted for the U.S. Customs Service by EG & G Dynatrend throughout the 50 states and Puerto Rico. Sales are conducted in the form of public auctions, with occasional open bids and negotiated sales. Regularly scheduled auctions are generally held every nine weeks at sales locations in Edison, New Jersey; Miami/Ft. Lauderdale, Florida; El Paso, Texas; Los Angeles, California; and Nogales, Arizona. Vehicle auctions are held at four week intervals in Otay Mesa, CA. Sales also may be held at other times and locations throughout the United States as the availability of merchandise warrants.

The U.S. Customs Service contractor, EG & G Dynatrend, advertises upcoming auctions through newspapers and trade publications for high-value aircraft and vessels. The U.S. Customs Support Division offers a catalog subscription program for individuals interested in receiving sales flyers. The sales flyer subscription is good for one year and provides information on all locations, dates, viewing and registration times, and a list of the property for sale. Nationwide subscriptions for sales in the continental U.S., Alaska and Puerto Rico, are available for $50. Eastern region subscriptions for sales held in states east of the Mississippi River and the western region for sales held west of the Mississippi River are $25 each. To become a subscriber, or to get more information about U.S. Customs Service Auctions, contact:

EG & G Dynatrend, Inc.,
U.S. Customs Service Support Division,
2300 Clarendon Avenue, Suite 705,
Arlington, VA 22201; (703) 351-7887.

You also can get information on the sales flyer subscription service, or receive a current flyer by calling the Public Auction Line at (703) 273-7373. The Public Auction Line is a 24-hour automated telephone information service that provides callers with immediate information on auctions throughout the United States. The Public Auction Line also provides details of upcoming sales, including sale dates and times, locations, and descriptions of the merchandise on sale.

U.S. MARSHAL'S SERVICE

Seized and forfeited property also is available to the general public through the U.S. Marshal's Service. Property that has been forfeited under laws enforced or administered by the Department of Justice and its investigative agencies is offered to the public through a variety of methods including sealed bid, auction and negotiation. Most forfeited property is sold by professional auctioneers and brokers under contract to the U.S. Marshal's Service. These local contractors sell a wide variety of items including residential and commercial real estate, business establishments, and a wide range of personal property, such as vehicles, boats, aircraft, art, jewelry, livestock, collectibles, and antiques.

The U.S. Marshal's Service advertises its sale of forfeited property in the classified sections of major newspapers in areas where the property is located. Major sales also are advertised the 3rd Wednesday of every month in the classified section of the "USA Today" national newspaper. Items of special interest also may appear in advertisements in trade publications and specialized publications.

The Marshal's Service doesn't maintain a mailing list to notify prospective buyers of upcoming sales. However, a list featuring names, locations and phone numbers of contract service providers and federal agencies who have been authorized to sell forfeited property for the Marshal's Service on a recurring basis is available. You can get the list for free by calling 1-800-688-9889. The list also is available on the Internet through the U.S. Consumer Information Center site at:

"http://www.pueblo.gsa.gov".

For general information on sales by the U.S. Marshal's Service, call or write the:

Office of Public Affairs, U.S. Marshal's Service, 600 Army Navy Drive, Arlington, VA 22201-4201; (202) 307-9087.

The Marshal's Service also has a site on the Internet at: "http://www.usdoj.gov/marshals/".

U.S. POSTAL SERVICE

Bargains from the post office? Believe it or not, the U.S. Postal Service does offer some bargains through the auction of various types of property. The Postal Service auctions "unclaimed loose-in-the-mail items" and postal equipment at a number of locations across the country. If you have the time to invest in tracking down and attending some of these auctions, you could come away with some really great buys.

Unclaimed loose-in-the-mail items may include an assortment of "undeliverable" merchandise, such as clocks, televisions, radios, tape recorders, compact discs, jewelry, VCRs, clothing, or any other items that are lost and unclaimed in the U.S. Mail. Auctions of unclaimed loose-in-the-mail items are held twice a year at each of the Postal Service's Mail Recovery Centers. Bulk Mail Center Managers are responsible for announcing when the auctions will be held. To find out when the auctions will be held, you should contact the General Managers of the Mail Recovery Centers listed below:

Atlanta Mail Recovery Center,
730 Great Southern West Parkway,
Atlanta, GA 30336-9590.

San Francisco Mail Recovery Center,
390 Main Street, San
Francisco, CA 94105-9602.

St. Paul Mail Recovery Center,
180 Kellogg Boulevard East, St.
Paul, MN 55101-9514.

The Postal Service also has sales programs that dispose of postal equipment, such as excess postal vehicles, computers, workroom and office furniture, electronic and hardware items for mailhandling equipment, and more. Auctions and sales of postal equipment are conducted locally to create community involvement and to reduce handling and transportation costs. Sales are announced in local newspapers and by notices posted on lobby bulletin boards at post offices where the sales will be held.

The Postal Service's Purchasing Service Centers maintain lists of people who are interested in making purchases. To have your name added to the list for an area, contact the Manager of the appropriate Purchasing Service Center from the following list:

Dallas Purchasing Service Center
(Texas, Louisiana, Oklahoma),
P.O. Box 667190,
Dallas, TX 75266.

Greensboro Purchasing Center
(West Virginia, Kentucky, Maryland,
Washington, DC, North Carolina,
South Carolina),
P.O. Box 2749,
Greensboro, NC 27495-1102.

Chicago Purchasing Service Center
(Michigan, Indiana, Illinois),
433 W. Van Buren Street,
Room 930,
Chicago, IL 60699-6260.

Denver Purchasing Service Center
(Washington, Oregon, Idaho, Montana,
Wyoming, Colorado, New Mexico, Arizona,
Nevada, Utah, Alaska),
8055 East Tufts Avenue Parkway, Suite 475,
Denver, CO 80237-2880.

Minneapolis Purchasing Service Center
(North Dakota, South Dakota, Nebraska,
Kansas, Missouri, Wisconsin, Minnesota, Iowa),
2051 Killebrew Drive,Suite 610,
Minneapolis, MN 55425-1880.

Memphis Purchasing Service Center
(Tennessee, Arkansas, Alabama, Georgia, Mississippi, Florida),
1407 Union Avenue,
Memphis, TN 38166-6260.

Philadelphia Purchasing Service Center
(Ohio, Pennsylvania, South New Jersey, Delaware), P.O. Box 8061,
Philadelphia, PA 19197-6260.

Newark Purchasing Service Center
(New York City metropolitan area,
North New Jersey, Puerto Rico, Virgin Islands),
60 Evergreen Place, 3rd Floor,
East Orange, NJ 07018-2114.

San Bruno Purchasing Service Center
(California and Hawaii),
850 Cherry Avenue,
San Bruno, CA 94099-6260.

Windsor Purchasing Service Center
(Maine, New Hampshire, Massachusetts, Rhode Island, Connecticut, New York —except New York metropolitan area, Vermont),
8 Griffin Road North,
Windsor, CT 06006-6260.

BUREAU OF LAND MANAGEMENT

If you're looking for land to build that "get-away-from-it-all" cabin on, the Bureau of Land Management (BLM) may have just what you want. The BLM is responsible for the management of nearly 300 million acres of public lands. Most of this land is in the 11 Western States— Alaska, Arizona, California, Colorado, Idaho, Montana, Nevada, New Mexico, Oregon, Utah, and Wyoming. There also are small parcels of land available in Alabama, Arkansas, Florida, Illinois, Kansas, Louisiana, Michigan, Minnesota, Missouri, Mississippi, Nebraska, North Dakota, Ohio, Oklahoma, South Dakota, Washington, and Wisconsin. Under certain conditions, this land is made available to the general public through direct sales and auctions.

If you're interested in investing in some of this land, you should first understand that it is unimproved or undeveloped land which has been deemed "unneeded" by the federal government. Available parcels are generally rural woodland, grassland, or desert. Some are small parcels of just a few acres, and some are several hundred acres in size. Since Congress repealed the Homestead Act, none of this public land is available free through homesteading. There are, however, some good bargains if you know where to look. Generally the BLM sells this public land at fair market value.

The BLM office with jurisdiction over the area you are interested in is the best source of information about public land that is going to be sold. BLM state offices (listed at the end of this chapter) can send you sale information including what sales are currently scheduled and what prospects are coming up. You can write, call or visit these offices periodically for the latest information. Sale information also is published and broadcast in local news media.

You also may find a bargain on state owned land. State governments sometimes offer state-owned land to the general public. Information on state land programs is available through the State Lands Office in each state capital. These offices should be listed in your phone directory.

INTERNAL REVENUE SERVICE (IRS)

Your friends at the IRS can make you a deal on a piece of property in California, a houseboat, a sportscar, a motorcycle, or a variety of other real and personal property. The IRS has such items available because there are some people who can't (or don't) pay their taxes. When that happens, the IRS seizes real and/or personal property to get what it believes is due in taxes. Delinquent taxpayers are given the first opportunity to come up with the tax money due and reclaim their property. If they can't (or don't), the IRS sells the seized property at public auctions.

IRS auctions feature a variety of items, such as real estate, motor vehicles, boats, antiques, art, jewelry, collectibles, luxury items, household goods, medical and dental equipment and supplies, commercial and industrial property, and much more. This property is offered for sale "where is" and "as is", with no guarantees. Items are sold by sealed bid and public auction.

The IRS has a number of district offices across the country, and each office maintains a mailing list of potential bidders. To get your name on such a list, contact the IRS district office nearest you (consult your phone directory). Make sure you specify what type of merchandise you're interested in purchasing. You also can contact the following IRS Sales Hotlines for information about IRS sales in your area.

Alaska (Pacific Northwest District)—
(907) 566-0616.

California
Los Angeles District— (213) 894-5777.
Northern California District— (415) 522-6029.

Florida
Jacksonville— (904) 279-1656.
Tampa— (813) 875-5918.
Orlando— (407) 660-5868.

Hawaii
(Pacific Northwest District)—
(808) 541-1104.

Indiana
Northern— (219) 736-4308.
Central— (317) 226-5946.
Southern— (812) 471-6605.

Iowa (Midwest District)—
(515) 284-4628.

Kentucky-Tennessee—
(800) 829-4933 Ext. 82967.

Nebraska (Midwest District)—
(515) 284-4628.

North Carolina— (910) 378-2073.

Oregon (Pacific Northwest District)—
(503) 326-7840.

Pennsylvania (Pennsylvania District)—
(412) 355-2534.

Washington (Pacific Northwest District)—
(206) 220-5461.

Wisconsin— (515) 284-4628.

DEPARTMENT OF VETERANS AFFAIRS (VA)

The Department of Veterans Affairs (VA) sells properties acquired through foreclosures on VA guaranteed loans. Sales are managed through the VA's 46 regional offices, with some offices issuing sales listings by direct mail, and others issuing sales listings in local newspapers. The properties, which include detached homes, townhouses and condominiums, are available for sale to the general public through private sector real estate brokers. The VA pays the sales commission for the services of participating real estate brokers. VA seller-financing, with competitive rates, terms and downpayments, also is available for most properties being offered for sale.

If you're interested in bidding on a VA property, you should contact a local participating real estate broker. Such a broker can provide information about VA sales procedures and assist you in finding, viewing and making an offer on a VA property. If you can't find a local participating broker, you may contact the Property Management Division of your nearest VA regional office (see listing at the end of this chapter) for referrals and general information about the VA property sales program.

FEDERAL DEPOSIT INSURANCE CORPORATION (FDIC)

When a bank fails, the Federal Deposit Insurance Corporation (FDIC) takes control of its assets and offers them for sale to the general public. These assets include loans, real estate such as undeveloped land, single-family homes, condominiums, and apartment complexes; and personal property including computers, phone systems, furniture, fixtures, plants, and specialty items such as crystal, china and antiques. The items are sold by brokers, sealed bid, and sometimes by auction.

The FDIC advertises its sales in "The Wall Street Journal", trade publications for specialized items, and local newspapers and broadcast media where the sales will be held. The regional FDIC offices listed below also can provide information on upcoming sales. To obtain this information, contact the FDIC, Asset Marketing, at the FDIC regional office where you are interested in buying property.

FDIC Regional Offices

NORTHEAST SERVICE CENTER
(CT, ME, MA, NH, NJ, NY, PA, RI, VT):
111 Founders Plaza,
East Hartford, CT 06108;
(800) 873-7785.

SOUTHEAST SERVICE CENTER
(AL, DE, District of Columbia, FL, GA, KY, LA, MD, MS, NC, SC, TN, VA, WV):
285 Peachtree Center Avenue,
NE, Marquis Tower II, Suite 300,
Atlanta, GA 30303;
(800) 765-3342.

MIDWEST SERVICE CENTER
(IA, IL, IN, KS, MI, MN, MO, ND, NE, OH, SD, WI):
30 S. Wacker Dr., 32nd Floor,
Chicago, IL 60606;
(800) 944-5343.

SOUTHWEST SERVICE CENTER
(AR, CO, NM, OK, TX):
5080 Spectrum
Drive, Suite 1000E,
Dallas, TX 75248;
(800) 319-1444.

WESTERN SERVICE CENTER:
(AK, AZ, CA, HI, ID, MT, NV, OR, UT, WA, WY):
25 Ecker Street, Suite 1900,
San Francisco, CA 94105;
(800) 756-3558.

GSA Regional Sales Offices

For information on GSA sales of used Federal personal property, or to be placed on a mailing list, write to Personal Property Sales, U.S. General Services Administration, at the address serving your location. Remember, mailing lists are for frequent purchasers. If you have access to the internet, you can reach the GSA through the World Wide Web on http://gas.gov:80/regions.htm. For recorded information about upcoming sales, call the hotline telephone number listed with address.

National Capitol Region
(Washington, DC Metropolitan area,
nearby Maryland and Virginia):
470 L'Enfant Plaza East, SW, Suite
8214, Washington, DC 20407;
(703) 557-7796.

Region I (CT, ME, MA, NH, RI, VT):
10 Causeway Street, 9th
Floor, Boston, MA 02222-1076;
(617) 565-7326.

Region II (NJ, NY, Puerto Rico, Virgin Islands):
Room-20-112, Box 10, 26 Federal Plaza,
New York, NY 10278; (212) 264-4823;
(800) 488-7253.

Region III (DE, MD and VA—except Metropolitan D.C. area— PA, WV):
P.O. Box 40657, Philadelphia, PA 19107—3396;
(215) 656-3400.

Region IV (AL, FL, GA, KY, MS, NC, SC, TN):
Peachtree Summit
Building, 401 West Peachtree Street,
Atlanta, GA 30365-2550;
(404) 331-5177.

Region V (IL, IN, MI, MN, OH, WI):
230 South Dearborn Street,
Chicago, IL 60604;
(312) 353-0246.

Region VI (IA, KS, MO, NE):
4400 College Boulevard, Suite 175,
Overland Park, KS 66211;
(816) 823-3714.

Region VII (AR, LA, NM, OK, TX):
819 Taylor Street, Room 6812,
Fort Worth, TX 76102-6105.

Region VIII (CO, MT, ND, SD, UT, WY):
P.O. Box 25506, Denver
Federal Building, Building 41,
Denver, CO 80225-0506; (303) 236-7705.

Region IX (AZ, CA, HI, NV):
450 Golden Gate Avenue,
San Francisco, CA 94102-3400;
(415) 522-2891; (415) 522-2891; (800) 676-8253.

Region X (AK, ID, OR, WA):
400 15th Street, SW, Room 1478,
Auburn, WA 98001-6599;
(206) 931-7566.

Bureau of Land Management State Offices

Alaska: 222 W. 7th Avenue, #13,
Anchorage, AK 99513-7599;
(907) 271-5555.

Arizona: 3707 North 7th Street,
P.O. Box 16563, Phoenix, AZ 85011;
(602) 640-5547.

California: 2800 Cottage Way, E-2841,
Sacramento, CA 95825-1899;
(916) 978-4754.

Colorado: 2850 Youngfield Street,
Lakewood, CO 80215-7076;
(303) 239-3705.

States East of the Mississippi River, plus Arkansas, Iowa, Louisiana, Minnesota, and Missouri: Eastern States Office,
7450 Boston Boulevard,

Springfield, VA 22153;
(703) 440-1600.

Idaho: 3380 American Terrace,
Boise, ID 83706;
(208) 384-3000.

Montana, North Dakota and South Dakota:
222 N. 32nd Street, P.O. Box 36800,
Billings, MT 59107;
(406) 255-2940.

Nevada:
850 Harvard Way,
P.O. Box 12000,
Reno, NV 89520-0006;
(702) 785-6501.

New Mexico, Kansas, Oklahoma, and Texas:
1474 Rodeo Road, P.O.
Box 27115, Santa Fe, NM 87502-0115;
438-7450.

Oregon and Washington:
1300 N.E. 44th Avenue, P.O. Box 2965,
Portland, OR 97208-2965;
(503) 280-7158.

Utah: CFS Financial Center- 301,
324 South State Street, P.O.
Box 45155, Salt Lake City, UT 84145-0155;

(801) 539-4100.

Wyoming and Nebraska:
2515 Warren Avenue, P.O. Box 1828,
Cheyenne, WY 82003;
(307) 775-6117.

Defense Reutilization and Marketing Service (DRMS) Retail Sales Outlet Stores

ALABAMA:
Huntsville— (205) 842-2570;
Montgomery— (334) 416-4196.

ALASKA: Fairbanks— (907) 353-7334;
Anchorage— (907) 552-3766.

ARIZONA: Huachuca— (520)533-7027;
Luke— (602) 856-7144.

ARKANSAS: Little Rock—(501) 988-3720.

CALIFORNIA: Alameda— (510) 869-8288;
Edwards— (805) 277-2209;
March Air Force Base— (909) 655-7118.

COLORADO:
Colorado Springs— (719) 526-4382.

CONNECTICUT: Groton— (203) 449-3523.

DELAWARE: Dover— (302) 677-3201.

FLORIDA: Elgin— (904) 882-2822;
Jacksonville— (904) 772-9249;
Patrick Air Force Base— (407) 494-6507;
Pensacola— (904) 452-2451;
Tampa— (813) 828-2872.

GEORGIA: Fort Benning— (706) 545-6020/3497;
Forest Park— (404) 363-5117/5118;
Fort Stewart— (912) 767-4645;
Warner Robins— (912) 2164/3437.

HAWAII: Barbers Point— (808) 474-6874.

IDAHO: Mountain Home— (208) 828-2306.

ILLINOIS: Great Lakes— (847) 688-3655;
Rock Island— (309) 782-1617;
Scott Air Force Base— (618) 452-4464.

INDIANA: Crane— (812) 854-1554/1728;
Indianapolis— (317) 377-5175.

KANSAS: Fort Riley— (913) 239-0535;
McConnell Air Force Base— (316) 652-4098.

KENTUCKY: Fort Campbell— (502) 798-4762.

LOUISIANA: Barksdale— (318) 456-8638;
Polk— (318) 531-4068.

MAINE: Brunswick NAS— (207) 921-2627.

MARYLAND: Aberdeen— (410) 278-4785;
Fort Meade— (301) 677-6366;
Patuxent River— (301) 826-3316.

MICHIGAN: Selfridge— (810) 307-5191.

MINNESOTA: Duluth— (218) 722-2536.

MISSISSIPPI: Columbus— (601) 434-7466.

MISSOURI: Leonard Wood— (314) 596-0390;
Whiteman Air Force Base— (816) 687-3308.

MONTANA: Great Falls— (406) 731-6347.

NEBRASKA: Offutt— (402) 294-4964.

NEVADA: Nellis Air Force Base— (702) 652-2005.

NEW HAMPSHIRE:
Portsmouth— (207) 438-4512.

NEW JERSEY: Lakehurst— (908) 323-4079.

NEW MEXICO— Cannon— (505) 784-2435;
Holloman— (505) 475-3749;
Kirtland— (505) 846-6396.

NEW YORK:
Watervliet Arsenal— (518) 266-4112.

NORTH CAROLINA:
Camp Lejeune— (910) 451-5613;
Cherry Point— (919) 466-5826;
Fort Bragg— (910) 396-5222;
Goldsboro— (919) 736-6695.

NORTH DAKOTA:
Grand Forks Air Force Base— (701) 747-3780.

OHIO: Columbus— (614) 692-3468;
Wright-Patterson— (513) 257-4291.

OKLAHOMA: Fort Sill— (405) 442-3415.

PENNSYLVANIA:
Mechanicsburg— (717) 790-3592;
Philadelphia— (215) 737-3723.

SOUTH CAROLINA:
Fort Jackson— (803) 751-7716;
Parris Island— (803) 525-2335;
Shaw— (803) 668-3556.

SOUTH DAKOTA:
Ellsworth Air Force Base— (605) 385-1021.

TEXAS: Fort Bliss— (915) 568-8582;

Dyess— (915) 696-5287;
Fort Hood— (817) 287-8824;
Reese— (602) 750-3320;
San Antonio—(210) 925-7766.

UTAH: Hill Air Force Base— (801) 777-6557.

VIRGINIA: Fort Belvoir— (703) 806-5501;
Norfolk— (757) 444-5366;
Richmond— (804) 279-4407;
St. Juliens Crk— (804) 396-0136;
Williamsburg— (804) 887-7261.

WASHINGTON: Fairchild— (509) 247-2350;
Whidby Island— (360) 257-2501.

WISCONSIN: Sparta— (608) 388-3685.

WYOMING: F.E. Warren— (307) 775-3970.

VA Regional Office Property Management Contacts

The following list of the 46 VA Regional Offices includes telephone numbers and, if available, the names of persons responsible for property management. These contacts may assist you in locating a local real estate broker who participates in VA sales programs. For mailing addresses of VA Regional Offices, see the Appendix at the end of this book.

ALASKA: Robert Orrin, Property Management Chief; (907) 257-4745.

ALABAMA: Ralph Strickland, Property Management Chief; (334) 213-3384.

ARIZONA & SOUTHERN NEVADA: Grant Singleton, Property Management Chief; (602) 640-4747.

ARKANSAS: Sharon Glanton, Property Management Chief; (501) 370-3763.

CALIFORNIA-Southern, except for San Diego Area: Randy Overbeck,
Property Management Chief; (310) 235-6143.

CALIFORNIA- Northern and Northern NEVADA: David Piersall, Property Management Chief; (510) 637-1066.

CALIFORNIA- San Diego Area: Nancy Higgins, Property Management Chief; (619) 680-4926.

COLORADO & WYOMING: Margo Keyser, Property Management Chief; (303) 914-5627.

CONNECTICUT— see New England

DELAWARE— see Pennsylvania- Eastern.

DISTRICT OF COLUMBIA & No. VIRGINIA: Wendy Bitner, Property Management Chief; (202) 418-4370.

GEORGIA: Mike Everett, Property Management Chief; (404) 347-4430.

FLORIDA: John Acosta, Property Management Chief; (813) 893-3516.

HAWAII: Sandy Luke, Property Management Chief; (808) 566-1475.

IDAHO: Kim Blackburn, Property Management Chief; (208) 334-1900.

ILLINOIS: David Kalish, Property Management Chief; (312) 353-2049.

INDIANA: Robert Amt, Property Management Chief; (317) 226-7827.

IOWA: Raymond Morris, Property Management Chief; (515) 284-4657.

KANSAS: James Goethe, Property Management Chief; (316) 688-6728.

KENTUCKY: Richard Sloan, Property Management Chief; (502) 582-5866.

LOUISIANA: Darryl Crum, Property Management Chief; (504) 589-6458.

MAINE— see New England.

MARYLAND: (410) 962-4250.

MASSACHUSETTS— see New England.

MICHIGAN: Jerry Weigold, Property Management Chief; (313) 226-7561.

MINNESOTA: Dennis Johnson, Property Management Chief; (612) 725-3827.

MISSISSIPPI: Bobbe Burkhalter, Property Management Chief; (601) 965-4975.

MISSOURI: George Marvin, Property Management Chief; (314) 342-9865.

MONTANA: Tom Murrin, Property Management Chief; (406) 442-6410.

NEBRASKA: Carol Swan, Property Management Chief; (402) 437-4020.

NEVADA-Northern— see California-Northern.

NEVADA-Southern— see Arizona.

NEW ENGLAND: Bill Marko, Property Management Chief; (603) 666-7484.

NEW HAMPSHIRE— see New England.

NEW MEXICO: Lynn Taylor, Property Management Chief; (505) 248-6680.

NEW JERSEY: (201) 645-3607.

NEW YORK- Western: Mike Meyer, Property Management Chief; (716) 846-5295.

NEW YORK- Eastern: William Rooney, Property Management Chief; (212) 807-7229.

NORTH CAROLINA: Jerry Farmer, Property Management Chief; (910) 631-5494.

NORTH DAKOTA— see Minnesota.

OKLAHOMA: Property Management Division; (918) 687-5494.

OHIO: Property Management Division; (216) 522-3583.

OREGON: Richard Lewis, Property Management Chief; (503) 326-2457.

PENNSYLVANIA—Western: Property Management Division; (412) 644-4508.

PENNSYLVANIA- Eastern: Janice DiBenedett, Property Management Chief; (215) 842-2000.

RHODE ISLAND—see New England.

SOUTH CAROLINA: Property Management Division; (803) 765-5154.

SOUTH DAKOTA— see Minnesota.

TENNESSEE: Property Management Division; (615) 736-5241.

TEXAS- Southern: Rosemary Kissel, Property Management Chief; (713) 791-1444.

TEXAS- Northern: Property Management Division; (817) 757-6869.

UTAH: Gerald Overstreet, Property Management Division; (801) 524-3411.

VERMONT— see New England.

VIRGINIA: except northern VA: Sam Saunders, Property Management Chief; (540) 857-2141.

WASHINGTON State: Cheryle Day, Property Management Chief; (206) 220-6167.

WEST VIRGINIA— see Virginia.

WISCONSIN: Property Management Division; (414) 382-5060.

WYOMING— see Colorado.

Chapter 9

More Free and Low Cost Travel For 50 Or Over

Travelers 50 or over can cash in on a number of travel deals available to them. Besides the special seniors only travel deals offered by Uncle Sam described in chapter 4, ("Free And Low-Cost Travel"), there also are a wealth of travel discounts available through travel clubs and seniors organizations. Special senior discounts of 50 percent and more also are available from many hotels, car rental agencies, and other travel providers.

On the following pages, you'll find a number of special travel programs offering discounts on everything from entrance fees to national parks and historic sites, to a free world travel program from Uncle Sam that allows senior travelers to see the world while sharing their experience and expertise with others. And the best part is that the minimum age requirement to take advantage of these travel bargains is, in most cases, a youthful 50!.

GOLDEN EAGLE PASSPORT

Here's your passport for savings while you tour the country, visiting the nation's natural wonders. The Golden Eagle Passport is an entrance to national parks, monuments, historic sites, recreation areas, and national wildlife refuges that charge an entrance fee. The Passport costs $50 and is good for one year from the date of purchase. It admits the passholder and any accompanying passengers in a private vehicle. If entry is not by private vehicle, the passport admits the passholder, spouse, children, and parents.

You can purchase a Golden Eagle Passport at any National Parks System entrance fee area or by mail. To purchase by mail, send a $50 check or money order to:

National Park Service,
1100 Ohio Drive, SW, Room 138,
Washington, DC 20242;
Attention: Golden Eagle Passport.

GOLDEN ACCESS PASSPORT

This is a lifetime entrance pass for persons who are blind or permanently disabled. It's available free at any entrance fee area by showing proof of medically determined disability and eligibility for receiving benefits under federal law.

With a Golden Access Passport, you and any accompanying passengers in a private vehicle will be admitted free to those national parks, historic sites, recreation areas , monuments, and national wildlife refuges that charge entrance fees. Where entry is not by private vehicle, the Passport admits the passholder, spouse, children, and parents.

The Golden Access Passport also provides a discount of 50 percent on federal use fees charged for facilities and services, such as fees for camping, swimming, parking, boat launching or cave tours. The Passport does not cover or reduce special recreation permit fees or fees charged by concessioners.

AMTRAK

If you're at least 62, you can "ride the rails" of AMTRAK and save up to 15%. AMTRAK offers senior travelers a 15% discount off the applicable adult rail fare on most of its trains. This includes sales fares, promotional fares, and all-aboard fares.

Call AMTRAK's toll-free hotline, 1-800-USA-RAIL, and receive a free travel planner which offers travel tips and services. You'll also receive a list of AMTRAK's special vacation packages. Contact:

AMTRAK,
60 Massachusetts Avenue, NW,
Washington, DC 20002.

ELDERHOSTEL

For around $340 you can combine travel across the world with an educational experience. That's about how much a week-long travel/education program costs through Elderhostel, a non-profit educational organization which caters to people age 60 or over.

Elderhostel offers inexpensive, short term academic programs hosted by educational institutions around the world. The organization has an international network of more than 2,300 participating institutions. Nearly a quarter million seniors enrolled in Elderhostel programs in 1996.

Most Elderhostel programs offer three academic courses for 1 1/2 hours each during a week-long (six nights) travel/education adventure. You'll have comfortable dormitory accommodations on college and university campuses in the United States and Canada, and plenty of free time to enjoy the cultural and recreational resources of the area you're visiting. Internationally, housing may be in dormitories, modest hotels, rural lodges, small ships, barges, or tents if you're on a hiking program.

International programs may last one to four weeks, including stays at different institutions and sometimes different countries each week. Besides classes, the tuition includes room, meals, and some extracurricular activities.

While Elderhostel's tuitions are relatively low, they still may be too steep for many people, especially those on fixed incomes. For those people, Elderhostel offers a limited number of scholarships called "Hostelships". These scholarships may be used only in the United States for programs that are 5 or 6 nights long. Scholarships or Hostelships for programs in Alaska and Hawaii only are available to residents of those states.

To be eligible for an Elderhostel program, you must be at least 60 years old. Participants' spouses of any age also are welcome. Companions of age-eligible participants must be at least 50. For more information, including a free Elderhostel catalog, or applications, write to:

Elderhostel,Inc.,
Catalog Department IH,
75 Federal Street,
Boston, MA 02110-1941;
(617) 426-8056.

PEACE CORPS

Let Uncle Sam pick up the tab as you travel the world fighting hunger, disease, illiteracy, poverty, and lack of opportunity. As a Peace Corps Volunteer, you can travel to the far corners of the world free of charge, and share your lifetime expertise with those less fortunate than you. And age is no deterrent. Over 500 seniors recently volunteered for Peace Corps assignments in Africa, Asia, the Pacific, Central and South America, the Carribean, Central and Eastern Europe, and former Soviet Union.

Peace Corps Volunteers work in agriculture, education, forestry, health, engineering, and skilled trades. Countries also are increasingly requesting help in new areas, including business, the environment, urban planning, youth development, and the teaching of English for commerce and technology. Assignments are, typically, for two years with volunteers living among native people, teaching and becoming part of the community. It's a great way to see the world at the government's expense, and serve your fellow man.

If you have the skills, motivation, and other qualities needed by Peace Corps Volunteers, contact your nearest Peace Corps Recruiting Office for information.

Peace Corps Recruiting Offices Recruiting offices are the primary source of information about the Peace Corps. If you want Volunteer information, contact the office that is responsible for your state. Along with your inquiry, you should provide the following information:

— Full Name
— Address
— Phone number
— Degree(s) held or skill area
— Years of experience in skill area

ATLANTA (AL, FL, GA, MS, SC, TN):
Peace Corps Recruiting Office,
100 Alabama Street, Suite 2R70,
Atlanta, GA 30303;
(404) 562-3455.

BOSTON (MA, VT, RI, ME, NH):
Peace Corps Recruiting Office,
Tip O'Neil Federal Building,
10 Causeway Street, Room 450,
Boston, MA;
(617) 565-5555.

CHICAGO (IL, IN, OH, MI):
Peace Corps Recruiting Office,
Xerox Center, 55 Monroe, Suite 450, Chicago,
IL 60603; (312) 353-4990.

DALLAS (NM, OK, LA, TX, AR):
Peace Corps Recruiting Office,
400 North Ervay Street, Room 230, P.O. Box 638,
Dallas, TX 75221;
(214) 767-5434.

DISTRICT OF COLUMBIA (DC, MD, NC, WV, VA): Peace Corps Recruiting Office,
1400 Wilson Boulevard, Suite 400,
Arlington, VA 22209;
(703) 235-9191.

DENVER (CO, MT, SD, ND, UT, WY):
Peace Corps Recruiting Office,
140 E. 19th Avenue, Suite 550,
Denver, CO 80203;
(303) 866-1057.

LOS ANGELES (AZ, Southern CA):
Peace Corps Recruiting Office,
11000 Wilshire Boulevard, Room 8104,
West Los Angeles, CA 90024;
(310) 235-7444.

MINNEAPOLIS (MN, WI):
Peace Corp Recruiting Office, 330 2nd Avenue, South, Room 420,
Minneapolis, MN 54401;
(612) 348-1480.

NEW YORK (NY, CT, NJ, PA):
Peace Corps Recruiting Office, 6
World Trade Center, Room 611,
New York, NY 10048-0900;
(212) 466-2477.

SEATTLE (AK, ID, OR, WA):
Peace Corps Recruiting Office,
2001 6th Avenue, Room 1776,
Seattle, WA 98121;
(206) 553-5490.

SAN FRANCISCO (HI, Northern CA, NV):
Peace Corps Recruiting Office,
211 Main Street, Room 533,
San Francisco, CA 94105;
(415) 977-8800.

For general information about the Peace Corps, contact the:

Peace Corps headquarters
1990 K Street, NW,
Washington, DC 20526;
(800) 424-8580.

SENIOR CITIZEN DISCOUNT AIRFARES

Virtually all major U.S. and Canadian airlines offer senior citizen discounts on airfare. While these discount programs vary from airline to airline, seniors 62 or over usually can get a 10 percent reduction off regular advertised airfare. This discount normally applies to all published fares from first class to coach/economy excursions. Always ask for your senior citizen discount before you fly.

You also should ask about other senior airfare discounts available. Some airlines' senior citizen clubs offer further fare discounts. For example, United's Silver Wings Plus is offered to seniors 55 or older. Continental Airlines offers a Golden Traveler's Club for seniors 60 and over, as well as "Freedom Passports" to travelers who are at least 62 years old. A single Freedom Passport program costs $999 and provides the holder with a 4-month pass for "off-peak" travel within the continental United States, St. Thomas, St. Croix, and Vancouver. Travel with the passport is restricted to "off-peak" times of from noon on Mondays through noon on Thursdays and all day on Saturdays. Contact your travel agent on individual airlines (listed below) for information about available senior discounts.

Other airfare discounts are available to all travelers, including "Off-Season" airfares and early-bird discounts. Off-season airfares are subject to the location you want to go to and whether or not it's peak tourist season. Most airlines limit the number of discounted seats on flights, but increase the number during off season. Your travel agent can give you information about these discounts.

Early-bird discounts provide the lowest fares if you buy your tickets in advance, typically either seven days or two weeks. Departure and return dates are fixed, so once you reserve these fares, you can't change your mind without risking the loss of a large portion of your ticket price.

Domestic Airlines

Air Canada: (800) 776-3000.
Air South: (800) 247-7688.
Alaska: (800) 426-0333.
Aloha: (800) 367-5250.
American: (800) 433-7300.
America West: (800) 247-5692.
Canadian International: (800) 426-7000.
Carnival: (800) 437-2110.
Continental: (800) 525-0280.
Delta: (800) 221-1212.
Frontier: (800) 432-1359.
Hawaiian: (800) 367-5320.
Horizon Air: (800) 547-9308.
Kiwi: (800) 538-5494.
Midway: (800) 446-4392.
Northwest: (800) 225-2525.
TWA: (800) 221-2000.
United: (800) 241-6522 (national);
(800) 538-2929 (international).
USAir: (800) 428-4322.
Vanguard: (800) 826-4827.
World Airways: (800) 967-5350.

SENIOR AIRLINE DISCOUNT COUPONS

Most major domestic airlines offer senior discount travel coupons for travelers age 62 or older. These coupons, which generally are available in books of four or eight, provide bargain-priced airfare for flights within the continental United States. In some cases, you can save 50 percent and more off regular fares by using senior coupons. Each coupon is good for a one-way flight, with two coupons often used for a round-trip ticket. You can use four coupons for a round-trip ticket to Alaska or Hawaii on some airlines.

Many airlines sell books of four senior discount coupons for $500 to $600, while books of eight coupons generally are priced around $1,000. Some airlines, such as TWA, sell discount coupon booklets to companions of any age who accompany qualifying seniors. Other airlines, while not offering companion coupons, offer a 10 percent discount to companions who are traveling with qualifying seniors.

If you plan to do a lot of flying, it may pay you to check out the deals available on senior discount coupons. The coupons are good for one year and generally are available to seniors aged 62 or older. In most cases, flights taken with airline discount coupons earn frequent flyer mileage. Some restrictions may apply, so you should be sure to check with your travel agent for the latest information and pricing before purchasing coupons.

Here are several airlines currently offering senior discount coupons (the information was accurate as of this writing— you should check with a travel agent or the airlines for current information and pricing):

Air Canada: Offers 4 coupons for $530; 8 coupons for $838. You must be at least 60 to qualify for this discount program, plus a travel companion of any age may purchase a coupon book for the same price. Coupons are valid for travel between the U.S. and Canada and within Canada.

America West: Offers 4 coupons for $495; 8 coupons for $920. Coupons are valid for flights to all U.S. cities served by America West.

American Airlines: Offers 4 coupons for $596; 8 coupons for $1032. Coupons are valid for flights within the continental United States, Puerto Rico, and the U.S. Virgin Islands. Two coupons are needed for a flight to Hawaii.

Continental: Offers 4 coupons for $579; 8 coupons for $999. Coupons are valid for travel to all U.S. cities. Two coupons are needed for flights to Alaska or Hawaii.

Delta: Offers 4 coupons for $596; 8 coupons for $1032. Coupons are valid for flights in the United States, Canada, St. Thomas, St. Croix, and Puerto Rico. Two coupons are required for travel to Alaska or Hawaii.

Northwest: Offers 4 coupons for $596; 8 coupons for $1032. Coupons are good for travel within the United States and Canada. Two coupons are needed for flights to Alaska or Hawaii.

TWA: Offers 4 coupons for $548. The offer includes a coupon for a 20 percent discount off a round-trip international flight. A travel companion of any age also may buy a book of 4 coupons for $648. Coupons are valid for travel in the continental United States. Two coupons are needed for travel to Hawaii.

United: Offers 4 coupons for $596; 8 coupons for $1032. Coupons, which are good for two years, are valid for travel in North America including the United States, Mexico, Canada and Puerto Rico. Two coupons are needed for Alaska or Hawaii.

USAir: Offers 4 coupons for $596; 8 coupons for $1032. Up to two children, ages 2-11, also may travel with qualifying seniors using the same coupon book. Coupons are valid for travel in the continental United States, Canada and Puerto Rico.

Hotel Discounts

Your status as a senior citizen also can get you a great deal on lodging. Most national hotel/motel chains offer senior discounts of 10 percent to 50 percent off regular rates. The minimum age requirement to qualify for these discounts varies from hotel to hotel, but in many cases travelers 50 and over are eligible. Most hotels require proof of age, and some also may require membership in their senior discount programs or proof of membership in travel clubs and organizations, such as AAA or AARP.

You can contact hotel chains through their toll-free national reservation numbers (listed below). Reservation staff can provide you with information about discounts and room availability. However, you'll usually have a wider choice of senior discounts and other promotions if you contact hotels directly.

The following national chains all offer senior discount programs. Discounts range from 10 percent to 50 percent, depending on the hotel and programs offered. While the prices and information listed were accurate at the time of writing, you should contact each hotel for current pricing and discount information.

Aston, (800) 922-7866. The Aston Sun Club provides travelers age 55 or older with a discount of 25 percent. Rental car discounts also are available.

Best Inns, P.O. Box 1719, Marion, IL 62959; (800) 237-8466. Best Inns' Senior First Club offers seniors age 50 and over a discount of up to 10 percent off regular room rates.

Best Western, Inc., P.O. Box 1023, Phoenix, AZ 85064-0203; (800) 603-2277. Best Western's 3,500 locations worldwide offer senior discounts of 10 percent off regular room rates. The discount is available to AARP members and anyone age 50 or older.

Choice Hotels, 10750 Columbia Pike, Silver Springs, MD 20901. Choice Hotels "Prime Time" savings program provides all travelers age 50 or over discounts of 10 percent to 30 percent. The discounts are available at all Sleep, Comfort, Quality, Clarion, EconoLodge, Rodeway and Friendship Inns. For information and reservations, call:

— Clarion; 1-800-252-7466
— Comfort; 1-800-228-5150
— Quality; 1-800-228-5151
— Rodeway; 1-800-228-2000
— Econo; 1-800-553-2666
— Friendship 1-800-453-4511
— Sleep; 1-800-627-5337

Days Inn, The September Days Club, P.O. Box 27287, Minneapolis, MN 55427-9741; (800) DAYS INN (329-7466). Day's Inn's "September Days Club" offers travelers 50 or over discounts of 15 percent to 50 percent off standard room rates. Membership also includes a 10 percent reduction on meals at participating Days Inns and up to 50 percent off at participating theme parks and entertainment attractions across the United States. A membership fee of $14 for one year; $23.50 for two years; $31.50 for three years; and $46.50 for five years is required.

Hampton Inns, 303 Madison Avenue, Memphis, TN 38103; (800) 426-7866. Under Hampton's Lifestyle 50 Benefits program, one to four persons can share a room for the price of one senior room. Minimum membership age is 50.

Hilton Hotels (U.S.), (800) 432-3600. Hilton's Senior Honors Program provides travelers age 60 and over savings of up to 50 percent off regular room rates, and 20 percent off dinner for two at U.S. Hilton Hotels. Other benefits include: free membership for your spouse, members-only toll-free reservation line, and free health club privileges at Hilton Hotels with health club facilities. Annual membership is $55; Lifetime membership is $290. For more information, call the Hilton Customer Service Center at (214) 788-0878.

Holiday Inn, (800) 258-6642. Holiday Inn provides a senior discount of 10 percent to AARP members. The chain also offers travel benefits to travelers age 60 and over through the Holiday Inn "Alumni Club". Members save 20 percent off the non-discounted individual room rates, and 10 percent off meals at participating hotels.

Howard Johnson, 3838 Van Buren, Phoenix, AZ 85038; (800) 547-7829. Howard Johnson's "Golden

Years Club" offers discounts of 15 percent to 50 percent to travelers 50 and older. Restaurant and car rental discounts also are available. Annual membership is $12.95.

Hyatt Hotels, (800) 233-1234. All seniors 62 and over can save up to 25 percent off regular room rates at Hyatt Hotels in the United States.

Embassy Suites, (800) 362-2799. The Embassy Suites hotel chain offers a 10 percent discount to all seniors 55 or older. Members of AARP who are at least 55 also get a 10 percent discount.

Ramada Inn, 3838 E. Van Buren, Phoenix, AZ 85038; (800) 2- RAMADA. Ramada's Best Years Club provides travelers age 60 or older with a discount of up to 25 percent off regular room rates. Ask at the front desk of any Ramada Inn for details.

Red Roof Inns, Inc., 4355 Davidson Road, Hilliard, OH 43026-2491; (800) 843-7663. Red Roof Inns' RediCard + 60 is available to travelers age 60 or older. Members receive a 10 percent discount at every Red Roof Inn. A lifetime membership in RediCard + 60 is $10.

Travelodge, (800) 522-1555. Travelodge's Classic Travel Club provides seniors 50 and over a discount of up to 15 percent off regular room rates. Participating hotels also offer a 15 percent discount to AARP members.

Vagabond Inns, (800) 522-1555. The Club 55 program offers discounts off regular room rates to travelers 55 and over. Minimum age, discount and/or program varies from hotel to hotel or season to season.

The best advice when it comes to lodging is to use your age to your advantage. The hotels listed above are just a few of the many chains that offer special discounts to guests 50 or over. Other chains that offer senior discounts include:

Budget Host Inns, P.O. Box 14341,
Arlington, TX 76094; (800) 283-4678.

Budgetel Inns,
250 E. Wisconsin Avenue, Suite 1750,
Milwaukee, WI 53202-4221; (800) 428-3438.
Cross Country Inns, 6077 Frantz Road,
Dublin, OH 43017;(800) 621-1429.

Economy Inns of America,
755 Raintree Drive, Suite 200,
Carlsbad, CA 92008; (800) 826-0778.

Excel Inns of America,
4706 E. Washington Avenue,
Madison, WI 53704; (800) 356-8013.

Shoney's Inns,
217 West Main Street,
Gallatin, TN 37066; (800) 222-2222.

Suisse Chalet,
One Chalet Drive,
Wilton, NH 03086; (800) 524-2538.

Super 8 Motels,
1910 Eith Ave., NE,
Aberdeen, SD 57401-3207; (800) 800-8000.

Car Rentals

Most major car-rental agencies— both national and international- offer discounts to seniors. Minimum age requirements vary from company to company, and some companies require membership in AARP or some other senior organizations. Car rental discounts for seniors, generally range from 5 percent to 10 percent off regular rates.

You might want to shop around to get the best deal possible. The following list features national and international car rental agencies. Contact the companies through their toll-free numbers for information about what, if any, senior discounts are available.

National/International Rental Companies

Agency Rent A Car, (800) 321-1972
Airways Rent A Car, (800) 952-9200
Alamo, (800) 327-9633
All Star Rent A Car, (800) 426-5243
American International Rent A Car,
(800) 527-0202
Auto Europe, (800) 223-5555
Avis, (800) 331-1212 (national);
(800) 831-2847 (international)
Avon, (800) 421-6808
Budget Rent A Car, (800) 527-0700
Dollar, (800)-800-4000
Enterprise Rent A Car, (800) 325-8007
European Car Reservations, (800) 535-3303
Europe By Car, (800) 223-1516;
(213) 272-0424 in CA; (212) 245-1713 in NY).
Exchange Car Rental, (800) 777-2836
Foremost Euro-Car, (800) 272-3299
Freedom Rent A Car, (800) 331-0777
General Rent A Car, (800) 327-7607
Hertz, (800) 654-3131
Kemwel, (800) 678-0678
National, (800) CAR-RENT(national);
(800) 227-3876 (international)
Payless, (800) 237-2804
Renault Eurodrive, (800) 221-1052
Thrifty, (800) 367-2277

Senior Travel Clubs and Organizations

Another money-saving option for travelers 50 or older is the travel services offered by specialized travel agencies and clubs and senior organizations. These sources can provide packages of discounts and benefits especially for seniors at many hotel chains, car-rental companies, on cruises and on airfare. For example, membership in the American Association of Retired Persons (AARP) entitles you to discounts of up to 50 percent at an extensive network of hotels, car rental agencies and other travel providers. United Airlines' Silver Wings Plus Club offers members a 10 percent discount on airfare, as well as discounts on hotel accommodations, car rentals, cruises and more. Your travel agent can provide you with more information about clubs and organizations offering special deals to the 50 or over crowd.

Over 50 Travel Clubs And Organizations

American Association of Retired Persons (AARP), 601 E. Street, NW, Washington, DC 20049; (202) 434-2760; (800) 523-5800. Membership in AARP entitles travelers age 50 or over to discounts of up to 50 percent at more than 30 well-known hotel and motel firms and three car rental companies with locations worldwide. Annual membership is $8.

Catholic Golden Age, 430 Penn Avenue, Scranton, PA 18503; (717) 342-3294; (800) 836-5699. This organization offers a number of services to older people including discounts on travel. Membership is $8 per year per couple; $19 for three years.

Grand Circle Travel, 347 Congress Street, Boston, MA 02110; (800) 221-2610. Grand Circle Travel specializes in providing reasonably-priced vacation packages directly to "active, mature Americans".

GrandTravel, 6900 Wisconsin Avenue, Suite 706, Checy Chase, MD 20815; (800) 247-7651. GrandTravel is a tour company that specializes in escorted domestic and international tours for grandparents who are travelling with their grandchildren. Recent vacation specials included tours to Washington, DC, the Pacific Northwest, Hawaii, the Grand Canyon, Alaska, and the Southwestern United States. Call the toll-free number for more information or to make reservations.

Greyhound's Ameripass, (800) 231-2222. Greyhound's Ameripass program offers customers unlimited travel throughout the continental United States, during a specified period of time at discounted prices. Greyhound also offers travelers 55 or over a senior citizen discount of 10% off the walk-up fare.

Mature Outlook, P.O. Box 10448, Des Moines, IA 50306-0448; (800) 336-6330. Mature Outlook is a program of special benefits offered by Sears Travel Service. Minimum membership age is 50 and members are entitled to additional discounts on Sears regular and sale-priced merchandise, half-price hotel discounts up to 50 percent and discounts on dining and car rental.

National Alliance of Senior Citizens, 1700 18th Street NW, Suite 401, Washington, DC 20009; (202) 986-0117. Membership in this seniors organization is $10 a year for individuals, $15 per couple; or $100 for a lifetime membership.

National Association of Retired Federal Employees (NARFE), 1533 New Hampshire Avenue, NW, Washington, DC 20036; (200) 234-0832 (general information); (800) 627-3394 (membership information). The NARFE offers a number of services to its members, including help in obtaining information about programs of other agencies such as Social Security and the Veterans Administration, as well as travel-related services. Membership is open to civilians who have at least five years vested service in any agency of the Federal or DC governments. The membership fee varies from chapter to chapter.

Saga Holidays, 222 Berkely Street, Boston, MA 02116; (800) 343-0273; Fax: (617) 375-5950. This travel club focuses on arranging travel packages for people 50 or over.

Seniors Abroad, 12533 Pacato Circle North, San Diego, CA 92128; (619) 485-1696. Seniors Abroad specializes in reasonably-priced vacation packages for senior travelers. Call or write for information.

United Airlines: Silver Wings Travel Club, P.O. Box 50159, Dallas, TX 75250; (214) 760-0022. Membership in United Airlines Silver Wings Plus Program, entitles travelers 62 or older a 10 percent discount on applicable published fares on United Express and Shuttle by United. Companions also get a 10 percent discount regardless of age. Members also receive discounts on Hertz rental cars, and at participating hotels. Call or write for more information.

Chapter 10

Late Addition: 50 More Federal Money Programs

This late addition to "Free Cash & Benefits For 50 Or Over" contains information from the recent update (December 1996) of the General Services Administration publication, "Catalog of Federal Domestic Assistance". The Catalog provides the latest information on all the 1,327 federal domestic assistance programs. Obviously, listing over 1,300 government assistance programs is beyond the scope of this book. What is included in this chapter is 50 additional federal "money" programs. The programs provide financial assistance in a number of ways: through grants, loans, loan guarantees, scholarships, mortgage loans, insurance, and other types of financial assistance. Most of the programs on the following pages are especially for the 50 or over age group.

Besides being available to individuals age 50 or over, the programs listed in this chapter all provide some sort of monetary assistance. Each listing contains the following:

1) The Administering Government Agency. For example, "Department of Housing And Urban Development".

2) Types of Assistance, which include:

— Grants: this is, in essence, free money, which does not have to be paid back. Grant money may include scholarships, fellowships, construction grants, and other types of financial assistance.

— Direct Payments for Specified Use: This is financial assistance from the federal government provided directly to, among others, individuals, to encourage or subsidize a particular activity, such as home repair and/or rehabilitation.

— Direct Payments with Unrestricted Use: This is money from the federal government paid directly to individuals who satisfy federal eligibility requirements with no restrictions imposed on the recipient as to how the money is spent. This type of assistance generally includes payments under retirement, pension, and compensation programs.

— Direct Loans: Financial assistance provided through the lending of federal money to individuals for a specified period of time, with a "reasonable expectation" of repayment. Direct loans may or may not require the payment of interest.

— Guaranteed/Insured Loans: This type of assistance is provided in programs in which the federal government arranges to indemnify a lender against part or all of any defaults by borrowers.

— Insurance: The government provides financial assistance to ensure reimbursement for losses sustained under specified conditions. The federal government may provide this coverage directly or it may be provided through private carriers. This coverage may or may not involve the payment of premiums.

3) Eligible Beneficiaries, which includes the ultimate beneficiaries of a specific assistance program. Generally, beneficiaries must satisfy specific criteria, such as being at least 60 or older, to be eligible for assistance.

4) Range of Assistance, includes, where available, the average and maximum amount of assistance. These figures are based on funds awarded in the past fiscal year and the current fiscal year to date. These figures are subject to change.

5) Contact. This section of each listing includes names and addresses of the office(s) at the local, state and/or headquarters level, where you can get information, eligibility requirements, and applications for specific assistance programs.

While the information in the following listings was accurate at the time of writing, you should keep in mind that individual programs are subject to change. Federal funding for specific programs may disappear, or eligibility requirements may change. However, with the number of programs offered by Uncle Sam, you should be able to find an assistance program for which you are eligible.

Department of Housing And Urban Development (HUD)

1. Rehabilitation Mortgage Insurance (203(k)

Type of Assistance: Guaranteed/Insured loans, which can be used to help families repair or improve, purchase and improve, or refinance and improve existing residential structures more than one year old.

Eligible Beneficiaries: Individual purchasers or investors.

Range of Assistance: Not Available (NA).

Contact: The nearest local HUD office (listed in your phone directory), or

Director, Single Family Development
Division, Office of Insured Single Family
Housing, Department of Housing and
Urban Development,
Washington, DC 20410;
(202) 708-2720.

2. Manufactured Home Loan Insurance: Financing Purchase of Manufactured Homes as Principal Residences of Borrowers (Title I)

Type of Assistance: Guaranteed and Insured Loans.

Eligible Beneficiaries: Individuals/families.

Range of Assistance: Maximum amount of loan is $48,000.

Contact: Director, Title I Insurance Division,
Department of Housing and
Urban Development,
490 L'Enfant Plaza East, Suite 3214,
Washington, DC 20024;
(202) 755-7400.

3. Mortgage Insurance: Homes (203 (b))

Type of Assistance: Guaranteed/Insured loans to help people undertake home ownership.

Eligible Beneficiaries: Individuals/families.

Range of Assistance: Maximum insurable loans up to $151,150.

Contact: Nearest local HUD office, or

Director, Single Family Development
Division, Office of Insured Single Family
Housing, Department of Housing and
Urban Development,
Washington, DC 20410;
(202) 708-2700.

4. Mortgage Insurance: Homes For Low and Moderate Income Families (221 (d) (2))

Type of Assistance: Guaranteed/Insured loans to help low-income and moderate income families undertake home ownership.

Eligible Beneficiaries: Individuals/families.

Range of Assistance: Maximum amount of loan $42,000 for a single-family home.

Contact: Nearest local HUD field office (see Appendix), or contact the HUD headquarters at the above address.

5. Mortgage Insurance: Homes in Outlying Areas (203 (i))

Type of Assistance: Guaranteed/Insured loans to help people purchase homes in rural areas.

Eligible Beneficiaries: Individuals/families.

Range of Assistance: NA

Contact: Nearest local HUD field office, or HUD headquarters at the above address.

6. Mortgage Insurance: Homes in Urban Renewal Areas (220 Homes)

Type of Assistance: Guaranteed /Insured loans to help families purchase or rehabilitate homes in urban renewal areas.

Eligible Beneficiaries: Individuals/families.

Range of Assistance: NA

Contact: Nearest local HUD field office, or HUD headquarters at the above address.

7. Mortgage Insurance: Purchase of Units in Condominiums (234 (c))

Type of Assistance: Guaranteed/Insured loans to help families
purchase units in condominium projects.

Eligible Beneficiaries: Individuals/families.

Range of Assistance: NA

Contact: Nearest local HUD field office, or HUD headquarters at above address.

8. Mortgage Insurance: Rental Housing (207)

Type of Assistance: Guaranteed/Insured loans to provide good quality rental housing for moderate income families.

Eligible Beneficiaries: Individuals/families.

Range of Assistance: NA

Contact: Nearest local HUD field office, or Policies and Procedures Division, Office of Insured

Multifamily Housing Development,
Department of Housing and
Urban Development,
Washington, DC 20410; (202) 708-2556.

9. Mortgage Insurance: Rental and Cooperative Housing for Moderate Income Families and Elderly, Market Interest Rate (221 (d) [3] and [4])

Type of Assistance: Guaranteed/Insured loans to provide good quality rental or cooperative housing for moderate income families and the elderly and handicapped.

Eligible Beneficiaries: All families are eligible—there are no income limits.

Range of Assistance: NA

Contact: Nearest local HUD field office, or HUD's Policies and procedures Division at the above address.

10. Mortgage Insurance: Rental Housing for the Elderly (231)

Type of Assistance: Guaranteed/Insured loans to provide good quality rental housing for the elderly.

Eligible Beneficiaries: All elderly or handicapped persons.

Range of Assistance: NA

Contact: Nearest local HUD field office, or HUD's Policies and Procedures Division at the above address.

11. Property Improvement Loan Insurance For Improving All Existing Structures and Building Of Nonresidential Structures (Title I)

Type of Assistance: Guaranteed/Insured loans to help finance improvements to homes and other existing structures and the building of new nonresidential structures.

Eligible Beneficiaries: Individuals/families.

Range of Assistance: Maximum amount of loan is $60,000.

Contact: Director, Title I Insurance Division,
Department of Housing and
Urban Development,
490 L'Enfant Plaza East, Suite
3214, Washington, DC 20024;
(800) 733-4633, or (202) 755-7400.

12. Mortgage Insurance: Homes For Members of the Armed Services (Section 222)

Type of Assistance: Guaranteed/Insured loans to help members of the armed services on active duty to purchase homes.

Eligible Beneficiaries: Individuals/families—members of U.S. armed services on active duty.

Range of Assistance: NA

Contact: Nearest local HUD field office, or
Director, Single Family Development Division,
Office of Insured Single Family Housing,
Department of Housing and
Urban Development,
Washington, DC 20410;
(202) 708-2700.

13. Mortgage Insurance: Growing Equity Mortgages (GEMS)

Type of Assistance: Guaranteed/Insured loans to help expand housing opportunities to the home buying public.

Eligible Beneficiaries: Individuals/families.

Range of Assistance: NA

Contact: Nearest local HUD field office, or HUD's Single Family Development Division at the above address.

14. Lower Income Housing Assistance Program: Section 8 New Construction / Substantial

Rehabilitation (Section 8 Housing Assistance Payments for Very Low Income Families)

Type Of Assistance: Direct payments to assist low-income families in obtaining decent, safe, and sanitary rental housing.

Eligible Beneficiaries: Low income families whose incomes meet program guidelines.

Range of Assistance: NA

Contact: Nearest local HUD office or
Director, Office of Multifamily Housing
Management, Housing Department of
Housing & Urban Development,
Washington, DC 20410;
(202) 708-3730.

15. Mortgage Insurance For Single Room Occupancy (SRO) Projects (221 (d) Single Room Occupancy)

Type of Assistance: Guaranteed/Insured loans.
Eligible Beneficiaries: Individuals/families— no income limits.

Range of Assistance: NA

Contact: Nearest local HUD field office, or
Policies and Procedures Division,

Office of Insured Multifamily Housing
Development,
Washington, DC 20410;
(202) 708-2556.

16. Lower Income Housing Assistance Program: Section 8 Moderate Rehabilitation

Type of Assistance: Direct Payments to assist low-income families in obtaining decent, safe and sanitary rental housing.

Eligible Beneficiaries: Low income families and low income elderly individuals.

Range of Assistance: Assisted families must pay the highest of 30% of their monthly adjusted family incomes; 10% of gross family income, or the portion of welfare assistance designated for housing toward rent.

Contact: Office of the Deputy Assistant
Secretary for Public and Assisted Housing
Operations, Office of Rental Assistance,
Department of Housing and
Urban Development,
Washington, DC 20410;
(202) 708-0477.

17. Section 8 Rental Certificate Program

Type of Assistance: Direct payments to aid low income families in obtaining decent, safe and sanitary housing.

Eligible Beneficiaries: Low income families.

Range of Assistance: NA

Contact: Office for Public and Assisted Housing Operations at the above address.

18. Adjustable Rate Mortgages (ARMS)

Type of Assistance: Guaranteed/Insured loans to be used to finance the purchase of proposed, under construction, or existing one-to-four-family housing as well as to finance indebtedness on existing homes.

Eligible Beneficiaries: Individuals/Families

Range of Assistance: NA

Contact: Nearest local HUD field office (see Appendix), or

Director, Single Family Development
Division, Office of Insured Single Family
Housing, Department of Housing and Urban
Development,
Washington, DC 20410; (202) 708-2700.

Veterans Benefits Administration

19. Pension To Veterans Surviving Spouses, and Children (Death Pension)

Type of Assistance: Direct payments to assist needy surviving spouses, and children of deceased war-time veterans whose deaths were not due to service.

Eligible Beneficiaries: Needy surviving spouses and children of war-time veterans.

Range of Assistance: Up to $8,466 annually.

Contact: The nearest Veterans Benefits Administration field office (see listing in the Appendix). For program information, contact:

Department of Veterans Affairs,
Washington, DC 20420;
(202) 273-7218.

20. Pension For Non-Service-Connected Disability For Veterans (Pension)

Type of Assistance: Direct payments (unrestricted use) to assist war-time veterans in need whose non-service-connected disabilities are permanent and total preventing them from following a substantially gainful occupation.

Eligible Beneficiaries: Disabled veterans whose disabilities are non-service-connected.

Range of Assistance: Up to $15,744 annually.

Contact: Nearest Veterans Benefits Administration field office.

21. Veteran's Compensation For Service-Connected Disability

Type of Assistance: Direct payments (unrestricted use) to compensate veterans for disabilities incurred or aggravated during military service.

Eligible Beneficiaries: Disabled veterans.

Range of Assistance: From $91 to $5,346 per month.

Contact: Nearest Veterans Benefits Administration field office.

22. Veterans Housing: Guaranteed and Insured Loans (VA Home Loans)

Type of Assistance: Guaranteed/ Insured loans to assist veterans, certain service personnel, and certain surviving spouses of veterans in obtaining credit for the purchase, construction or improvement of homes on more liberal terms than are typically available to non-veterans.

Eligible Beneficiaries: Veterans, service personnel, unremarried surviving spouses of veterans.

Range of Assistance: NA

Contact: Nearest Veterans Benefits Administration field office.

23. Survivors and Dependents Educational Assistance

Type of Assistance: Direct Monthly Payments to be used for tuition, books, subsistence, etc.

Eligible Beneficiaries: Spouses, surviving spouses, and children of veterans who died or who are permanently and totally disabled due to military service.

Range of Assistance: Up to $404 per month for institutional training; up to $1,200 tutorial assistance.

Contact: Nearest Veterans Benefits Administration field office, or

Department of Veterans Affairs,
Central Office,
Washington, DC 20402;
(202) 273-7132.

Health Care Financing Administration (HCFA)

24. Medicare: Hospital Insurance

Type of Assistance: Direct payments to provide hospital insurance protection for covered services to persons 65 or older.

Eligible Beneficiaries: Persons age 65 or over and qualified disabled persons.

Range of Assistance: NA

Contact: Director, Bureau of Program
Operations, Health Care Financing
Administration, Room S2-01-09,
7500 Security Boulevard,
Baltimore, MD 21444;
(410) 786-8050.

25. Medicare: Supplementary Medical Insurance

Type of Assistance: Direct payments to provide medical insurance protection for covered services to persons age 65 or over.

Eligible Beneficiaries: Persons 65 and over, and persons under age 65 who qualify for hospital insurance benefits.

Range of Assistance: The beneficiary must meet an annual $100 deductible before benefits begin— thereafter, Medicare pays 80% of the fee schedule amount or the "reasonable" costs for covered services.

Contact: Bureau of Program Operations, HCFA at above address.

U.S. Department of Agriculture

26. Commodity Loans and Purchases (Price Supports)

Type of Assistance: Direct payments (unrestricted use); Direct loans— to be used to improve and stabilize farm income, to assist in bringing about a better balance between supply and demand of the commodities, and to assist farmers in the marketing of their crops.

Eligible Beneficiaries: Owners, landlords, tenants, or sharecroppers on farms that have produced eligible commodities, and meets other program requirements as announced by the Secretary of Agriculture.

Range of Assistance: Direct Payments (Purchases): NA; Average loans $24,288.

Contact: Consult your local phone directory for

the location of the Farm Service Agency (FSA) county office. If no county office is listed, contact the appropriate FSA state office, listed under "Farm Service Agency" in the government section of your phone directory, or contact:

Department of Agriculture,
Farm Service Agency,
Price Support Division, Ag Box 0512,
Washington, DC 20013-2415;
(202) 720-7641.

For general information about the FSA and its programs, contact:

USDA FSA Public Affairs Staff,
P.O. Box 2415, Stop 0506,
Washington, DC 20013;
(202) 720-5237.

27. Agricultural Conservation Program (ACP)

Type of Assistance: Direct payments to be used to assist soil, water, energy, woodland, and pollution abatement programs on farms and ranches.

Eligible Beneficiaries: Any owner, landlord, tenant, or sharecropper on a farm or ranch who bears a part of the cost of an approved conservation practice.

Range of Assistance: Average assistance $1,600.

Contact: Nearest FSA office, or

Department of Agriculture,
Farm Service Agency, Ag Box 0520,
Washington, DC 20013;
(202) 720-6221.

28. Forestry Incentives Program (FIP)

Type of Assistance: Direct payments to be used for tree planting, timber stand improvement, and site preparation for the natural regeneration of land.

Eligible Beneficiaries: Private individuals who own "non-industrial" private forest lands capable of producing industrial wood crops.

Range of Assistance: Average Direct payments of $1,600.

Contact: Consult your phone directory for the location of the Natural Resources Conservation Service (NCRS) office where your land is located. If no local office is listed, contact your state NRCS office, or

NRCS, Department of Agriculture,
P.O. Box 2890,
Washington, DC 20013;
(202) 720-1870.

29. Farm Operating Loans

Type of Assistance: Direct loans; Guaranteed/Insured loans— to help family farmers make more efficient use of their land, labor, and other resources.

Eligible Beneficiaries: Individuals/ families who are farmers or ranchers and who meet program requirements.

Range of Assistance: Average Direct Loan, about $41,000; average Guaranteed loan, about $108,000.

Contact: Your local or state Farm Service Agency, or

Department of Agriculture,
Farm Service Agency, Director,
Loan Making Division, Ag Box 0522,
Washington, DC 20250;
(202) 720-1632.

30. Emergency Loans

Type of Assistance: Direct loans to be used to repair, restore, or replace damaged or destroyed farm property and supplies which were lost or damaged as a direct result of a natural disaster.

Eligible Beneficiaries: Individuals/families who are farmers or ranchers.

Range of Assistance: Average loan is $45,000.

Contact: Appropriate FSA local or state office, or

Department of Agriculture,
Farm Service Agency, Director,
Loan Making Division, Ag Box 0522,
Washington, DC 20250;
(202) 720-1632.

31. Conservation Reserve Program (CRP)

Type of Assistance: Direct annual payments in return for the implementation of a conservation plan approved by the local conservation district for converting highly erodible cropland or "environmentally sensitive" land to a less intensive use. For example, cropland might be planted with a vegetative cover, such as perennial grasses, legumes, shrubs, or trees.

Eligible Beneficiaries: Individuals (and others) owning or operating private croplands.

Range of Assistance: Average annual payment, $5,324.

Contact: Nearest county or state FSA office, or

Department of Agriculture,
Farm Service Agency, Ag Box 0513,
Washington, DC 20013;
(202) 720-6221.

32. Interest Assistance Program

Type of Assistance: Guaranteed/ Insured loans to aid family sized farms in obtaining credit when they are temporarily unable to project a positive cash flow without a reduction in the interest rate.

Eligible Beneficiaries: Individuals/families.

Range of Assistance: Average loans, $115,000.

Contact: Nearest local or State FSA office, or

Department of Agriculture,
Farm Service Agency, Director,
Loan Making Division, Ag Box 0522,
Washington, DC 20250;
(202) 720-1632.

Social Security Administration (SSA)

33. Social Security Disability Insurance

Type of Assistance: Direct payments (unrestricted and specified use) to replace part of the earnings lost due to a physical or mental impairment severe enough to prevent an individual from working.

Eligible Beneficiaries: Qualified disabled workers under the age of 65.

Range of Assistance: Monthly cash benefits for a worker disabled in 1996, range up to a maximum of $1,462 based on the level of the worker's earnings and the age at which a worker becomes disabled.

Contact: Your nearest local SSA office listed in the phone directory, or:

Office of Public Inquiry,
Room 4100, Annex,
Social Security Administration,
Baltimore, MD 21235;
(410) 965-2736.

34. Social Security: Retirement Insurance

Type of Assistance: Direct monthly payments to replace part of earnings lost due to retirement.

Eligible Beneficiaries: Retired workers age 62 and over who have worked the required number of years under Social Security, and to certain family members.

Range of Assistance: Monthly cash benefits for a worker retiring at age 65 in 1966, range up to $1,248 and to a maximum of $2,183 for a family of such a worker receiving benefits.

Contact: Your nearest local SSA office, or SSA's Office of Public Inquiry at the above address.

35. Supplemental Security Income (SSI)

Type of Assistance: Direct payments to assure a minimum level of income to persons who have attained age 65 or are blind or disabled, whose income and resources are below specified levels.

Eligible Beneficiaries: Persons who are 65 or older, or who are blind or disabled and who continue to meet the income and resource tests.

Range of Assistance: Up to $705 per month.

Contact: Nearest SSA office, or SSA's Office of Public Inquiry at the above address.

36. Social Security: Special Benefits for Persons Aged 72 and over

Type of Assistance: Direct payments (with unrestricted use) to assure some regular income to certain persons age 72 and over who had little or no opportunity to earn Social Security protection during their working years.

Eligible Beneficiaries: Individuals who reached age 72 before 1968 and those who reached age 72 after 1967 through 1971 who have Social Security work credits.

Range of Assistance: The payment was $188.80 for each qualifying individual as of December 1995.

Contact: Your local SSA office, or the SSA's Office of Public Affairs at the above address.

Department of Education

37. Douglas Teacher Scholarships

Type of Assistance: Scholarship assistance to support postsecondary study that leads to a teaching certificate.

Eligible Beneficiaries: Individuals who wish to pursue teaching careers at the preschool, elementary or secondary level.

Range of Assistance: Scholarship assistance amounts up to $5,000 each year for up to four years. The scholarship cannot exceed the recipients cost of attendance. Scholarship recipients also must fulfill teaching requirements or pay back the scholarship with interest.

Contact: The Douglas Teacher Scholarships Program is administered by the Department of Education headquarters office. Program descriptions are available at regional offices, which are listed at the end of this chapter. You also can contact:

Department of Education,
Office of the Assistant Secretary for
Postsecondary Education,
Division of Higher Education
Incentives Program,
600 Independence Avenue, SW,
Washington, DC 20202-5329.
Contact Valerie Hurry; (202) 260-3392.

38. State School Incentives Grants

Type of Assistance: Grants to be used for full-time attendance by students with substantial financial need who are enrolled at postsecondary institutions.

Eligible Beneficiaries: Postsecondary education students with substantial financial need.

Range of Assistance: Grants up to $5,000 for full-time attendance.

Contact: Program descriptions and a list of state student scholarships or assistance agencies (listed at the end of this chapter). You also can contact:

Division of Policy Development,
Policy, Training, and Analysis Service,
Student Financial Assistance Programs,
Office of Assistant Secretary For
Postsecondary Education,
Department of Education,
Pell and State Grant Section,
600 Independence Avenue, SW,
Washington, DC 20202-5447.
Contact: Fred H. Sellers; (202) 708-4607.

39. Federal Supplemental Educational Opportunity Grants (SEOG)

Type of Assistance: Direct payments to be used for undergraduate postsecondary study.

Eligible Beneficiaries: Individuals enrolled or accepted for enrollment as regular students, and who have financial need.

Range of Assistance: Grants to students range from $200 to $4,000 per year. Estimated average award to students, $705.

Contact: You should contact the educational institution(s) you plan to attend. For general information about the program, contact:

Policy Development Division,
Student Financial Assistance Programs,

Office of Assistant Secretary for
Postsecondary Education,
Department of Education,
600 Independence Avenue, SW,
Washington, DC 20202-5446.
Contact: Harold McCollough,
Chief, Campus-Based Programs Section,
Grants Branch; (202) 708-4690.
40. Federal Family Education Loans

Type of Assistance: Guaranteed/Insured loans to help defray costs of education at participating schools.

Eligible Beneficiaries: Generally, any person who is enrolled or accepted for enrollment in a degree or certificate program on at least a half-time basis at a postsecondary school.

Range of Assistance: Under the Federal Stafford Loan Program, the maximum may not exceed $2,625 for the first academic year of undergraduate study; $3,500 for the second academic year; and $5,500 for each remaining year of undergraduate education. Total undergraduate loans outstanding may not exceed $23,000. Under the Subsidized Stafford program, an undergraduate may borrow an aggregate loan maximum of $23,000.

Contact: The Department of Education regional office in your area (listed at the end of this chapter), or the

Division of Policy Development,
Policy, Training, and Analysis Service,
Office of the Assistant Secretary for
Postsecondary Education,
Department of Education,
Washington, DC 20202.
Contact: Pamela A. Moran;
(202) 798-8242.

41. Federal Pell Grant Program (Pell Grants)

Type of Assistance: Direct Payments to help eligible undergraduate postsecondary students meet educational expenses.

Eligible Beneficiaries: Undergraduate students who have demonstrated financial need and who meet financial need criteria.

Range of Assistance: Grants range from $400 to $2,340. Average award is around $1,500.

Contact: Federal Student Aid Information Center, 1-800-433-3243. Regional Director, Office of Student Financial Assistance, the Director of Student Financial Aid at the institution you plan to attend, high school guidance counselors, or directors of State Departments of Education (see listing at the end of this chapter).

Corporation For National And Community Service

42. Senior Companion Program (SCP)

Type of Assistance: Grants to be used for Senior Companion stipends, transportation, physical examinations, insurance, meals, etc.

Eligible Beneficiaries: Persons 60 years of age or over, with incomes within limits determined by the CEO of the Corporation for National Service, interested in serving special-needs adults, especially the frail-elderly, and must be physically, mentally and emotionally capable and willing to serve on a person-to-person basis.

Range of Assistance: NA

Contact: Senior Companion Program,
Corporation for National Service,
1201 New York Avenue, NW,
Washington, DC 20525;
(202) 606-5000.

Employment And Training Administration

43. Unemployment Insurance

Type of Assistance: Grants and Direct Payments to assist eligible workers.

Eligible Beneficiaries: All workers whose wages are subject to State unemployment insurance loans.

Range of Assistance: NA

Contact: Local office of the State Employment Service; local office of the State Unemployment Service; Employment and Training Administration regional offices (see Appendix). For program information, contact:

Director, Unemployment Insurance Service,
Employment and Training Administration,
Department of Labor,
Washington, DC 20210;
(202) 219-7831.

44. Senior Community Service Employment Program (SCSEP— Older Worker Program)

Type of Assistance: Grants to be used to create and pay for part-time community service job positions for eligible persons 55 and over.

Eligible Beneficiaries: Individuals 55 years or older with a family income at or below the specified levels.

Range of Assistance: NA

Contact: Office of Special Targeted Programs,
Employment and Training Administration,
Department of Labor, Room N4641,
200 Constitution Avenue, NW,
Washington, DC 20210;
(202) 219-5500.

Federal Emergency Management Agency (FEMA)

45. Disaster Assistance

Type of Assistance: Direct payments (unrestricted use) to assist individuals and families adversely affected by declared disasters. Assistance may include disaster housing, assistance to unemployed, individual and family grants for disaster-related necessary expenses or serious needs.

Eligible Beneficiaries: Individual disaster victims in designated emergency or major disaster areas.

Range of Assistance: NA

Contact: Nearest FEMA regional office, listed at the end of this chapter, or

Patricia Stahlschmidt, Federal Emergency
Assistance Agency, Response and Recovery
Directorate,
Washington, DC 20472; (202) 646-4066.

Food And Consumer Service

46. Food Stamps

Type of Assistance: Direct payments in the form of a coupon allotment which may be used in participating retail stores to buy food for home consumption and garden seeds and plants to produce food for personal consumption.

Eligible Beneficiaries: Households are certified individually by local welfare offices based on national eligibility standards, with verification as required by regulation.

Range of Assistance: Varies by income and family size. Averaged $73,32 per month, per person in 1996.

Contact: Food and Consumer Regional Office, listed in your phone directory, or

Deputy Administrator, Food Stamp Program,
Food and Consumer Services,
Department of Agriculture,
Alexandria, VA 22302;
(703) 305-2026.

Pension Benefit Guaranty Corporation (PBGC)

47. Pension Plan Termination Insurance

Type of Assistance: Insurance to protect pension benefits in ongoing plans to provide for the timely and uninterrupted payment benefits to participants and beneficiaries of covered plans, and to maintain premiums charged by the PBGC at the lowest level possible.

Eligible Beneficiaries: All participants of covered single-employer pension plans.

Range of Assistance: Average monthly benefit per retiree, $335.

Contact: Nearest Department of Labor, Pension Welfare Administration Field Office (see chapter 2, "Free Help Getting A Job Or Going To College"), or contact:

Pension Benefit Guaranty Corporation,
1200 K Street, NW,
Washington, DC 20005-4026;
(202) 326-4000.

Small Business Administration (SBA)

48. Small Business Loans (Regular Business Loans: 7 (a) loans)

Type of Assistance: Guaranteed/Insured loans to be used to construct, expand, or convert facilities; to purchase building equipment or materials; and for working capital.

Eligible Beneficiaries: Small businesses, including those owned by low-income and handicapped individuals, or located in high unemployment areas.

Range of Assistance: Guaranteed loans up to $500,000.

Contact: Initial contact should be with the SBA district office in your area. Consult your phone directory for SBA listings. For program information, contact:

Director, Loan Policy and Procedures Branch,
Small Business Administration,
409 Third Street, SW,
Washington, DC 20416;
(202) 205-6570

49. Loans For Small Businesses (Direct Loan Program, Low-Income/ High-Unemployed Areas.

Type of Assistance: Direct loans to assist in

establishing , preserving, and strengthening small businesses owned by low-income persons or located in areas of high unemployment.

Eligible Beneficiaries: Credit worthy individuals with income below basic needs or small businesses located in areas of high unemployment, or business located in areas with a high percentage of low-income individuals.

Range of Assistance: Average direct loan, $61,778.

Contact: Nearest SBA Field Office, or Loan Policy and Procedures Branch at the above address.

50. Veterans Loan Program

Type of Assistance: Direct loans to assist small businesses owned by Vietnam-era and disabled veterans.

Eligible Beneficiaries: Vietnam-era and disabled veterans who own small businesses.

Range of Assistance: Average loan, $75,845.

Contact: Nearest SBA field office, or Loan Policy and Procedures Branch at the above address.

Department of Education Regional Offices

Each of the Department of Education's 10 regions covers several states. The following list gives the state responsibilities of each region as well as the points of contact in each region:

Region I (Connecticut, Maine, Massachusetts, New Hampshire, Rhode Island, Vermont):
Jan L. Paschal, 540 McCormack Courthouse,
Post Office Square,
Boston, MA 02109-4557;
(617) 223-9317; Fax: (617) 223-9324.

Region II (New Jersey, New York, Puerto Rico, Virgin Islands):
W. Wilson Goode (acting),
75 Park Place, 12th Floor, New York, NY 10007;
(212) 264-7005,
or Patricia Parisi, Deputy; (212) 637-6284;
Fax: (212) 264-4427.

Region III (Delaware, District of Columbia, Maryland, Pennsylvania, Virginia, West Virginia):
W. Wilson Goode, 3535 Market Street,
Room 16350, Philadelphia, PA 19104-3398;
(215) 596-1001; Fax: (215) 596-1094.

Region IV (Alabama, Florida, Georgia, Kentucky, Mississippi, North Carolina, South Carolina, Tennessee):

Stanley Williams,
P.O. Box 1777,
101 Marietta Tower Building, Suite 2221,
Atlanta, GA 30323;
(404) 331-2502; Fax: (404) 841-5382.

Region V (Illinois, Indiana, Michigan, Minnesota, Ohio, Wisconsin):
Stephanie J. Jones,
401 South State Street, Suite 700A,
Chicago, IL 60605-1225;
886-8215; Fax: (312) 353-5147.

Region VI (Arkansas, Louisiana, New Mexico, Oklahoma, Texas):
Sally H. Cain,
1200 Main Tower Building, Room 2125,
Dallas, TX 75202-4309;
(214) 767-3626; Fax: (214) 729-3634.

Region VII (Iowa, Kansas, Missouri, Nebraska):
Sandra V. Walker,
10220 N. Executive Hills Boulevard, Suite 720,
Kansas City, MO 64153-1367;
(816) 880-4000; Fax: (816) 891-0578.

Region VIII (Colorado, Montana, North Dakota, South Dakota, Utah, Wyoming):
Lynn Osborn Simons, Regional Office,
Federal Building,

1244 Speer Boulevard, Suite 310,
Denver, CO 80204-3582;
(303) 844-3544; Fax: (303) 564-2524.

Region IX (Arizona, California, Hawaii, Nevada):
Loni Hancock,
50 United Nations Plaza, Room 205,
San Francisco, CA 94102-4987;
(415) 437-7520; (415) 437-7540.

Region X (Alaska, Idaho, Oregon, Washington):
Carla Nuxoll,
Office of the SRR, Jackson Federal Building,
Room 3362, 915 Second Avenue,
Seattle, WA 98174-1099;
(206) 220-7800; Fax: (206) 220-7806.

Federal Emergency Management Agency (FEMA) Regional Offices

FEMA has 10 regional offices. Each region serves several states, and regional staff work directly with the states to help plan for disasters, develop mitigation programs, and meet needs when major disasters occur.

Region I (Connecticut, Massachusetts, Maine, New Hampshire, Rhode Island, Vermont):
Louis A Elisa, II, Regional Director,
Federal Emergency Management Agency,

JW McCormack Post Office and
Courthouse Building, Room 442,
Boston, MA 02109-4595;
(617) 223-9540; Fax: (617) 223-9519.

Region II (New Jersey, New York, Puerto Rico, Virgin Islands):
Lynn G. Canton, Regional Director,
Federal Emergency Management Agency,
26 Federal Plaza, Room 1337,
New York, NY 10278-0002;
(212) 225-7209; Fax: (212) 225-7281.

Region III (District of Columbia, Delaware, Maryland, Pennsylvania, Virginia, West Virginia):
Rita A. Calvan, Regional Director, Federal Emergency Management Agency,
Liberty Square Building,
Second Floor, 105 South Seventh Street,
Philadelphia, PA 19106-3316;
(215) 931-5608; Fax: (215) 931-5261.

Region IV (Alabama, Florida, Georgia, Kentucky, Mississippi, North Carolina, South Carolina, Tennessee):
Kenneth D. Hutchison, Regional Director,
Federal Emergency Management Agency,
3003 Chamblee-Tucker Road,
Atlanta, GA 30341;

(770) 220-5200; Fax: (770) 220-5230.

Region V (Illinois, Indiana, Michigan, Minnesota, Ohio, Wisconsin):
Michelle M. Burkett, Regional Director,
Federal Emergency Management Agency,
175 W. Jackson Boulevard, Fourth Floor,
Chicago, IL 60604-2698;
(312) 408-5501/5503; Fax: (312) 408-5234.

Region VI (Arkansas, Louisiana, New Mexico, Oklahoma, Texas):
Gary E. Jones, Acting Regional Director,
Federal Emergency Management Agency,
Federal Regional Center, 800 N. Loop 288,
Denton, TX 76201-3698;
(817) 898-5104; Fax: (817) 898-5325.

Region VII (Iowa, Kansas, Missouri, Nebraska):
John A. Miller, Regional Director,
Federal Emergency Management Agency,
2323 Grand Boulevard, Suite 900,
City, MO 64108-2670;
(816) 283-7061; Fax: (816) 283-7582.

Region VIII (Colorado, Montana, North Dakota, South Dakota, Utah, Wyoming):
Michael J. Armstrong, Regional Director,
Federal Emergency Management Agency,
Denver Federal Center, Building 710, Box 25267,

Denver, CO 80255-0267;
(303) 235-4812; Fax: (303) 235-0267.

Region IX (Arizona, California, Guam, Hawaii, Nevada):
Shirley Mattingly, Regional Director,
Federal Emergency Management Agency,
Building 105, Presdio of San Francisco,
San Francisco, CA 94129;
(415) 923-7100; Fax: (415) 923-7112.

Region X (Alaska, Idaho, Oregon, Washington):
David L. de Courcy, Regional Director,
Federal Emergency Management Agency,
Federal Regional Center, 130 228th Street, SW,
Bothell, WA 98021-9796;
(206) 487-4604; Fax: (206) 487-4622.

State Higher Education Agencies

ALABAMA: Alabama Commission on Higher Education, Suite 205, 3465 Norman Bridge Road, Montgomery, AL 36105-2310; (334) 281-1998.

State Department of Education, Gordon Persons Office Building, 50 North Ripley Street, Montgomery, AL 36130-3901; (205) 242-8082.

ALASKA: Alaska Commission on Postsecondary Education, 3030 Vintage Boulevard, Juneau, AK 99801-7109; (907) 465-2962. State

Department of Education, Goldbelt Place, 801 West 10th Street, Suite 200, Juneau, AK 99801-1894; (907) 465-8715.

ARIZONA: Arizona Commission for Postsecondary Education, 2020 North Central Ave., Suite 275, Phoenix, AZ 85004-4503; (602) 229-2531. State Department of Education, 1535 West Jefferson, Phoenix, AZ 85007; (602) 542-2147.

ARKANSAS: Arkansas Department of Higher Education, 114 East Capitol, Little Rock, AR 72201-3818; (501) 324-9300. Arkansas Department of Education, 4 State Capitol Mall, Room 304A, Little Rock, AR 72201-1071; (501) 682-4474.

CALIFORNIA: California Student Aid Commission, P.O. Box 510845, Sacramento, CA 94245-0845; (916) 445-0880, or 1515 South Street, North Building, Suite 500, P.O. Box 510845, Sacramento, CA 94245-0621; (916) 322-2294. California Department of Education, 721 Capitol Mall, Sacramento, CA 95814; (916) 657-2451.

COLORADO: Colorado Commission on Higher Education, Colorado Heritage Center, 1300 Broadway, 2nd Floor, Denver, CO 80203; (303) 866-2723. State Department of Education, 201 East Colfax Avenue, Denver, CO 80203-1705; (303) 866-6779.

CONNECTICUT: Connecticut Department of Higher Education, 61 Woodland Street, Hartford, CT 06105-2391. Connecticut Department of Education, 165 Capitol Avenue, P.O. Box 2219, Hartford, CT 06106-1630.

DELAWARE: Delaware Higher Education Commission, Carvel State Office Building, Fourth Floor, 820 North French Street, Wilmington, DE 19801; (302) 577-3240. State Department of Public Instruction, Townsend Building #279, Federal and Lockerman Streets, P.O. Box 1402, Dover, DE 19903-1402; (302) 739-4583.

DISTRICT OF COLUMBIA: Department of Human Services, Office of Postsecondary Education, Research and Assistance, 2100 Martin Luther King Jr., Avenue, SE, Suite 401, Washington, DC 20020; (202) 727-3685. District of Columbia Public Schools, Division of Student Services, 4501 Lee Street, N.E., Washington, DC 20019; (202) 724-4934.

FLORIDA: Florida Department of Education, Office of Student Financial Assistance, 1344 Florida Education Center, 325 West Gaines Street, Tallahassee, FL 32399-0400; (904) 487-0649.

GEORGIA: Georgia Student Finance Authority, State Loans and Grants Division, Suite 245, 2082 East Exchange Place, Tucker, GA 30084; (404) 414-3000. State Department of Education, 2054 Twin Towers

East, 205 Butler Street, Atlanta, GA 30334-5040; (404) 656-5812.

HAWAII: Hawaii State Postsecondary Education Commission, 2444 Dole Street, Room 202, Honolulu, HI 96822-2394; (808) 956-8213. Hawaii Department of Education, 2530 10th Avenue, Room A12, Honolulu, HI 96816; (808) 733-9103.

IDAHO: Idaho Board of Education, P.O. Box 83720, Boise, ID 83720-0037; (208) 334-2270. State Department of Education, 650 West State Street, Boise, ID 83720; (208) 334-2113.

ILLINOIS: Illinois Student Assistance Commission, 1755 Lake Cook Road, Deerfield, IL 60015-5209; (708) 948-8500.

INDIANA: State Student Assistance Commission of Indiana, Suite 500, 150 West Market Street, Indianapolis, IN 46204-2811; (317) 232-2350. Indiana Department of Education, Room 229 - State House, Center for Schools Improvement and Performance, Indianapolis, IN 46204-2798; (317) 232-2305.

IOWA: Iowa College Student Aid Commission, 914 Grand Avenue, Suite 201, Des Moines, IA 50309-2824; (800) 383-4222.

KANSAS: Kansas Board of Regents, 700 S.W. Harrison, Suite 1410, Topeka, KS 66603-3760; (913) 296-3517. State Department of Education, Kansas State Education Building, 120 East Tenth Street, Topeka, KS 66612-1103; (913) 296-4876.

KENTUCKY: Kentucky Higher Education Assistance Authority, Suite 102, 10050 U.S. 127 South, Frankfort, KY 40601-4323; (800) 928-8926. State Department of Education, 500 Metro Street, 1919 Capital Plaza Tower, Frankfort, KY 40601; (502) 564-3421.

LOUISIANA: Louisiana Student Financial Assistance Commission, Office of Student Financial Assistance, P.O. Box 91202, Baton Rouge, LA 70821-9202; (800) 259-5626. State Department of Education, P.O. Box 94064, 626 North 4th Street, 12th Floor, Baton Rouge, LA 70804-9064; (504) 342-2098.

MAINE: Finance Authority of Maine, P.O. Box 949, Augusta, ME 04333-0949; (207) 287-3263. Maine Department of Education, 23 State House Station, Augusta, ME 04333-0023; (207) 287-5800.

MARYLAND: Maryland Higher Education Commission, Jeffrey Building, 16 Francis Street, Annapolis, MD 21401-1781; (410) 974-2971. Maryland State Department of Education, 200 West Baltimore Street, Baltimore, MD 21201-2595; (410) 767-0480.

MASSACHUSETTS: Massachusetts Higher Education Coordinating Council, 330 Stuart Street, Boston, MA 02116; (617) 727-9420. State Department of Education, 350 Main Street, Malden, MA 02148-5023; (617) 388-3300. Massachusetts Higher Education Information Center, 666 Boylston Street, Boston, MA 02116; (617) 536-0200.

MICHIGAN: Michigan Higher Education Assistance Authority, Office of Scholarships and Grants, P.O. Box 30462, Lansing, MI 48909-7962; (517) 373-3394. Michigan Department of Education, 608 West Allegan Street, Hannah Building, Lansing, MI 48909; (517) 373-3324.

MINNESOTA: Minnesota Higher Education Coordinating Board, Suite 400, Capital Square Building, 550 Cedar Street, St. Paul, MN 55101-2292; (800) 657-3866. Department of Children, Families and Learning, 712 Capitol Square Building, 550 Cedar Street, St. Paul, MN 55101; (612) 296-6104.

MISSISSIPPI: Mississippi Postsecondary Education, Financial Assistance Board, 3825 Ridgewood Road, Jackson, MS 39211-6453; (601) 982-6663. State Department of Education, P.O. Box 771, Jackson, MS 39205-0771; (601) 359-3768.

MISSOURI: Missouri Coordinating Board For Higher Education, 3515 Amazonas Drive, Jefferson City, MO 65109-5717; (314) 751-2361. Missouri State

Department of Elementary and Secondary Education, P.O. Box 480, 205 Jefferson Street, Sixth Floor, Jefferson City, MO 65102-0480; (314) 751-2931.

MONTANA: Montana University System, 2500 Broadway, Helena, MT 59620-3103; (406) 444-6570 State Office of Public Instruction, State Capitol, Room 106, Helena, MT 59620; (406) 444-4422.

NEBRASKA: Coordinating Commission for Postsecondary Education, P.O. Box 95005, Lincoln, NE 68509-5005; (402) 471-2847. Nebraska Department of Education, P.O. Box 94987, 301 Centennial Mall South, Lincoln, NE 68509-4987; (402) 471-2784.

NEVADA: Nevada Department of Education, 400 West King Street, Capitol Complex, Carson City, NV 89710; (702) 687-5915.

NEW HAMPSHIRE: New Hampshire Postsecondary Education Commission, 2 Industrial Park Drive, Concord, NH 03301-8512; (603) 271-2555. State Department of Education, State Office Park South, 101 Pleasant Street, Concord, NH 03301; (603) 271-2632.

NEW JERSEY: Office of Student Financial Assistance, 4 Quakerbridge Plaza, CN 540, Trenton, NJ 08625; (800) 792-8670. State Department of Education, 225 West State Street, Trenton, NJ 08625-

0500; (609) 984-6409.

NEW MEXICO: New Mexico Commission on Higher Education, 1068 Cerrillos Road, Santa Fe , New Mexico 87501-4925; (505) 827-7383. State Department of Education, Education Building, 300 Don Gaspar, Santa Fe, New Mexico 87501-2786; (505) 827-6648.

NEW YORK: New York State Higher Education Services Corporation, One Commerce Plaza, Albany, NY 12255; (518) 474-5642. State Education Department, 111 Education Building, Washington Avenue, Albany, NY 12234; (518) 474-5705.

NORTH CAROLINA: North Carolina State Education Assistance Authority, P.O. Box 2688, Chapel Hill, NC 27515-2688; (919) 821-4771
State Department of Public Instruction, Education Building, Division of Teacher Education, 116 West Edenton Street, Raleigh, NC 27603-1712; (919) 733-0701.

NORTH DAKOTA: North Dakota University System, North Dakota Student Financial Assistance Program, 600 East Boulevard Avenue, Bismarck, ND 58505-0230; (701) 224-4114. State Department of Public Instruction, State Capitol Building, 11th Floor, 600 East Boulevard Avenue, Bismarck, ND 58505-0164; (701) 224-2271.

OHIO: Ohio Student Aid Commission, P.O. Box 182452, 309 South Fourth Street, Columbus, OH 43218-2452; (800) 837-6752. State Department of Education, 65 South Front Street, Room 1005, Columbus, OH 43266-0308; (614) 466-2761.

OKLAHOMA: Oklahoma State Regents for Higher Education, Oklahoma Guaranteed Student Loan Program, P.O. Box 300, Oklahoma City, OK 73101-3000; (405) 858-4300; (800) 247-0420. State Department of Education, Oliver Hodge Memorial Education Building, 2500 North Lincoln Boulevard, Oklahoma City, OK 73105-4599; (405) 521-4122.

OREGON: Oregon State Scholarship Commission, Suite 100, 1500 Valley River Drive, Eugene, Oregon 97401-2130; (503) 687-7400. Oregon State System of Higher Education, 700 Pringle Parkway, SE, Salem, OR 97310-0290; (503) 378-5585.

Oregon Department of Education, 255 Capitol Street NE, Salem, OR 97310-0203.

PENNSYLVANIA: Pennsylvania Higher Education Assistance Agency, 1200 North Seventh Street, Harrisburg, PA 17102-1444; (800) 692-7435, or P.O. Box 8114, Harrisburg, PA 17105-8114; (717) 720-2075.

RHODE ISLAND: Rhode Island Board of Governors for Higher Education & Rhode Island Office of Higher Education, 301 Promenade Street,

Providence, RI 02908-5720; (401) 277-6560. Rhode Island Higher Education Assistance Authority, 560 Jefferson Boulevard, Warwick, RI 02886; (800) 922-9855. State Department of Education, 22 Hayes Street, Providence, RI 02908; (401) 277-3126.

SOUTH CAROLINA: South Carolina Higher Education Tuition Grants Commission, 1310 Lady Street, Suite 811, P.O. Box 12159, Columbia, SC 29201; (803) 734-1200. State Department of Education, 803-a Rutledge Building, 1429 Senate Street, Columbia, SC 29201; (803) 734-8364.

SOUTH DAKOTA: Department of Education and Cultural Affairs, Office of the Secretary, 700 Governors Drive, Pierre, SD 57501-2291; (605) 773-3134.

TENNESSEE: Tennessee Higher Education Commission, 404 James Robertson Parkway, Suite 1900, Nashville, TN 37243-0820; (615) 741-3605. State Department of Education, 100 Cordell Hull Building, Nashville, TN 37219-5335; (615) 741-1346 or (800) 342-1663 (in TN).

TEXAS: Texas Higher Education Coordinating Board, P.O. Box 12788, Capitol Station, Austin, TX 78711; (800) 242-3062.

UTAH: Utah State Board of Regents, Utah System of Higher Education, 355 West North Temple,

#3 Triad Center, Suite 550, Salt Lake City, UT 84180-1205; (801) 321-7205. Utah State Office of Education, 250 East 500 South Salt Lake City, UT 84111; (801) 538-7779.

VERMONT: Vermont Student Assistance Corporation, Champlain Mill, P.O. Box 2000, Winooski, VT 05404-2601; (800) 642-3177. Vermont Department of Education, 120 State Street, Montpelier, VT 05620-2501; (802) 828-3147.

VIRGINIA: State Council of Higher Education for Virginia, James Monroe Building, 101 North Fourteenth Street, Richmond, VA 23219; (804) 786-1690. State Department of Education, P.O. Box 2120, James Monroe Building, 14th and Franklin Streets, Richmond, VA 23216-2120; (804) 225-2072.

WASHINGTON: Washington State Higher Education Coordinating Board, P.O. Box 43430, 917 Lakeridge Way, SW, Olympia, WA 98504-3430; (206) 753-7850 State Department of Public Instruction, Old Capitol Building, P.O. Box FG 11, Olympia, WA 98504-3211; (206) 753-2858.

WEST VIRGINIA: State Department of Education, 1900 Washington Street, Building B, Room 358, Charleston, WV 25305; (304) 588-2691 State College & University Systems of West Virginia Central Office, 1018 Kanawha Boulevard East, Suite 700, Charleston, WV 25301-2827; (304) 558-4016.

WISCONSIN: Higher Education Aids Board, P.O. Box 7885, Madison, WI 53707-7885; (608) 267-2206. State Department of Public Instruction, 125 South Wester Street, P.O. 7841, Madison, WI 53707-7814; (608) 266-2364.

WYOMING: Wyoming State Department of Education, Hathaway Building, 2300 Capitol Avenue, 2nd Floor, Cheyenne, WY 82002-0050; (307) 777-6265. Wyoming Community College Commission, 2020 Carey Avenue, 8th Floor, Cheyenne, WY 82002; (307) 777-7763.

NOTES

Chapter 11

Free Stuff For 50 or Over And Their Grandkids

Throughout this edition of "Free Cash & Benefits" we've described scores of government programs offering money and benefits to qualified seniors. In this final chapter, it's time to take a look at hundreds of sources of other free items for seniors.

Besides the free goodies from Uncle Sam, there are hundreds of things you can get free from non-government sources as well. For example, many companies offer free samples of their products—everything from coffee to shampoo. Scores of groups and organizations also offer free items including information in the form of educational and instructural booklets, pamphlets and brochures. If you know where to look, you actually can save hundreds of dollars you might have spent on gifts for the grandkids or on "experts" to help you with your taxes, for needed eye care, housing information and advice, and much more.

So how do you get all this free stuff? In most cases, all you have to do is write a letter (or make a toll-free phone call) and ask for it. Some offers will require that you submit a small fee for postage and handling, along with a specified size self-addressed, stamped envelope (SASE), but the items themselves are free. In most cases, the items you receive will be worth many times the amount you spend on postage and handling.

In this chapter, we've listed more free offers from a number of government agencies— everything from free help with your taxes to information on how to get free or low cost eye care. We've also listed hundreds of "free" offers from non-government sources, such as companies promoting their products with free samples, and professional sports teams which offer free "fan mail" packages on request. Many of the offers are especially for people 50 or over, but we've included a section of free things for your grandkids as well— everything from coloring books to posters and stickers.

Before you begin your search for free stuff, you should keep in mind the following:

1) Most free offers have expiration dates. Publications go out of print, product samples are

available in limited quantities only, and offers may be for a specified time only. While every effort was made to ensure that the listings in this chapter were accurate and valid at the time of this writing, some of the free items and offers may no longer be available by the time you read this book.

2) Since most free items are usually available in limited quantities only, you should send for the items you want right away.

3) When responding to any free offer, you should follow all directions and instructions precisely. Make sure you include the proper size SASE and any required postage and handling fees with each written request.

4) It usually takes at least three to six weeks before you receive a free item you've sent for, so be patient.

FREE FROM UNCLE SAM

"Protecting Older Americans Against Overpayment of Income Tax".

This booklet provides information to help older Americans claim their rightful income tax deductions, exemptions, and tax credits. The booklet is updated every January and includes information on the latest tax law changes.

To get a free copy, contact the:

Special Committee on Aging,
U.S. Senate, Washington,
DC 20410; (202) 224-5364.

Single copies of the following Federal Deposit Insurance Corporation (FDIC) and Resolution Trust Corporation (RTC) publications are available by contacting the:

Federal Deposit Insurance Corporation,
Public Information Center, 801 Seventeenth
Street, NW, Room 100,
Washington, DC 20434; (800) 276-6003;
Fax: (202) 416-2076.

— **"Insured or Not Insured"**: this pamphlet describes what is not protected by FDIC insurance.

— **"Your Insured Deposit"**: this pamphlet provides examples of FDIC insurance coverage on certain types of accounts commonly held by depositors in FDIC-insured banks.

— **" A Dream Realized"**: this is a pamphlet explaining how to obtain afforable housing.

— **"How To Buy Real Estate".**

— **"Complete Guide to the RTC".**

— "Buying A Single-Family Home Through the RTC's Affordable Housing Disposition Program".

— "General Financing Guidelines For Real Estate".

The Social Security Administration publishes many pamphlets and factsheets explaining its programs and benefits. The following publications are available by calling Social Security's toll-free number, 1-800-772-1213. If you have access to the internet, you also can find free Social Security publications at http://www.ssa.gov.

— "Social Security: 24-Hour Telephone Service", Publication #05-10082.

— "Social Security: What Every Woman Should Know", Pub. # 05-10127.

— "Social Security: Basic Facts", Pub. # 05-10080.

— "Social Security: Understanding The Benefits", Pub. 05-10024.

— "Social Security: How You Earn Credits", Pub. # 05-10072.

— "Social Security: Your Taxes— What They are Paying For And Where The Money Goes", Pub. # 05-10010.

— "Social Security: What You Need To Know When You Get Retirement or Survivor Benefits", Pub. # 05-10077.

— "How Your Retirement Benefit Is Figured", Pub. # 05-10070.

— "Supplemental Security Income", Pub. # 05-11000

— "Social Security: You May Be Able To Get SSI", Pub. # 05-110-69.

— "Receiving Your Benefits By Direct Deposit"

The Internal Revenue Service (IRS) may not be your favorite government agency, but it does provide a wealth of free tax information. The IRS produces many free publications to help taxpayers fill out their tax returns and answer tax questions. All IRS publications can be ordered at no charge by calling the IRS at 1-800-829-3676. Here are several free publications available from the IRS:

— Publication 1, "Your Rights as a Taxpayer": this publication explains taxpayers' rights at each step in the tax process.

— Publication 17, "Your Federal Income Tax (For Individuals)": this publication provides help in preparing individual tax returns. Each step of the tax return is explained in detail.

— Publication 334, "Tax Guide for Small Businesses": identifies federal tax laws that apply to businesses and the tax responsibilities of the four major forms of business organizations— sole proprietorship, partnership, corporation, and S corporation.

— Publication 463, "Travel, Entertainment, and Gift Expenses": explains business-related travel, entertainment, gift, and local transportation expenses that may be deductible.

— Publication 502, "Medical And Dental Expenses": explains which medical and dental expenses are deductible, how to deduct them, and how to treat reimbursements you receive for medical care.

— Publication 521, "Moving Expenses": explains whether or not certain expenses of moving are deductible. For example, if you change job locations or start a new job, you may be able to deduct your moving expenses.

— Publication 523, "Selling Your Home": explains how to treat any gain or loss from selling your main home.

— Publication 524, "Credit for the Elderly or Disabled": this publication explains that you may be able to claim this credit if you are 65 or older or if you're retired on permanent and total disability. It also explains how to figure this credit.

— Publication 525, "Taxable and Nontaxable Income": explains the difference between taxable and nontaxable income.

— Publication 526, "Charitable Contributions": describes organizations that are qualified to receive charitable contributions. The publication also describes contributions you can (and cannot) deduct. It also explains deduction limits.

— Publication 527 "Residential Rental Property": explains rental income and expenses and how to report them on your return. The publication also defines the sale of rental property and other special rules that apply to rental activity.

— Publication 529, "Miscellaneous Deductions": identifies expenses that may qualify as miscellaneous deductions on Form 1040 (Schedule A), such as employee business expenses and expenses of producing income. Itemized deductions, such as those for charitable contributions, moving expenses, interest, taxes, or medical and dental expenses, are not discussed in this publication, but are explained in separate IRS publications.

— Publication 533, "Self-Employment Tax": explains the self-employment tax, which is a Social Security and Medicare tax for people who work for themselves.

— Publication 550, "Investment Income and Expenses".

— Publication 559, "Survivors, Executors, and Administrators": provides helpful information for reporting and paying the proper federal income tax if you are responsible for settling a decedent's estate. The publication also answers many questions that a spouse or other survivor faces when a person dies.

— Publication 560, "Retirement Plans For The Self-Employed": explains tax considerations relevant to retirement plans available to self-employed employers, such as the simplified employee pensions (SEPs) and Keogh plans.

— Publication 564, "Mutual Fund Distribution": explains the tax treatment of distributions paid or allocated to an individual shareholder of a mutual fund and explains how to figure gain or loss on the sale of mutual fund shares.

— Publication 575, "Pension and Annuity Income": explains how to report pension and annuity income and discusses the optional tax treatment you can choose to use for lump-sum distributions from pension, stock bonus, or profit-sharing plans. Also discusses rollovers from qualified retirement plans.

— Publication 590, "Individual Retirement Arrangements (IRAs)": explains the tax rules that apply to IRAs and the penalties for not following them. Included are rules that affect contributions, deductions, transfers (including rollovers) and withdrawals. It also includes tax rules for simplified employee pension (SEP) plans.

— Publication 596, "Earned Income Credit": explains who may receive the Earned Income Credit, how to figure and claim the credit, and how to receive advance payments of the credit.

— Publication 915, "Social Security and Equivalent Railroad Retirement Benefits".

— Publication 924, "Reporting of Real Estate Transactions to IRS": defines information that sellers of certain real estate must provide to individuals who report real estate transactions to the IRS on Form 1099-S.

— Publication 936, "Home Mortgage Interest"

— Publication 939, "Pension General Rule (Nonsimplified Method)": discusses the General Rule for the taxation of pensions and annuities, which must be used if the Simplified General Rules does not apply or is not chosen. The publication contains needed actuarial tables.

The Federal Trade Commission offers a number of free consumer publications dealing with everything from saving money to treatments for varicose veins. Here are some of the publications available upon request by contacting:

Public Reference Branch,
Room 130, Federal Trade Commission,
Washington, DC 20580; (202) 326-2222.

— "66 Ways To Save Money"
— "Coping With A Temporary Loss of Income"
— "How To Resolve Consumer Disputes"
— "Solving Consumer Problems"
— "Building A Better Credit Record"
— "Choosing And Using Credit Cards"
— "Credit Repair: Self Help May Be Best"
— "Credit And Older Americans"
— "Varicose Vein Treatments"
— "The Skinny On Dieting"
— "Energy Guide To Home Heating And Cooling"
— "Personal Emergency Response Systems"

"A Citizens Guide To Radon"— this booklet provides information about the dangers of radon. To get a free copy, contact:

Public Information Center,
Environmental Protection Agency,
401 M. Street, SW, PM-211B,
Washington, DC 20460.

The Federal Emergency Management Administration (FEMA) offers a free booklet explaining how to clean up after a flood. To get a copy, write to:

FEMA,
P.O. Box 70274,
Washington, DC 20024.

The United States Department of Labor Occupational Safety and Health Administration (OSHA) has a number of free publications available upon written request. To get any of the following publications, write to:

OSHA Publications Office, U.S.
Department of Labor,
200 Constitution Avenue, NW, Room N3101,
Washington, DC 20201.

— "Access to Medical Exposure Records": describes OSHA requirements for employee access to employer-maintained exposure and medical records regarding the detection, treatment, and prevention of occupational diseases caused by toxic substances or harmful physical agents.

— "Employee Workplace Rights": explains employee workplace rights under the Occupational Safety and Health Act of 1970, including right to know, access to exposure and medical records, inspections, variances, and confidentially.

— "How To Prepare for Workplace Emergencies": details the basic steps for handling emergencies, such as accidental release of toxic gases, chemical spills, fires, explosions, and personal injuries.

— "OSHA Publications and Audiovisual Programs": lists OSHA's publications and audiovisual programs.

The Health Care Financing Administration (HCFA), a federal agency within the Department of Health and Human Services, administers the Medicare and Medicaid programs— two national health care programs that benefit more than 72 million beneficiaries. While the HCFA acts mainly as a purchaser of health care services for the Medicare and Medicaid beneficiaries, it also produces a number of publications about both health care programs. These publications are available free upon request from the:

HCFA,
7500 Security Boulevard,
Baltimore, MD 21244. HCFA

Publications also are available via the Internet at http://www.hcfa.gov/about.htm#whatis.

Here are some of the HCFA publications currently available:

— "The 1996 Medicare Handbook": summary of Medicare benefits, rights and obligations, and obligations, and answers to the most frequently asked questions about Medicare.

— "1996 Guide to Health Insurance for People With Medicare": provides information on how to choose a Medigap plan.

— "Guide To Choosing A Nursing Home": a step-by-step process and key resources to help you choose a nursing home.

— "Medicare Hospice Benefits": information on hospice benefits under Medicare Hospital Insurance (Part A).

— "Savings for Qualified Beneficiaries": provides information on programs that can help people pay their Medicare expenses.

— "Medicare and Home Health Care": explains how to qualify for home health care and provides information on what services Medicare covers.

— "Medicare Kidney Coverage": explains Medicare coverage of kidney dialysis and kidney transplant services.

The National Eye Institute (NEI) conducts and supports research, training, health information dissemination, and other programs with respect to blinding eye diseases, visual disorders, preservation of sight, and the special health problems and requirements of the blind. The NEI disseminates a number of publications, including brochures, booklets, and fact sheets for the general public. All of the NEI's publications, including those listed below, are available at no charge. To order any of the following publications, contact the:

National Eye Institute,
National Institutes of Health,
Building 31, Room 6A03, 31 Center Drive,
MSC 2510, Bethesda, MD 20892-2510.

The following brochures are intended for people who are at higher risk for specific eye diseases.

— "Don't Lose Sight of Age-Related Macular Degeneration"
— "Don't Lose Sight of Cataracts"
— "Don't Lose Sight of Diabetic Eye Disease"
— "Don't Lose Sight of Glaucoma"

The following fact sheets also are available at no charge from the NEI.

— "Cornea and Corneal Disease": provides information on common corneal diseases and highlights of National Eye Institute-supported research.

— "Selected Resources for People with Low Vision": lists resources to help individuals with visual impairments make the most of their remaining sight.

— "Financial Aid for Eye Care": provides information on financial assistance available through selected national organizations.

— "Finding an Eye Care Professional": offers strategies and resources for finding an eye care professional.

The Office on Smoking and Health (OSH) a division of the Centers for Disease Control and Prevention, develops and distributes the annual Surgeon General's report on smoking and health. The OSH also coordinates a national public information and education program on tobacco use and health, an effort which includes the distribution of consumer publications on smoking and pregnancy, smoking and teenagers, and smoking cessation. The OSH publications are available free by contacting the:

Office on Smoking And Health,
Centers for Disease Control and Prevention,
Mail Stop K-50, 4770 Buford Highway, NE,
Atlanta, GA 30341-3724;
(404) 488-5705; (800) CDC-1311;
Fax: (404) 488-5939.

Here are some of the OSH publications you can order:

— "Good News For Smokers 50 and Older"
— "Health Benefits of Smoking Cessation"
— "Clearing The Air"
— "Out of the Ashes"
— "Review and Evaluation of Smoking Cessation Methods"

"Participate in Archaeology": this free brochure provides some basic information on archaeology. It also lists other sources of additional information, including books, magazines, videos, and agencies and organizations. To get a free copy, contact the:

National Park Service,
Archaeological Assistance Division, U.S. Department of the Interior,
P.O. Box 37127,
Washington, DC 20013-7127;
(202) 208-4747.

"Introduction to Stamp Collecting": here's a free brochure that provides information to help beginners learn how to start and maintain a collection. A copy of the brochure is available from the:

U.S. Postal Service,
475 L'Enfant Plaza West, SW,
Washington, DC 20260.

The National Institute of Allergy and Infectious Diseases can provide a number of free publications dealing with allergies and treatments. Contact the:

National Institute of Allergy and
Infectious Diseases, Office of Communications,
Building 31, Room 7A50, 9000 Rockville Pike,
Bethesda, MD 20892; (301) 496-5717.

The U.S. Consumer Product Safety Commission (CPSC) bears the responsibility of protecting the public from the unreasonable risk of injury or death from 15,000 types of consumer products. One of the ways the CPSC does that is through the distribution of publications which describe the hazards associated with the use of consumer products. The CPSC also recommends ways to avoid those hazards in its publications, which include fact sheets, brochures, and other materials developed for use by consumers.

The following publications are all available free upon request. Send a post card to:

Publication Request,
Office of Information and Public Affairs, U.S. Consumer Product Safety Commission,
Washington, DC 20207.

Be sure to include the publication item numbers with your order.

— "For Kids Sake, Think Toy Safety" (281)
— "Toy Safety Coloring Book" (283)
— "Which Toy For Which Child" (birth -five years of age). (285)
— "Which Toy For Which Child" (6-12 years of age). (286)
— "Choking Hazard Label Fact Sheet" (282)
— "Ten Smart Routes To Bike Safety" (343)
— "Poison Prevention Poster" (388)
— "CPSC Guide To Home Wiring Hazards" (518)
— "Home Fire Safety Checklist" (556)
— "Furnaces Fact Sheet" (079)
— "Home Safety Checklist For Older Consumers" (701)
— "The Inside Story: A Guide To Indoor Air Quality" (450)
— "Biological Pollutants in Your Home" (426)

These and other CPSC publications also may be requested from the Commission's Regional Offices:

— Central Regional Center,
230 South Dearborn Street, Room 2944,
Chicago, IL 60604-1601.

— Eastern Regional Office,
6 World Trade Center, Versey Street, Room 350,
New York, NY 10049-0950.

— Western Regional Center,
600 Harrison Street, Room 245,
San Francisco, CA 94107-1370.

Many CPSC publications also are available free of charge on the Internet from the CPSC's gopher server. The gopher address is "gopher://cpsc.gov".

The Department of Housing And Urban Development (HUD) provides free information on housing and its many housing programs. By calling The following toll-free 800 numbers, you can get free booklets and brochures, referrals, and othr HUD information.

— HUD Homes Hotline: 800-766-4483. Leave your address and HUD will send you a free brochure detailing how to buy a HUD owned home.

— Housing Counseling Line: 800-697-6967. Provides information pertaining to mortgages that were recently sold by HUD, or refers callers to local HUD offices.

— Fair Housing Information Clearinghouse: 800-343-3442; 800-795-7915. Distributes information and materials about Federal fair housing laws and HUD fair housing programs and initiatives.

— HUD Homes Information System: 800-366-4582. Provides listings for HUD homes in Alabama, Florida, Georgia, Mississippi, North Carolina, South Carolina, Tennessee, and the Caribbean.

— HUD Homes Information System: 800-827-1240. Provides listings for HUD homes in Arkansas, Louisiana, New Mexico, Oklahoma, and Texas.

— Multifamily Housing Clearinghouse: 800-685-8470. Assists local residents and others on issues such as resident rights and programs for the elderly and disabled. Also distributes application packets for those programs.

— Single Family Housing: 800-800-3088. Refers consumers interested in the HUD Pre-foreclosure Sale Program to their lenders for more information. HUD offers homeowners with FHA insured mortgages the opportunity to sell their homes at less than the amount owed to the mortgage company.

— Title I Insurance Program: 800-733-4663. Provides names of Title I Loans for property improvements.

— Debt Management Service Center-
Seattle, WA: 800-347-3731.

Agents work with consumers who have defaulted on Title I Property Improvement or Mobile Home Loans to facilitate collection.

— Debt Management Service Center-
Albany, NY: 800-669-5152.
Provides services same as above.

— Debt Management Service Center-
Chicago, IL: 800-735-4849.
Provides services same as above.

— Office of Manufactured Housing Voice Mail System: 800-927-2891. Serves as a Consumer Complaint Hotline. Calls are returned within 24 hours.

— Homeownership for Women: 888-466-3487. Provides homeownership information for women with a goal of helping them overcome obstacles to owning a home.

The Food And Drug Administration (FDA) offers scores of free consumer publications dealing with a number of health-related topics. To order any of the FDA's free publications, including those listed below, contact the FDA's Office of Consumer Inquiries:

FDA, HFE-88, 5600 Fishers Lane,
Rockville, MD 20857;
(301) 443-3170.

Many FDA publications also are available free via the Internet and the FDA home page at http://www.fda.gov.

— "Boning Up On Osteoporosis"
— "Losing Weight Safely"
— "Surviving Cold And Flu Season"
— "Truth About Choosing Medical Treatments"
— "FDA Highlights: Health Care For The Elderly"
— "It's Spring Again And Allergies Are In Bloom"

The U.S. Office of Consumer Affairs now offers a toll-free Helpline for consumer complaints. If you have a complaint with a government agency or a business— the Helpline will serve as a central resource in the nation's capital providing toll-free consumer information and referrals.

The Helpline is the first nationwide federal clearinghouse for consumer complaint handling. You can obtain person-to-person assistance simply by dialing 1-800-664-4435 between 10:00 a.m. and 2:00 p.m. Monday through Friday. The line is accessible from all 50 states, the District of Columbia, Puerto Rico, and the U.S. Virgin Islands.

The U.S. Railroad Retirement Board (RRB) offers a number of free publications dealing with retirement matters. The publications include booklets and brochures, which you can download free of charge from RRB's Internet site at http://www,rrb.gov/. The publications also are available at all RRB field offices. Look in your phone directory under "government agencies".

Here are some of the publications available from the RRB:

— "How Earnings Affect Payment of Retirement Annuities"
— "Conditions Under Which a Person is Eligible for A Railroad Retirement Annuity"
— "Railroad Retirement and Survivor Benefits"
— "Guide To Finding The Right Job"
— "Railroad Unemployment and Sickness Benefits"

The Consumer Information Center (CIC) publishes the Consumer Information Catalog, which lists scores of federal government consumer publications. The CIC Catalog lists government publications on a wide range of consumer topics, including health, food, automobiles, nutrition, money management, housing, employment, and education. Many of the publications, including those listed below, are available free of charge. To order a free CIC Catalog, write to the:

Consumer Information Center,
P.O. Box 100,
Pueblo, CO 81009.

If you have access to the Internet, you also can find the CIC Catalog at http://www.pueblo.gsa.gov.

Here are some of the free government publications listed in a recent Consumer Information Catalog:

— "Enjoying Retirement", Publication 606D: This 10-page booklet from the Administration On Aging lists items to think about and plan before retirement, including daily activities, exercise, diet, finances, and more.

— "Dealing With A Disability", Publication 603D: This is a 12-page booklet that discusses options for housing, health care, financial benefits, work, and legal rights. The booklet also offers advice for families and friends, including sources of assistance.

— "A Consumer's Guide To Postal Services and Products", Publication 604D: Everything you want to know about the Postal Service is in this 40-page booklet from the U.S. Postal Service. The booklet describes many special mailing services that can save you time and money.

— "1997 Consumer's Resource Handbook", Publication 623D: This 127 page book lists contacts to help with consumer problems and complaints. Included are corporate programs, automobile manufacturers, government agencies, how to write an effective complaint letter, smart shopping tips, and much more.

— "A Guide To Disability Rights Law", Publication 622D. This 14-page booklet from the Department of Justice describes your rights regarding fair housing, public accommodations, telecommunications, education and employment.

— "Taking Legal Action", Publication 607D: This is a 10-page publication that discusses when legal action may be appropriate, how to file in small claims court, and when to consider hiring a lawyer.

— "Health Information On-Line", Publication 613D: Access to a wide assortment of health and medical information is available on the Internet. Some of that information is fraudulent and false. This 5-page booklet from the Food and Drug Administration provides tips to help determine if a site is reliable. It also tells you where to find reputable sites.

— "Lifting The Clouds of Cataracts", Publication 543D: This 4-page Food and Drug Administration booklet (FDA) explains how cataracts develop and discusses symptoms and treatment options.

— "The Sun, UV, and You", Publication 546D: This is a 12-page publication from the EPA that explains what the ultraviolet radiation (UV) index is and how you can use it to avoid skin cancer, cataracts, and premature aging of the skin.

— "Aspirin: A New Look at an Old Drug", Publication 547D: This 3-page booklet from the FDA explains how aspirin can help in the prevention and treatment of cardiovascular disease.

— "FDA's Tips for Taking Medicines", Publication 551D: A 5-page booklet that explains how to get the most benefit with the fewest risks. It also provides suggestions for long-term medication use.

— "Unproven Medical Treatments Lure Elderly", Publication 560D: This 5-page FDA publication takes a look at unproven medical treatments and explains why they can be dangerous. The booklet also tells you how to avoid fraud.

— "Making It Easier To Read Prescriptions", Publication 554D: This 3-page booklet gives an example of a typical prescription and defines common symbols and terms so you'll know what you're getting.

— "Nonprescription Medicines: What's Right for You", Publication 556D: This 12-page FDA publication provides important advice on choosing over-the-counter (OTC) medicines and how to avoid harmful interactions.

— "Alzheimer's Disease", Publication 561D: This 36-page booklet explains how Alzheimer's is diagnosed and discusses possible causes and current treatments. It also lists references and various sources of help.

— "Coping With Arthritis In Its Many Forms", Publication 562D: This 5-page booklet describes proven treatments for the most common types of arthritis, and how to avoid being a target for "fraudulent cures".

— "Prostate Cancer", Publication 563D: Learn how prostate cancer is detected, what treatments are available, and where to get more information in this 5-page FDA booklet.

— "Anxiety Disorders", Publication 567D: This 24-page booklet describes treatments available and lists resources to contact for more information on panic phobias, stress, obsessive-compulsive, and other anxiety disorders.

— "Plain Talk About Depression", Publication 573D: Learn how depression is diagnosed and treated in this 4-page booklet, which also discusses how to get help.

— "Food Allergies: Rare But Risky", Publication 528D: This 6-page FDA booklet explains the differences between food allergies and food intolerance. It also provides information on diagnosis and tips on preventing and treating certain allergic reactions.

— "Protect Your Family From Lead In Your Home", Publication 578D: Learn how to check your home and reduce the hazards of lead in this 15-page publication from the EPA.

— "Energy Efficient Mortgage Home Owner Guide", Publication 609D: If you're buying, selling, refinancing, or remodeling your home, you can save money with a mortgage that encourages energy conservation. This 9-page booklet from the Department of Energy explains who qualifies for such a mortgage, the process, and more.

— "How To Buy A Home With A Low Down Payment", Publication 574D: This 12-page booklet describes private and federal options for obtaining a low down payment mortgage, how to qualify, how to determine what you can afford, and more.

— "Progress in Blood Supply Safety", Publication 544D: This 4-page FDA booklet discusses how the blood industry is regulated. It also explains the test now performed on all donated blood.

— "Choosing Medical Treatments", Publication 549D: This 5-page booklet from the FDA explains how to decide if alternative therapy such as hypnosis, acupuncture, herbs, or biofeedback is right for you. You'll also learn how to avoid fraudulent, unproven health treatments.

— "Taming Tummy Turmoil", Publication 559D: This 4-page booklet lists OTC medications for motion sickness, heartburn, indigestion and overindulgence. Possible side effects of these OTC medications also are discussed in this booklet.

— "Healthful Snacks for the Chip & Dip Crowd", Publication 532D: This 5-page booklet produced by the FDA provides tips on choosing what snacks are best for you and your diet.

— "The HUD Homebuying Guide", Publication 575D: This 11-page booklet provides step-by-step instructions for finding and financing a HUD home. The booklet includes charts to help you estimate mortgage payments.

— "Deputy Fire Marshal Kit", Publication 587C: This kit includes stickers, a badge and colorful certificate to help teach your grandkids the "cool rules" of fire safety.

— "Growing Up Drug Free", Publication 504C: This 33-page booklet shows parents what children should know about drugs, including alcohol and tobacco, at each age level.

— "Telecommute America", Publication 590C: This 8-page booklet, produced by the Department of Labor, describes the kinds of jobs appropriate for work at home or in satellite offices. It also lists benefits, requirements and skills needed, and how to present work at home proposals to management.

— "Collecting Used Oil For Recycling Use", Publication 502C: This is a 2-page EPA publication which contains tips on how to change your own motor oil. It also explains why recycling oil helps the environment and saves energy.

FREE OR LOW-COST FOOD AND NUTRITION MATERIALS

The following nutritional, medical, and health organizations offer a wide assortment of food and nutrition materials to consumers.

Most of the materials are available in the form of informational booklets, pamphlets, brochures, reports and other consumer-oriented publications. You can call or write any of these organizations and request a publications list. Many of the publications offered are free— some ave available for a small fee.

American Academy of Allergies— Asthma and Immunology, 611 East Wells Street, Milwaukee, WI 53202; (414) 272-6071; (800) 822-2762.

American Allergy Association, 1100 Industrial #9, San Carlos, CA 94070; (415) 322-1663.

The Food Allergy Network, 10400 Eaton Place, Suite 107, Fairfax, VA 22030; (703) 691-3179; (800) 929-4040; Fax: (703) 691-2713; Internet: http://www.foodallergy.org/

National Clearinghouse for Alcohol and Drug Information, Information Specialist, P.O. Box 2345, Rockville, MD 20847-2345; (301) 468-2600; (800) 729-6686; Fax: (301) 468-6433; Internet: http://www.health.org/

National Institute of Dental Research, Public Information and Reports Section, Building 31, Room 2C35, 31 Center Drive MSC 2290, Bethesda, MD 20892-2290; (301) 496-9988; Internet: http://www.nidr.nih.gov/.

Arthritis Foundation Information Line, P.O. Box 7669, Atlanta, GA 30326; (404) 872-7100; (800) 283-7800; Fax: (404) 872-0457; Internet: http://www.arthritis.org/.

Celiac Disease Foundation, 13251 Ventura Boulevard, Suite 1, Studio City, CA 91604; (818) 990-2379.

Celiac Sprue Association/United States of America, Inc., P.O. Box 31700, Omaha, NE 68131-0700; (402) 558-0600; Fax: (402) 558-1347.

Crohn's and Colitis Foundation of America, Inc., 386 Park Avenue, South, 17th Floor, New York, NY 10016-8804; (212) 685-3440; (800) 932-2423; Fax: (212) 779-4098; Internet: http://www.ccfa.org./

The Gluten Intolerance Group of North America, P.O. Box 23-53, Seattle, WA 98102-0353; (206) 325-6980.

Food and Drug Administration, Seafood Hotline; (202) 205-2314; (800) FDA-4010; Fax: (202) 401-3532; Internet: http://vm.cfsan.fda.gov/seafood1.html.

Food Safety And Inspection Service, Meat and Poultry Hotline/USDA, 14th Street, SW, Room 2925-S, Washington, DC 20250; (202) 720-3333; (800) 535-4555; Fax: (202) 690-3754; Internet: http://www.usda.gov/fsis/.

American Medical Association, 515 N. State Street, Chicago, IL 60610; (312) 464-5000; (800) 621-8335; Fax: (312) 464-5600; Internet: http://www.ama-assn.org/

National Council Against Health Fraud, Inc., P.O. Box 1276, Loma Linda, CA 92354; (909) 824-4690; Fax: (909) 824-4838; (816) 228-4595 (in Kansas City,

Mo); Internet: http://www.ncahf.org/.

ODPHP (Operation of Disease Prevention and Health Promotion) National Health Information Center, P.O. Box 1133, Washington, DC 20013-1133; (301) 565-4167; (800) 336-4797; Internet: http:nhic-nt.health.org/.

Public Voice For Food and Health Policy, 1101 14th Street, NW, Suite 710, Washington, DC 20005; (202) 371-1840; Fax: (202) 371-1910; Internet: http://www.publicvoice.org/pvoice.html.

North American Menopause Society, University Hospitals, Department of OB/GYN, 1100 Euclid Avenue, Suite 7024, Cleveland, OH 44106; (216) 844-8748; Fax: (216) 844-8708; Internet: http://www.menopause.org/.

Osteoporosis & Related Bone Disease, National Resource Center, 1150 17th Street, NW, Suite 500, Washington, DC 20036-4603; (202) 223-0344; (800) 624-BONE; Fax: (202) 223-2234.

American Dairy Products Institutes, 130 N. Franklin Street, Chicago, IL 60606; (312) 782-4888; Fax: (312) 782-5299.

Dairy Management, Inc., National Dairy Council, O'Hare International Center, Nutrition Education Research, 10255 West Higgins Road, Suite 900, Rosemont, IL 60018-5616; (847) 803-2000; (800)

426-8271; Fax: (800) 974-6455.

California Dry Bean Advisory Board, 531-D N. Alta Avenue, Dinuba, CA 93618; (209) 591-4866; Fax: (209) 591-5744.

American Meat Institute, P.O. Box 3556, Washington, DC 20007; (703) 841-2400; Fax: (703) 527-0938; Internet: http://www.meatami.org/.

National Pork Producers Council, P.O. Box 10383, Des Moines, IA 50306; (515) 223-2600; Fax: (515) 223-2646; Internet: http://www.nppc.org.

Calorie Control Council, 5775 Peachtree-Dunwoody Road, Suite 500-G, Atlanta, GA 30342; (404) 252-3663; Fax: (404) 252-0774.

International Food Information Council, 1100 Connecticut Avenue, NW, Suite 430, Washington, DC 20036; (202) 296-6540; Fax: (202) 296-6547; Internet: http://www.ificinfo.health.org.

National Pasta Association, 2101 Wilson Blvd., Suite 920, Arlington, VA 22201; (703) 841-0818; Fax: (703) 528-6507; Internet: http://www.1lovepasta.org.

Idaho Potato Commission, P.O. Box 1068, Boise, ID 83701; (208) 334-2350; (800) 824-4605; Fax: (208) 334-2274; Internet: http://www.famouspotatoes.org/.

USA Rice Council, P.O. Box 740121, Houston, TX 777274; (713) 270-6699; (800) 888-7423; Fax: (713) 270-9021; Internet:http://www.usarice.com/.

Produce Marketing Association, 1500 Casho Mill Road, Newark, DE 19714-6036; (302) 738-7100; Fax: (302) 731-2409; Internet: http://www.pma.com/.

FREE RECIPES

To get a free 24-page booklet with a nutritional plan, healthy recipes, and exercise tips send a long SASE to:

Sunkist Growers, Consumer Affairs,
P.O. Box 7888,
Van Nuys, CA 92409-7888.

A free booklet with recipes for meat, fish and poultry is available from Lea & Perrins, the makers of Worcestershire Sauce. For a free copy of the recipe booklet, write to:

Lea & Perrins,
Fairlawn, NY 07410.

If you're interested in "cooking light", write to:
Healthy Choice Cooking Light Recipe Offer,
P.O. Box, 44043,
El Paso,TX 88544-0043.

You'll receive a a booklet with several "light' recipes.

For quick and easy recipes using beef, send a SASE to the:

National Council of Beef,
Ad Department,
444 North Michigan Avenue,
Chicago, IL 60611.

Rice is nice, and you can get 10 free recipes using rice, by contacting the:

USA Rice Council,
P.O. Box 740121,
Houston, TX 77274.

Ask for: "Brown Rice: The Whole Grain", booklet. Include a SASE.

Tofu lovers can get a recipe collection using tofu to create tasty treats. To get the recipe collection, send a SASE to:

Soy Deli,
161 Beacon Street,
South San Francisco, CA 940870.

To get a recipe booklet using peanuts as the main ingredient, contact:

Peanut Classics,
195 North Park Place, Suite 525,
Atlanta, GA 30339.
Include a SASE.

To receive a recipe booklet using figs, send a SASE to:

California Fig Advisory Board,
Fresno, CA 93712.

Free "Prize Winning Chicken Recipes" are available from the:

Delmarva Poultry Industry,
RD 2, Box 47,
Georgetown, DL 19947.
Include a business size SASE with your request.

Make your next barbeque a success with a free "Stage a Year Round Redhot Barbeque Bash" kit. The kit includes recipes, tips for a successful barbeque, and a 2.5 ounce bottle of hot sauce.

To get the kit, contact:
Frank's Original Redhot Sauce,
P.O. Box 307,
Coventry, CT 06238.
Include a 3x5 index card with your request.

Want to learn how to make the perfect sandwich? You may find the perfect sandwich recipe in a free 20-page booklet from the makers of Ziplock Sandwich Bags. The recipes are from winners of a national kid's sandwich-making contest. To get the recipe booklet, send a postcard to:

Bread Winners c/o Ziplock Sandwich Bags,
P.O. Box 78890,
New Augusta, IN 46278.
Request the "Bread Winners Booklet".

Get your grandkids a free "Kids-Can-Do-It" cookbook from Kelloggs. The cookbook features more than a dozen tasty recipes for main course meals and desserts made from cereal. To get the cookbook, send a postcard to the:

Kellogg Company,
Department G-9, One Kellogg Square,
Battle Creek, MI 49016.
Ask for "Kellogg's Cereal Recipe Collection".

The American Egg Board offers a free recipe booklet. The booklet features recipes and tips for creating tasty dishes using eggs. For a free copy of the recipe booklet, send a business size SASE to the:

American Egg Board,
1460 Renaissance,
Park Ridge, IL 60068.
Ask for the "Egg Cooking Recipe" booklet.

Return to your "salad days" with a free recipe booklet containing unique ideas for salads. To get a free copy, write to:

Salad Tour of the USA, H.J. Heinz Co.,
P.O. Box 57,
Pittsburgh, PA 15230.

Turn pasta into award winning meals using the recipes you'll find in the "Endless Pastabilities Recipes" booklet. To get a free copy, send a business size SASE to:

Mueller's Endless Pastabilities,
P.O. Box 307,
Coventry, CT 06238.

The makers of Uncle Ben's Rice offers 14 gourmet recipes free of charge. To get these gourmet recipes, send a postcard to:

Uncle Ben's Country Inn Recipes,
P.O. Box 11166,
Chicago, IL 60611.
Ask for the "Country Inn Recipe Packet".

Spice up your meals with 10 spicy tomato sauce recipes. To get these 10 free recipes, write :

Free Pace Recipe Cards,
Box 169,
El Paso, TX 79977.

Best Foods offers 24 different recipe books featuring tasty treats for all occasions. To get your free copies, write to:

Best Foods,
Department LL, Box 307,
Coventry, CT 06238.

"29 Apple Juice Recipes": this booklet features 29 recipes using apple juice for meats, salads and desserts. To get the recipes, write to:

Speas Co.,
2400 Nicholson Avenue,
Kansas City, MO 64120.

Ocean Spray offers a free recipe booklet featuring recipes for cranberry and grapefruit drinks and desserts. To get the booklet, write to:

Ocean Spray,
P.O. Box 237B,
Hilliard, OH 43026.

To get several delicious recipes using soy sauce, send a SASE to:

Kikkoman International, Inc.,
Department CS8Q,
P.O. Box 427084,
San Francisco, CA 94142-0784.

"Sensible Delicious Recipes": this booklet features several tasty recipes using Nestle Toll House Morsels. To get a free copy, write to:

Sensibly Delicious Recipes,
P.O. Box 1898,
Young America, MN 55594-1898.

You can get 30 delicious chicken recipes by sending a postcard to:

Perdue Cookbook,
P.O. Box 1537,
Salisbury, MD 21801.
Ask for "Thirty Delicious Chicken Recipes".

Prepare meals with a Mexican and Tex-Mex flavor with free recipes from:

Pace Recipe Cards,
P.O. Box NB 169, El Paso, TX 79977.

20 delicious Italian recipes are available free upon request from:

Prego's Easy Intalian Cooking,
Box 964,
Bensalem, PA 19020.

To get a selection of recipes using tomatoes, send a SASE to:

Favorite Tomato Recipes,
Florida Tomato Committee,
Box 140533, Suite CL,
Orlando, FL 32814-0533.

The National Turkey Federation has a number of great recipes using turkey. To get a collection of these free turkey recipes, write to the:

National Turkey Federation,
Consumer Department,
11319 Sunset Hills Road,
Reston, VA 22090.

You can get a free recipe booklet featuring dishes prepared with prunes by writing to:

Prune Recipe Ideas,
P.O. Box 882168,
San Francisco, CA 94188-2168.

FREE PRODUCT SAMPLES

Protect yourself from the sun and bugs with this free offer from Coppertone. Send a postcard for up to $7.00 in samples and coupons to :

Coppertone Bug 'N Sun Try Me Free Offer,
P.O. Box 7995,
Young America, MN 55573-7995.

Perfume Sample: get a free sample of Sunshine Perfume— the newest perfume from the makers of "Charlie" perfume. Call 1-800-99-SUNSHINE to request your free sample.

Hair Color Kit: To get a free Clairol Natural Instincts Color Kit, call 1-800-993-3612. Be prepared to answer a few short questions when you call.

"Crunchy Nacho Cheese": The makers of Cheetos offer a free 8 ounce sample of their new snack. Call 1-800-445-5555 and provide requested information. Allow up to a month for delivery of your free snack.

Sugar Substitute: Get a free sample of "Equal Sweetener" sugar substitute. Call 1-800-323-5316 and ask for the "107 Sample Pack".

Coffee Sample: Get a free sample of "Alan's Blend" coffee— medium to strong— by sending a SASE and your brewer details to:

Coffee Connoisseurs,
267 Glenferrie Road,
Malvern, VIC 3144.

Dried Fruit Sample: To get a free sample of dried fruit, send a business size SASE to:

Naturally Nuts & Fruity Too,
Mail Distribution Center,
2831 Sheridan Way,
Stockton, CA 95207.
Allow 4 to 6 weeks for delivery.

Free Skin Cream: Do you have a problem with dry hands? If so, you might want to check out this free sample of AAA Dry Hand Skin Cream. To get the sample, send a SASE to:

AAA Dry Hand Skin Cream,
Suite 500, 1225 E. Sunset Drive,
Bellingham, WA 98226-3529.

Include a letter with your age, sex, occupation and when your dry hand symptoms started. Allow at least 3 weeks for delivery.

Carpet And Upholstery Cleaner: To get a free sample of Supercleans Carpet and Upholstery Cleaner, send a SASE to:

Laakkonen, Inc.,
3401 Old Creek Road,
Chesterfield, VA 23832.

Free Skin Care Product: Take care of your skin with T'rific skin care products. To try them out, send for the free sample— you'll get a color brochure with product information, one Splasher Handi-Pack, and one Clear Z'it Up Handi-Pack. To get the sample, send a #10 SASE to:

T'rific Sample Offer,
P.O. Box 6866,
Westlake Village, CA 91359.

Allow 2-3 weeks to process your sample request.

FREE STUFF FOR THE GRANDKIDS

Emergency and First Aid Chart: this free chart is designed to help kids identify emergencies and learn basic first aid. It provides step-by-step instructions for treating the most common emergencies. To get the chart, send a postcard to:

Council on Family Health,
420 Lexington Avenue,
New York, NY 10017.
Ask for the "First Aid Wall Chart".

"How To Enjoy A Symphony": this is a music appreciation booklet for children. The booklet will help children learn the fundamentals of symphonic music appreciation. To get a free copy of the booklet, send a business size SASE to:

How To Enjoy A Symphony
c/o Hershey Chocolate USA,
P.O. Box 800,
Hershey, PA 17033-0800.

"Introduction to Scale Model Railroading": this free booklet will provide everything you need to know about scale model railroading. To get the booklet, contact:

Model Railroader Magazine,
1027 North 7th Street,
Milwaukee, WI 53233.
Ask for the booklet by name.

Free Coloring Book: this 26-page coloring book begins with baby teeth and ends with the proper way to brush your teeth. To get the coloring book, send $.32 for postage to:

American Dental Association,
211 E. Chicago Avenue,
Chicago, IL 60611.
Ask for the "ABC's of Good Oral Health".

"How To Respect And Display Our Flag": this free 32-page booklet tells all about the United States Flag. To get a copy of the booklet, send a postcard to:

U.S. Marine Corps, Department of the Navy,
Washington, DC 20380.
Ask for the booklet by name.

Pet Coloring book: a free coloring book and poster depicting various types of pets is available by sending a postcard to:

Pets Are Wonderful Council,
500 North Michigan Avenue, Suite 200,
Chicago, IL 60611.
Request "Pets Are Wonderful Companions".

Kid's Fun Pak: The fun pak includes games, puzzles, and crafts just for kids. The fun pak includes over 40 fun things to do. To get the fun pak, send a business size SASE to:

Kid's Fun Pak, The Children's Museum,
533 16th Street, Bettendorf, IA 52722.

Yo-Yo Tricks Pamphlet: this free pamphlet provides step-by-step instructions for several Yo-Yo tricks. To get a free copy of the pamphlet, send a business size SASE to:

Duncan Toys Company,
P.O. Box 165,
Baraboo, WI 53913.

Bicycle Care And Safety Guide: this free guide provides tips for taking care of your bike. It also discusses safety rules for bike riders. To get the guide, send a business size SASE to:

Aetna Life & Casualty,
Consumer Information Department,
151 Farmington Avenue,
Hartford, CT 06156.

Ask for the Bicycle Safety Pamphlet.

Free Coloring Books: Your grandkids will love these free coloring books which show the nutritional value of various foods. To request these coloring books, write to:

Public Information, Food and Nutrition Service, 500 12th Street, SW #764,
Washington, DC 20250.

Pet Care Bookmarker: Want a bookmark depicting your favorite pet? You can get one by sending a business size SASE to:

Animal Protection,
P.O. Box 22505,
Sacramento, CA 95822.

Be sure to specify which pet bookmark you want.

Free Stamps: Kids 12 years of age or younger may request free stamps by sending a SASE to:

Free Stamps For Kids,
P.O. Box 8073,
Asheville, NC 28814.

You'll receive 50 different World Wide stamps in 3 to 4 weeks.

"How To Collect Stamps": This free booklet will help you get started in the fascinating hobby of stamp collecting. To get a free copy, send a postcard to:

Littleton/Mystic Stamp Company,
96 Main Street, Camden, NY 13316.

Free Conifer Seedling: Plant a tree with a free seedling courtesy of the Georgia Pacific Company. To get your free seedling, call 1-800-522-2359, ext. 1129.

Coolman Sticker: The sticker reads "COOLMAN WUZ HERE" and is available free by sending a SASE to:

Coolman,
P.O. Box 1213, Mankato, MN 56002.

"Smokey Bear Fire Ranger Kit": To get this free kit and to become an Honorary Junior Fire Ranger, send a postcard to:

Smokey Bear Headquarters,
Washington, DC 20252.

George Washington Slept Here: You can get a free illustrated book that tells of the life of our nation's first president, George Washington. The book is available by sending a postcard to:

Washington National Insurance Company,
Consumer Education Department,
Evanston, IL 60201.

Free National Geographic World For Kids Magazine: To get a free sample copy of National Geographic World Magazine for Kids, send a postcard to:

National Geographic World,
17th and "M" Streets, Suite 687,
Washington, DC 20036.

Become a chessmaster with a free 32-page booklet that tells you how to play. To get a copy of the booklet, send a postcard to:

Dover Publications, Inc.,
31 East Second Street,
Mineola, NY 11501.
Ask for the beginners chess booklet.

Roller Skating Booklets: You can get two free booklets— "How To Roller Skate" and "Fun & Games On Roller Skates— which feature safety tips, hints, stunts and games, by sending a postcard to:

Chicago Roller Skate Company,
4458 West Lake Street,
Chicago, IL 60424.

"What's The Weather": Here's a free booklet that explains everything you want to know about the weather and how it affects our loves. To get a copy of the booklet, send a business size SASE to:

Air France Distributing Center,
2039 Ninth Avenue,
Ronkonkoma, NY 11779.

Noise News: How much noise is too much? Take the quiz in the free Noise Quiz book and find out. You'll also get a free coloring book when you send your request to the:

Office of Noise Abatement and Control,
Environmental Protection Agency, ANR 471,
Washington, DC 20460.

"Play It Safe Coloring Book": This coloring book is available free by sending a business size SASE to:

Aetna Life & Casualty Company,
Consumer Information Department,
151 Farmington Avenue,
Hartford, CT 06156.

"Traveling With Your Pet": Make traveling with your pet more enjoyable with the information and tips in this free brochure. Send a business size SASE to:

American Veterinarian Association,
930 North Meacham Road,
Shaumburg, IL 60196.

Scouting Information: Free information on becoming a girl scout is available by writing to: Girls Scouts of the U.S.A., 830 Third Avenue, New York, NY 10022. To get free information on joining the boy scouts, write to:

Boy Scouts of America,
1325 Walnut Hill Lane,
Irving, TX 75062.

Publish A School Newspaper: Get a free booklet explaining different printing methods, picture-taking and aspects of publishing a school newspaper. Write to:

Eastman Kodak,
343 State Street,
Rochester, NY 14650.

FREE SAMPLE CHILDREN'S MAGAZINES

You can encourage your grandkids to read by presenting them with copies of popular children's magazines. Many children's magazine publishers provide sample copies of their products. In most cases, you'll be required to send a SAE (signed, addressed envelope) and sufficient postage. Your request for a free sample copy will not obligate you to purchase subscription, and the sample copy is yours to keep. The following children's magazines all provide free sample copies :

BREAD FOR GOD'S CHILDREN— this magazine is "designed as a teaching tool for Christian families", with its focus mainly on the juvenile market. To get three (3) sample copies send a 9 x 12 SAE and 6 first-class stamps to:

Bread For God's Children,
Bread Ministries, Inc., P.O. Box 1017,
Arcadia, FL 33821.

CHALLENGE— contains youth interests, crafts, sports, sports personalities, and religious articles. A free sample copy is available for a #10 SAE and three (3) first-class stamps. Write to:

Challenge, Brotherhood Commission, SBC,
1548 Poplar Avenue,
Memphis, TN 38104.

EXPLORING— published four times a year, this magazine is published for members of the Boy Scouts of America's Exploring Program. To get a sample copy, send a business size SAE and five (5) first-class stamps to:

Exploring, Boy Scouts of America, 1325
W. Walnut Hill Lane, P.O. Box 152079,
Irving, TX 75015-2079.

FALCON MAGAZINE— this bimonthly magazine is designed for "young conservationists". A sample copy is available for a business size SAE. Write to:

Falcon Magazine, Falcon Press,
48 Last Chance Gulch, P.O. Box 1718,
Helena, MT 59624.

CHRISTIAN GUIDE MAGAZINE— this is a weekly "Christian journal" aimed at middle readers and young adults. A sample copy is available free with a 5 x 9 SAE and two (2) first-class stamps. Write to:

Guide Magazine,
Review and Herald Publishing Association,
55 W. Oak Ridge Drive, Hagerstown, MD 21740.

HIGH ADVENTURE— published monthly, this magazine is designed to provide boys with "worthwhile, enjoyable, leisure reading". A sample copy is available free with a 9 x 12 SASE.

JUNIOR SCHOLASTIC— published biweekly during the school year, this magazine is designed for students in grades 6-8. To get a free sample copy, send a 9 x 11 SAE to:

Junior Scholastic, Scholastic Inc.,
555 Broadway,
New York, NY 10012-3999.

JUNIOR TRAILS— this is an "8-page take home paper for fifth and sixth graders", featuring fiction of a contemporary or historical nature. To get a free sample copy, send a 9 x 12 SAE and two (2) first-class stamps to:

Junior Trails, Gospel Publishing House,
1445 Boonville Avenue,
Springfield, MO 65802.

ON COURSE, A Magazine for Teens— this quarterly magazine features fiction and nonfiction for young adults. A free sample copy is available for a 9 x 11 SAE. Write to:

On Course,
General Council of the Assemblies of God,
1445 Boonville Avenue,
Springfield, MO 65802-1894.

ON THE LINE— published "monthly in weekly parts", this magazine provides fiction and nonfiction for middle readers and young adults. To get a free sample copy send a 7 x 10 SAE to:

On The Line, Mennonite Publishing House,
616 Walnut Avenue,
Scottdale, PA 15683.

SCHOOL MATES, USCF's Magazine for Beginning Chess Players— this magazine for beginning chess players features instructional articles, features on famous chess players, games, puzzles, and other chess-related articles. A free sample copy is available for a 9 x 12 SAE and two (2) first-class stamps.

SCIENCELAND, To Nuture Scientific Thinking— this is a "content reading picture-book" designed for readers in grades 1-3. A sample copy is available free with a 9 x 12 SASE. Write to:

Scienceland, To Nurture Scientific Thinking,
Scienceland, Inc., 501 Fifth Avenue, $2108,
New York, NY 10017-6165.

SOCCER JR., The Soccer Magazine for Kids— published bimonthly, this magazine is for soccer players 8 to 16 years old. For a free sample copy, send a 9 x 12 SAE and five (5) first-class stamps to:

Soccer JR., Triplepoint Inc.,
27 Unquowa Road,
Fairfield, CT 06430.

STRAIGHT— this magazine published "quarterly in weekly parts" is designed for Christian teenagers. A sample copy is available free with a business size SASE. Write to:

Straight,
Standard Publishing,
8121 Hamilton Avenue,
Cincinnati, OH 45231.

TEEN LIFE— this is a quarterly newspaper with articles slanted toward the 15 to 19 year old teen. It's a Christian publication with articles focusing on "Christian responses to life". Two sample copies are available free with a 6 x 9 SASE. Write to:

Teen Life,
Gospel Publishing House,
1445 Boonville Avenue,
Springfield, MO 65802-1894.

TIME FOR KIDS— this weekly publication from the publishers of "Time", is a news magazine for kids in grades 4 through 6. A sample copy is available for an 8 x 10 SAE and two (2) first-class stamps. Write to:

Time For Kids,
1271 Avenue of the Americas,
23rd Floor,
New York, NY 10020.

MORE FREE STUFF

"From Credit Despair to Credit Repair": this free booklet features advice and tips on improving your financial health. To get a copy, send your request to

Credit Repair,
P.O. Box 310,
Sacramento, CA 95802.

"A Handi Guide To Planning A Family Reunion": this free booklet is a helpful planner featuring tips and recipes for a successful family reunion. To get a free copy, send your request to Handi Wrap, P.O. Box 78980, New Augusta, IN 46278. Be sure to ask for the booklet by name.

Get a free pamphlet, "Exercise and Fitness Guide: A Guide for Women" by writing to the:

American College of Obstetricians and
Gynecologists, Resource Center/AP045,
P.O. Box 96920,
Washington, DC 20090-6920.
Include a business-size SASE with your request.

"How To Avoid Plumbing Problems": this free booklet may save you a bundle in plumbing bills. To get a free copy, write to:

Copper Development Association, Inc.,
Greenwich Office, Park 2, Box 1840,
Greenwich, CT 06836-1840.

"Safety Tips For Your Travel": this free booklet includes information on preparing your home before you leave, packing, and airport safety. To get a copy of the booklet, send a business size SASE to:

American Society of Travel Agents,
1101 King Street,
Alexandria, VA 22314.

Mini-Sewing Kit: This kit is great to have on hand in the event of "sewing emergencies". It includes everything needed to fix a button, safety pins, needles, thread, a needle threader, and a measuring tape. To get a mini-sewing kit, send $1.00 for postage and handling to:

Assiduity Industries,
Box 1147,
Willits, CA 95490.

Insulin-dependent diabetics can get a free business size card that provides information to help adjust the levels of insulin while traveling by air. The guide is for those diabetics requiring 2 injections per day. Send a SASE to:

The Diabetic Traveler,
P.O. Box 8223-RWS,
Stamford, CT 06905.

"Househunter's Scorecard": this free booklet provides advice on how to choose the house that's right for you. It discusses the house itself, the neighborhood, financial considerations, and more. For a free copy, write to:

Chicago Title Insurance Company,
Consumer Affairs, 111 West Washington Street,
Chicago, IL 60602.

The makers of Alberto VO5 offer a free booklet featuring a number of ideas on unique things to do with their hair care products, other than using them on your hair. For example, the hair care products also are useful for protecting shoes from winter salt. To get a free copy of this booklet, write to:

Alberto VO5,
P.O. Box 1588,
Melrose Park, IL 60160.

If you wear a wig or toupee, you can send for a free video and brochure from:

The Wig Company,
Department 9093, Box 112650,
Pittsburgh, PA 15241 or call 1-800-433-5599.

Free Healthy Lifestyle Information: The makers of Quaker Oats will send you some free information about healthy eating, physical fitness and well-being. To get the information, call the Quaker Oats Company at 1-800-476-2242.

Coffee House Sticker: Here's a free sticker for your computer, modem, car, briefcase, notebook, etc. The sticker says, "Carpe Diem" and is available by sending a SASE to:

Carpe Diem Artist Management International,
Coffee House Sticker, 1019 Due West Avenue,
Madison, TN 37115-3405.

Free project Sheets: These free project sheets use Beacon Liquid Laminate and show you how to create unusual ornament shapes, picture frames, and much more. Send a SASE to:

Signature Marketing and Manufacturing, Inc.,
P.O. Box 427,
Wyckoff, NJ 07481.

Ceramic Tips and Ideas Booklet: Get a free sample of Soft Tints the blended look of ceramic along with tips and an idea booklet by sending a SASE to:

Delta Technical Coatings, Inc.,
2550 Pellissier Place,
Whittier, CA 90601.

Covered Button Creativity: Get free tips and ideas for turning covered buttons into jewelry, wearable art, and much more. Contact the:

Prym-Dritz Corporation,
P.O. Box 692,
Spartanburg, SC 29304-0692.

Quilt Pattern: To get a free school days quilt pattern, send a SASE to:

Fabric Traditions, 1
350 Broadway,
New York, NY 10018.

"A Patients Guide To Cataract In Adults": To get a free copy of this booklet, contact:

Agency for Health Care Policy and Research,
Publications Clearinghouse, P.O. Box 8547,
Silver Spring, MD 20907, or call (800) 358-9295.

Sewing Caddy: If you love to sew, you'll love this free reversible sewing caddy that features an oversize pin cushion. It's available by sending a SASE to the:

Singer Sewing Company,
P.O. Box 1909, Department PIN,
Edison, NJ 08837.

Free Poster: Want to watch the sun set every evening? You can with this free sunset poster available from:

Lifetime Products, Customer Service,
P.O. Box 1525,
Clearfield, UT 84016.

Vitamin C Booklet: This free booklet contains information on vitamin C and provides ideas on planning menus featuring foods rich in vitamin C. The booklet is available upon request from:

Vitamin C,
P.O. Box 148, Department A,
Lakeland, FL 33802-0145.

Jog and run safely with these free tips from the:

American Running & Fitness Association,
9310 Old Georgetown Road,
Bethesda, MD 20814.

Ask for "Safety Tips For A Safe Workout". Include a business size SASE with your request.

Free Eyecare For Seniors: Senior citizens who meet specified income requirements can get free eye care by calling 1-800-222-3927. Doctors who are members of the American Academy of Ophhthalmology provide comprehensive eye examination and care for any diagnosed eye condition. The examination and care is free (does not cover prescription drugs, hospital care, or eyeglasses) to any U.S. citizen or resident 65 or older.

Free Craft and Decorating Booklet: This booklet includes craft ideas, home improvements and refinishing projects. To get a free copy, send a SASE to:

Thompson & Formby's, Inc.,
825 Crossover Lane,
Memphis, TN 38117.

"Cold Sores, Fever Blisters & Canker Sores": Whatever you call them, they're a nuisance and a pain. Find out what you can do about these nasty sores by sending for a free booklet. Send a business size SASE to:

American Academy of Otolaryngology-Head and Neck Surgery, "Fever Blisters",
One Prince Street,
Alexandria, VA 22314.

"How To Hold A Garage Sale": This free booklet will show you how to hold a money-making garage sale. To get a free copy, send a business size SASE to:

United Van Lines,
Consumer Services Department,
One United Drive,
Fenton, MO 63026.

Free Tickets To Your Favorite TV Shows: To find out about getting free tickets, contact the following:

ABC, 1330 Avenue of the Americas,
New York, NY 10019;

NBC, 30 Rockefeller,
New York, NY 10020;

and

CBS, 51 West 52nd Street,
New York, NY 10019.

Crochet Pattern: Get a free crochet pattern for a pinwheel potholder and a catalog of over 100 other crochet patterns by sending a SASE to:

Crocheting Forever,
20021 Fox Street,
Cassopolis, MI 49031.

Bowling For Fun: If you're looking for a fun and inexpensive form of relaxation, you might consider bowling. You can get a free beginners booklet, "Tips for Young Bowlers", by sending a business size SASE to:

American Bowler's Association,
5301 South
76th Street, Greendale,
WI 53129.

Basketball Hall of Fame Pamphlet: If basketball is your game, this free pamphlet will tell you how you can take a tour through the professional Basketball Hall of Fame. For a free copy of the pamphlet, write to:

Basketball Hall of Fame,
1150 West Columbus Avenue,
Springfield, MA 01105.

FREE STUFF FROM YOUR FAVORITE SPORTS TEAMS

Most professional sports teams offer free fan-mail packages, which include team decals, team photos, and other team-related items.

Here are the contact addresses for Major League Baseball (MLB), The National Football League (NFL) and The National Basketball Association (NBA).

You can contact your favorite team(s) and ask what fan-mail packages are available.

Major League Baseball

— American League

Baltimore Orioles, 333 W. Camden Street, Baltimore, MD 21201; (410) 685-9800; Fax: (410) 547-6767; Official Web Site: http://www.theorioles.com/.

Boston Red Sox, Fenway Park, 4 Yawkey Way, Boston, MA 02215; (617) 267-9440; Fax: (617) 236-6797; Web site: http://www.redsox.com/.

Anaheim Angels, Anaheim Stadium, P.O. Box 2000, Anaheim, CA 92803; (714) 9397-7200; Fax: (714) 937-7277.

Chicago White Sox, 333 W 35th Street, Chicago, IL 60616; (312) 451-5116; Web site: http://www.chisox.com/.

Cleveland Indians, Jacobs Field, 2401 Ontario Street, Cleveland, OH 44115; (216) 420-4200; Fax: (216) 420-4396; Web site: http://www.indians.com/.

Detroit Tigers, Tiger Stadium, 2121 Trumbull Avenue, Detroit, MI 48216; (313) 962-4000; Fax: (313) 962-1128.

Kansas City Royals, P.O. Box 419969, Kansas City, MO 64141; (816) 921-2200; Fax: (816) 921-5775; Web site: http://www.kcroyals.com/.

Milwaukee Brewers, P.O. Box 3099, Milwaukee, WI 53201; (414) 933-4114; Fax: (414) 933-7323; Web site: http://www.milwaukeebrewers.com/.

Minnesota Twins, 501 Chicago Avenue S., Minneapolis, MN 55415; (612) 375-1366; Fax: (612) 375-7473; Web site:
http://www.wcco.com/sports/twins/.

New York Yankees, Yankee Stadium, Bronx, NY 10451; (718) 293-4300; Fax: (718) 293-8341; Web site: http://www.yankees.com/.

Oakland Athletics, Oakland-Alameda County Coliseum, Oakland, CA 94621; (510) 638-4937; Web site: http://www.oaklandathletics.com/.

Seattle Mariners, P.O. Box 4100, Seattle, WA 98104; (206) 628-3555; Fax: (206) 628-3340; Web site: http://www.mariners.org/.

Texas Rangers, P.O. Box 90111, Arlington, TX 76004; (817) 273-5222; Fax: (817) 273-5206; Web site: http://www.texasrangers.com/.

Toronto Blue Jays, One Blue Jays Way, Suite 3200, Skydome, Toronto, Ontario M5V 1J1, Canada; (416) 341-1000; Fax: (416) 341-1250; Web site: http://www.bluejays.ca/bluejays/.

— National League

Atlanta Braves, P.O. Box 4064, Atlanta, GA 30302; (404) 614-1391; Web Site: http://www.atlantabraves.com/.

Chicago Cubs, Wrigley Field, 1060 West Addison Street, Chicago, IL 60613; (312) 404-2827; Fax: (312) 404-4129.

Cincinnati Reds, Cynergy Field, 100 Riverfront Stadium, Cincinnati, OH 45202; (513) 421-5410; Fax: (513) 421-7342.

Colorado Rockies, 2001 Blake Street, Denver, CO 80205; (303) 292-0200; Fax: (303) 312-2319.

Florida Marlins, Joe Robbie Stadium, 2267 NW 199th Street, Miami, FL 33056; (305) 626-7400; Fax: (305) 626-7302; Web site: http://www.flamarlins.com/.

Houston Astros, P.O. Box 77001, Houston, TX 77001; (713) 799-9500; Fax: (713) 799-9562; Web site: http://www.astros.com/.

Los Angeles Dodgers, 1000 Elysian Park Avenue, Los Angeles, CA 90012; (213) 224-1500; Fax: (213) 224-1269; Web site: http://www.dodgers.com/.

Montreal Expos, P.O. Box 500, Station M, Montreal, Quebec H1V 3P2, Canada; (514) 253-3434; Fax: (514) 253-8282; Web site: http://wwwmontrealexpos.com/.

New York Mets, Shea Stadium, 126th Street & Roosevelt Avenue, Flushing, NY 11368; (718) 507-6387; Fax: (718) 565-4382.

Philadelphia Phillies, P.O. Box 7575, Philadelphia, PA 19101; (215) 463-6000; Fax: (215) 389-3050.

Pittsburgh Pirates, P.O. Box 7000, Pittsburgh, PA 15212; (412) 323-1724; Web site: http://www.pirateball.com/.

St. Louis Cardinals, 250 Stadium Plaza, St. Louis, MO 63102; (314) 421-3060; Fax: (314) 425-0640; Web site: http://www.stlcardinals.com/.

San Diego Padres, P.O. Box 2000, San Diego, CA 92112; (619) 283-4494; Fax: (619) 282-2228; Web site: http://www.padres.org/.

San Francisco Giants, 3COM Park, San Francisco, CA 94124; (415) 468-3700; Fax: (415) 467-0485; Web site: http://www.sfgiants.com/.

Expansion Teams (will begin play in 1998)

Arizona Diamondbacks, P.O. Box 2095, Phoenix, AZ 85001; (602) 514-8500; Fax: (602) 514-8599; Web site: http://ww.azdiamondbacks.com/.

Tampa Bay Devil Rays, The Thunderdome, One Stadium Drive, St. Petersburg, FL 33705; (813) 825-3137; Fax: (813) 825-3300.

National Basketball Association

Atlanta Hawks, One CNN Center, Suite 405, South Tower, Atlanta, GA 30303; (404) 827-3865.

Boston Celtics, 151 Merrimac Street, 4th Floor, Boston, MA 02114; (617) 523-3030.

Charlotte Hornets, 100 Hive Drive, Charlotte, NC 28217; (704) 357-0489.

Chicago Bulls, 1901 West Madison, Chicago, IL 60612; (312) 455-4000.

Cleveland Cavaliers, Gund Arena, One Center Court, Cleveland, OH 44115; (216) 420-CAVS.

Dallas Mavericks, Reunion Arena, 777 Sports Street, Dallas, TX 75207; (214) 939-2800.

Denver Nuggets, 1635 Clay Street, Denver, CO 80204; (303) 893-DUNK.

Detroit Pistons, The Palace of Auburn Hills, Two Championship Drive, Auburn Hills, MI 48326; (810) 377-0100.

Golden State Warriors, Oakland Coliseum Arena, 7000 Coliseum Way, Oakland, CA 94621; (510) 638-6300.

Houston Rockets, 10 Greenway Plaza, Houston, TX 77046; (713) 627-DUNK.

Indiana Pacers, Market Square Arena, 300 East Market Street, Indianapolis, IN 46204; (317) 263-2100.

Los Angeles Clippers, LA Sports Arena, 3939 South Figueroa Street, Los Angeles, CA 90037; (213) 745-0500.

Los Angeles Lakers, Great Western Forum, P.O. Box 10, Inglewood, CA 90306; (310) 419-3182.

Miami Heat, Sun Trust International Center, One Southeast Third Avenue, Suite 2300, Miami, FL 33131; (305) 577-HEAT.

Milwaukee Bucks, 1001 North Fourth Street, Milwaukee, WI 53203; (414) 227-0500.

Minnesota Timberwolves, 600 First Avenue North, Minneapolis, MN 55403; (612) 337-DUNK.

New Jersey Nets, 405 Murray Hill Parkway, East Rutherford, NJ 07073; (201) 935-8888.

New York Knicks, Madison Square Garden, Four Pennsylvania Plaza, New York, NY 10121; (212) 465-JUMP.

Orlando Magic, P.O. Box 76, Orlando, FL 32802; (407) 89M-AGIC.

Philadelphia 76ers, Veterans Stadium, P.O. Box 25050, Philadelphia, PA 19147; (215) 339-7676.

Portland Trailblazers, 1 Center Court, Suite 200, Portland, OR 97227; (503) 797-9783.

Sacramento Kings, ARCO Arena, One Sports Parkway, Sacramento, CA 95834; (916) 928-6900.

San Antonio Spurs, 100 Montana Street, San Antonio, TX 78203-1031; (210) 554-7773.

Seattle Sonics, 190 Queen Anne Avenue North, P.O. Box 900911, Seattle, WA 98109-9711; (206) 283-DUNK.

Toronto Raptors, 20 Bay Street, Suite 1702, Toronto, Ontario M5J 2N8, Canada; (416) 366-DUNK.

Utah Jazz, Delta Center, 301 West South Temple, Salt Lake City, UT 84101; (801) 355-DUNK.

Vancouver Grizzlies, General Motors Place, 800 Griffiths Way, Vancouver, BC V6B 6G1, Canada: (604)

899-4667.

Washington Bullets, USAir Arena, One Harry S. Truman Drive, Lanover, MD 20785; (301) NBA-DUNK.

National Football League

Arizona Cardinals, P.O. Box 888, Phoenix, AZ 85001-0888; (602) 379-0101.

Atlanta Falcons, 2745 Burnette Road, Suwanee, GA 30174; (404) 945-1111.

Baltimore Ravens, 11001 Owings Mills Blvd., Owings Mills, MD 21117; (410) 654-6200.

Buffalo Bills, One Bills Drive, Orchard Park, NY 14127; (716) 648-1800.

Carolina Panthers, 227 West Trade Street, Suite 1600, Charlotte, NC 28202; (704) 358-7000.

Chicago Bears, 250 North Washington Road, Lake Forest, IL 60045; (708) 295-6600.

Cincinnati Bengals, 200 Cynergy Field, Riverfront Stadium, Cincinnati, OH 45202; (513) 621-3550.

Dallas Cowboys, One Cowboys Parkway, Irving, TX 75063; (214) 556-9900.

Denver Broncos, 13655 Broncos Parkway, Englewood, CO 80112; (303) 649-9000.

Detroit Lions, Pontiac Silverdome, 1200 Featherstone Road, Pontiac, MI 48324; (313) 335-4131

Green Bay Packers, 1265 Lombardi Avenue, Green Bay, WI 54304; (414) 496-5700.

Houston Oilers, 6910 Fannin Street, Houston, TX 770030; (713) 797-9111.

Indianapolis Colts, P.O. Box 535000, Indianapolis, IN 46253; (317) 297-2658.

Jacksonville Jaguars, One Stadium Place, Jacksonville, FL 32202; (904) 633-6000.

Kansas City Chiefs, One Arrowhead Drive, Kansas City, MO 64129; (816) 924-9300.

Miami Dolphins, 2269 N..W. 199th Street, Miami, FL 33056; (305) 650-5000.

Minnesota Vikings, 9520 Viking Drive, Eden Prairie, MN 55344; (612) 828-6500.

New England Patriots, 60 Washington Street, Foxboro, MA 02035; (508) 543-8200; Web site: http://www.patriots.com/.

New Orleans Saints, 6928 Saints Drive, Metairie, LA 70003; (504) 733-0255.

New York Giants, Giants Stadium, East Rutherford, NJ 07073; (201) 935-8111.

New York Jets, 1000 Fulton Avenue, Hempstead, NY 11550; (516) 538-6600.

Oakland Raiders, 332 Center Street, El Segundo, CA 90245; (310) 332-3451.

Philadelphia Eagles, 3501 South Broad Street, Philadelphia, PA 19148; (215) 463-2500.

Pittsburgh Steelers, 300 Stadium Circle, Pittsburgh, PA 15212; (412) 323-1200.

St. Louis Rams, 100 North Broadway, St. Louis, MO 63102.

San Francisco 49ers, 4949 Centennial Boulevard, Santa Clara, CA 92160; (408) 562-4949.

San Diego Chargers, P.O. Box 609609, San Diego, CA 92160; (619) 280-2111.

Seattle Seahawks, 11220 N..E. 53rd Street, Kirkland, WA 98033; (206) 827-9777.

Tampa Bay Buccaneers, One Buccaneer Place, Tampa, FL 33607; (813) 870-2700.

Washington Redskins, 21300 Redskin Park Drive, Ashburn, VA 22011; (703) 478-8900.

Appendix

DEPARTMENT OF HOUSING AND URBAN DEVELOPMENT (HUD) REGIONAL AND FIELD OFFICES

Region 1 (CT., ME, MA, NH, RI, VT—includes Massachusetts office)—Room 375 O'Neill Federal Office Bldg., 10 Causeway St., Boston, MA 02222-1092; (617) 565-5234.

Connecticut Office— 330 Main St., Hartford, CT 0106-1860; (203) 240-4523.

Maine Office— 99 Franklin Street, Suite 302, Bangor, ME 04401-4925; (207) 945-0467.

New Hampshire Office— Cotton Federal Building, 275 Chestnut St., Manchester, NH 03101-2487; (603) 666-7681.

Rhode Island Office — Sixth Floor, 10 Weybosset St., Providence, RI 02903-3254; (401) 528-5351.

Vermont Office— Room 244 Federal Building, 11 Elmwood Ave., P.O. Box 879, Burlington, VT 05402-0879; (802) 951-6290.

Region 2 (NY, NJ— includes New York City Office)— 26 Federal Plaza, New York, NY 10278-0068; (212) 264-6500.

Northern New York State Office— 52 Corporate Circle, Albany, NY 12203-5121; (518) 464-4200.

Western New York State Office— Lafayette Court, 5th Floor, 465 Main St., Buffalo, NY 14203-1780; (716) 846-5752.

Southern New Jersey Office— Hudson Building, 2nd Floor, 800 Hudson Square, Camden, NJ 08102-1156; (609) 757-5081.

Northern New Jersey Office— One Newark Center, 13th Floor, Newark, NJ 07102-5260; (201) 622-7900.

Region 3 (DL, District of Columbia, MD, PA, VA, WV)— Liberty Square Building, 105 S. 7th St., Philadelphia, PA 19106-3392; (215) 597-2560.

Delaware Office— 824 Market St., Suite 850, Wilmington, DE 19801-3016; (302) 573-6300.

Maryland (except Montgomery and Prince George counties) Office— City Crescent Building, 5th Floor, 10 S. Howard St., Baltimore, MD 21201; (301) 962-2520.

West Virginia Office— Kanawha Valley Building, 405 Capitol Street, Suite 708, Charleston, WV 25301-1795; (304) 347-7000.

Western Pennsylvania, West Virginia Office— 339 Sixth Ave., Pittsburgh, PA 15222-2515; (412) 644-6428.

Virginia Office— 3600 W. Broad St., P.O. Box 90331, Richmond, VA 23230-0331; (804) 278-4507.

Washington, DC Office— 820 First St. NE, Washington, DC 20002-4205; (202) 275-9200.

Region 4 (AL, FL, GA, KY, MS, NC, SC, TN— includes Georgia office)— Russell Federal Building, 75 Spring St. SW, Atlanta, GA 30303-3388; (404) 331-5136.

Alabama Office— 600 Beacon Pkwy., Suite 300, Birmingham, AL 35209-3144; (205) 290-7617.

Central Florida (Orlando) Office— Suite 270, Langley Bldg., 3751 Maguire Blvd., Orlando, FL 32803-

3032; (407) 648-6441.

Central Florida (Tampa) Office— Timberlake Federal Building Annex, 501 E Polk St., Suite 700, Tampa, FL 33602-3945; (813) 228-2504.

Central Tennessee Office— 251 Cumberland Bend Dr., Nashville, TN 37228-1803; (615) 736-5213.

Florida (Jacksonville) Office— Suite 2200 Southern Bell Tower, 301 W. Bay St., Jacksonville, FL 32202-5121; (904) 232-2627.

Kentucky Office— Gene Snyder Customs & Courthouse, 601 West Broadway, Louisville, KY 40201-1044; (502) 582-5251.

Mississippi Office— Room 910 McCoy Federal Building, 100 W. Capitol St., Jackson, MS 39269-1096; (601) 965-5308.

North Carolina Office— 2306 West Meadowview Road, Greensboro, NC 27407-3707; (910) 547-4000.

South Carolina Office— Strom Thurmond Federal Building, 1835 Assembly St., Columbia, SC 29201-2480; (803) 765-5592.

Southern Florida Office— 1320 S. Dixie Hwy., 5th Floor, Coral Gables, FL 33146-2911; (305) 662-4510.

Tennessee (Knoxville) Office— Duncan Federal Building, 3rd Floor, 710 Locust St. SW, Knoxville, TN 37902-2526; (423) 545-4384.

Western Tennessee Office— One Memphis Place, Suite 1200, 200 Jefferson Ave, Memphis, TN 38103-2335; (901) 544-3367.

Region 5 (IL, IN, MI, MN, OH, WI— includes Chicago Area Office)– 77 W. Jackson Blvd., Chicago, IL 60604-3507; (312) 353-5680.

Central & Southern Illinois— 509 West Capitol St., Suite 206, Springfield, IL 62704-1906; (217) 492-4085.

Eastern Michigan Office— Manager, 605 N. Saginaw St., Suite 200, Flint, MI 48502-1953; (313) 766-5112.

Indiana Office— 151 North Delaware St., Indianapolis, IN 46204-2526; (317) 226-6303.

Michigan Office— McNamara Federal Building, 477 Michigan Ave., Detroit, MI 48226-2592; (313) 766-5122.

Minnesota Office— Bridge Place Building, 220 Second St. S., Minneapolis, MN 55401-2195; (612) 370-3000.

Northern Ohio Office— 1350 Euclid Ave., Suite 500, Cleveland, OH 44115-1815; (216) 522-4058

Ohio Office— 200 N. High St., Columbus, OH 43215-2499; (614) 469-5737.

Southwestern Ohio Office— 525 Vine Street, 7th Floor, Cincinnati, OH 45202-3188; (513) 684-2884.

Western & Northern Michigan Office— Third Floor, Trade Center Building, 50 Louis St., NW, Grand Rapids, MI 49503-2648; (616) 456-2100.

Wisconsin Office— 310 W. Wisconsin Ave., Suite 1380, Milwaukee, WI 53203-2289; (414) 297-3214.

Region 6 (AR, LA, NM, OK, TX)— 1600 Throckmorton, P.O. Box 2905, Fort Worth, TX 76113-2905; (817) 885-5401.

Arkansas Office— 425 W. Capitol Ave., TCBY Tower, Suite 900, Little Rock, AR 72201-3488: (501) 324-5931.

East Central Texas Office— Suite 200 Norfolk Tower, 2211 Norfolk, Houston, TX 77098-4096; (713) 653-3274.

Eastern, Northern, Western Texas and New Mexico Office— 525 Griffin St., Room 860, Dallas, TX 75202-5007; (214) 767-8359.

Eastern Oklahoma Office— 50 East 15th Street, Tulsa, OK 74119; (918) 581-7434.

Louisiana Office— Hale Boggs Federal Building, 501 Magazine St. 9th Floor, New Orleans, LA 70130-3099; (504) 589-7200.

New Mexico Office— 625 Truman St. NE, Albuquerque, NM 87110-6443; (505) 262-6463.

Northern Louisiana Office— 401 Edwards Street, Suite 1510, Shreveport, LA 71101-3289: (318) 676-3385.

Northwest Texas Office— Federal Office Building, 1205 Texas Ave., Lubbock, TX 79401-4093; (806) 743-7265.

Oklahoma Office— 500 W. Main Street, Suite 400, Oklahoma City, OK 73102-3202; (405) 231-4181.

Southwest Texas— Washington Sq. Building, 800 Dolorosa, San Antonio, TX 78207-4563; (512) 229-6800.

Region 7 (IA, KS, MO, NB— includes Kansas City Area Office)— Room 200 Gateway Tower II, 400 State Ave, Kansas City, KS 66101-2406; (913) 551-5462.

Eastern Missouri Office— Robert A. Young Federal Building, 1222 Spruce St., Room 3207, St. Louis, MO 63103-2836; (314) 539-6583.

Iowa Office— 210 Walnut Street, Room 239, Des Moines, IA 50309-2155; (515) 284-4512.

Nebraska Office— Executive Tower Center, 10909 Mill Valley Rd., Omaha, NE 68154-3955; (402) 492-3101.

Region 8 (CO, MT, ND, SD, UT, WY— includes Denver Office)— First Interstate Tower North, 633 17th St., Denver, CO 80202-3607; (303) 672-5281.

Montana Office— Room 340 Federal Bldg., 301 S. Park, Helena, MT 59626-0095: (406) 449-5027.

North Dakota Office— Federal Building, 657 2nd Ave, 58108-2483; (701) 239-5136.

South Dakota Office— 2400 W. 49th St., Suite I-201, Sioux Falls, SD 57105-6558; (605) 330-4223.

Utah Office— 257 E. 200 South, Suite 550, Salt Lake City, UT 84111-2048: (801) 524-5379.

Wyoming Office— 4225 Federal Building, 100 E. B St., P.O. Box 120, Casper, WY 82602-1918; (307) 261-5252.

Region 9 (AZ, CA, HI, NV, — includes San Francisco area)— 450 Golden Gate Ave., P.O. Box 36003, San Francisco, CA 94102-3448; (415) 436-6532.

Arizona Office— Two Arizona Center, 400 N. 5th St., Suite 600, Phoenix, AZ 85004-2361; (602) 379-4434.

Arizona (Tucson) Office— 33 N. Stone Ave., Suite 700, Tucson, AZ 85701-1467; (520) 670-6207.

California Office— 1630 E. Shaw Ave., Suite 138, Fresno, CA 93710-8193; (209) 487-5033.

California (San Diego) Office— Suite 300, Mission City Corporate Center, 2365 Northside Drive, San Diego, CA 92108-2712; (619) 557-6296

Hawaii Office— 7 Waterfront Plaza, Suite 500, 500 Ala Moana Blvd., Honolulu, HI 96813-4918; (808) 541-1323.

Nevada (Las Vegas) Office— Atrium Building, 333 North Rancho Drive, Suite 700, Las Vegas, NV 89106-3714: (702) 388-6500.

Nevada (Reno) Office— 1575 DeLucchi Lane, Suite 114, P.O. Box 30050, Reno, NV 89502-6581; (702) 784-5356.

Northeastern California Office— 777 12th St., Suite 200, Sacramento, CA 95814-1977; (916) 498-5220.

Southern California Office— 611 W. Sixth Street, Suite 80, Los Angeles, CA 90017; (213) 894-8000.

Region 10 (AK, ID, OR, WA)— Suite 200 Seattle Federal Office Building, 909 First Ave, Seattle, WA 98104-1000; (206) 220-5270.

Alaska Office— Suite 401 University Plaza Building, 949 E. 36th Ave., Anchorage, AK 99508-4135; (907) 271-4170.

Eastern Washington Office— Farm Credit Bank Building, 8th Floor-east, W. 601 First Ave., Spokane, WA 99204-0317; (509) 353-2510.

Oregon Office— 400 Southwest Sixth Ave., Seventh Floor, Portland, OR 97204-1632; (503) 326-2561.

Washington (Seattle) Office- Federal Office Building, 909 1st Ave., Suite 200, Seattle, WA 98104-1000; (206) 220-5406.

West-Central Idaho Office— Suite 220, Plaza IV, 800 Park Blvd., Boise, ID 83712-7243; (208) 334-1990 ext. 3007.

EQUAL EMPLOYMENT OPPORTUNITY COMMISSION

District Offices

ALABAMA: 1900 Third Ave. N.- Ste. 101, Birmingham, AL 35203-2397; (205) 731-0082.

ARIZONA: 4520 N. Central Ave- Ste. 300, Phoenix, AZ 85012-1848; (602) 640-5000.

CALIFORNIA: 255 E. Temple Avenue, 4th Floor, Los Angeles, CA 90012; (213) 894-1000; 901 Market Street- Ste. 500, San Francisco, CA 94103; (415) 744-6500.

COLORADO: 303 E. 17th Ave- Ste. 510, Denver, CO 80203-9634; (303) 866-1300.

DISTRICT OF COLUMBIA: 1400 L ST. NW- Ste. 200, Washington, DC 20005; (202) 275-7377.

FLORIDA: One Biscayne Tower- Ste. 2700, Miami, FL 33131; (305) 536-4491.

GEORGIA: Ste. 1100, Citizens Trust Building, 75 Piedmont Ave., NE, Atlanta, GA 30335.

ILLINOIS: 500 W. Madison St.- Ste. 2800, Chicago, IL 60661; (312) 353-2713.

INDIANA: Ste. 1900, Federal Building, 101 W. Ohio Street, Indianapolis, IN 46204; (317) 226-7212.

LOUISIANA: 701 Loyola Ave.- Ste. 600, New Orleans, LA 70113-9936; (504) 589-2329.

MARYLAND: City Crescent Building, 3rd Floor, 10 S. Howard, Baltimore, MD 21201; (410) 962-3932.

MICHIGAN: Ste. 1540 McNamara Federal Building, 477 Michigan Ave., Detroit, MI 48226-9704; (313) 226-7636.

MISSOURI: 625 N. Euclid St., 5th Floor, St. Louis, MO 63108; (314) 425-6585.

NEW MEXICO: 505 Marquette NW- Ste. 900, Albuquerque, NM 87102-2189; (505) 766-2061.

NEW YORK: 7 World Trade Center, 18th Floor, New York, NY 10048-0948; (212) 748-8500.

NORTH CAROLINA: 5500 Central Avenue, Charlotte, NC 28121-2708; (704) 567-7100.

OHIO: Ste. 850 Tower City, Skylight Office Tower, 1660 W. 2nd Street, Cleveland, OH 44113-1454; (216) 522-2001.

PENNSYLVANIA: 1421 Cherry Street, 10th Floor, Philadelphia, PA 19102; (215) 656-7000.

TENNESSEE: 1407 Union Avenue- Ste. 621, Memphis, TN 38104; (901) 722-2617.

TEXAS: 207 S. Houston St., Dallas, TX 75202-4726; (214) 655-3355; Concorde Tower, 7th Floor, 1919 Smith St., Houston, TX 77002; (713) 653-3377; Ste. 200 Mockingbird Plaza II, 5410 Fredericksburg Rd., San Antonio, TX 78229-3555; (512) 229-4810.

WASHINGTON: 909 First Street- Ste. 400, Seattle, WA 98121-1061; (206) 220-6883.

WISCONSIN: Ste. 800 Reuss Federal Plaza, 310 W. Wisconsin Ave., Milwaukee, WI 53203-2293; (414) 297-1111.

Area Offices

ARKANSAS: 425 W. Capitol Ave.- Ste. 621, Little Rock, AR 72201; (501) 324-5060.

FLORIDA: 501 E. Polk Street, Room 1020, Tampa, FL 33602: (813) 228-2310.

KENTUCKY: Room 268, U.S. Post Office & Courthouse, 600 Martin Luther King Jr. Pl., Louisville, KY 40202; (502) 582-6082.

MASSACHUSETTS: One Congress Street, 10th Floor, Boston, MA 02114; (617) 565-3200.

MINNESOTA: 4330 S. Second Ave.- Ste. 430, Minneapolis, MN 55401-2224; (612) 335-4040.

MISSISSIPPI: Cross Road Plaza Complex, 207 W. Amite St., Jackson, MS (601) 965-4537.

MISSOURI: 911 Walnut, 10th Floor, Kansas City, MO 64106; (816) 426-5773.

NEW JERSEY: One Newark Center, 21st Floor, Newark, NJ 07102-5233; (201) 645-6383.

NORTH CAROLINA: 1309 Annapolis Drive, Raleigh, NC 27608-2129; (919) 856-4064.

OHIO: 525 Vine Street, Room 810, Cincinnati, OH 45202-3122; (513) 684-2851.

OKLAHOMA: 531 Couch Drive, Oklahoma City, OK 73102-2265; (405) 231-4911.

PENNSYLVANIA: Room 2038A Federal Building, 1000 Liberty Ave, Pittsburgh, PA 15222; (412) 644-3444.

TENNESSEE: 50 Vantage Way- Ste. 202, Nashville, TN 37228; (615) 736-5820.

TEXAS: Ste. 100 The Commons Building, 4171 N. Mesa St., El Paso, TX 79902; (915) 534-6550.

VIRGINIA: Federal Building, 1st Floor, 252 Monticello Avenue, Norfolk, VA 23510; (804) 441-3470; 3600 Broad Street, Room 229, Richmond, VA 23240; (804) 771-2692.

Local Offices

CALIFORNIA: 1265 W. Shaw Ave.- Ste. 103, Fresno, CA 93711; (209) 487-5793; 1301 Clay Street-Ste. 1170-N, Oakland, CA 94612-5217; (510) 637-5217;

401 B St.- Ste. 1550, San Diego, CA 92101; (619) 637-3230; 96 N. Third St.- Ste. 200, San Jose, CA 95112; (408) 291-7352.

GEORGIA: 10 Mall Blvd.- Ste. G, Savannah, GA 31406; (912) 652-4234.

HAWAII: 677 Ala Moana Blvd.- Ste. 404, P.O. Box 50082, Honolulu, HI 96813; (808) 541-3120.

NEW YORK: 6 Fountain Plaza- Ste. 350, Buffalo, NY 14203; (716) 846-4441.

NORTH CAROLINA: 801 Summit Ave., Greensboro, NC 27405-7813; (919) 333-5174.

SOUTH CAROLINA: Room 530 Southern National Bank Building, 15 S. Main Street, Greenville, SC 29601; (803) 241-4400.

FEDERAL INFORMATION CENTER

The Federal Information Center (FIC), administered by the General Services Administration (GSA), can help you find information about the Federal government's agencies, services and programs. The FIC also can tell you which office to contact for help with problems. Simply dial (800) 688-9889 if you are calling from one of the following metropolitan areas. If you are not in one of the areas listed, please call (301) 722-9000. If you use a Telecommunications

Device for the Deaf (TDD/TTY), you may call toll-free from anywhere in the United States by dialing (800) 326-2996.

Call 1-800-688-9889 for the following metropolitan areas:

Birmingham and Mobile, Alabama

Anchorage, Alaska

Phoenix, Arizona

Little Rock, Arkansas

Los Angeles, San Diego, Santa Ana, and Sacramento, California

Colorado Springs, Denver and Pueblo, Colorado

Hartford and New Haven, Connecticut.

Wilmington, Delaware

Fort Lauderdale, Jacksonville, Miami, Orlando, St. Petersburg, Tampa, and West Palm Beach, Florida

Atlanta, Georgia

Honolulu, Hawaii

Boise, Idaho

Chicago, Illinois

Gary and Indianapolis, Indiana

Iowa (all locations)
Kansas (all locations)

Louisville, Kentucky

New Orleans, Louisiana

Portland, Maine

Baltimore, Maryland

Boston, Massachusetts

Detroit and Grand Rapids, Michigan

Minneapolis-St. Paul, Minnesota

Jackson, Mississippi

Missouri (all locations)

Billings, Montana

Nebraska (all locations)

Las Vegas, Nevada

Portsmouth, New Hampshire

Newark and Trenton, New Jersey

Albuquerque, New Mexico
Albany, Buffalo, New York City, Rochester, and Syracuse, New York

Charlotte, North Carolina

Fargo, North Dakota

Akron, Cincinnati, Cleveland, Columbus, Dayton, and Toledo, Ohio

Oklahoma City and Tulsa, Oklahoma

Portland, Oregon

Philadelphia and Pittsburgh, Pennsylvania

Providence, Rhode Island

Greenville, South Carolina

Sioux Falls, South Dakota

Chattanooga, Memphis and Nashville, Tennessee

Austin, Dallas, Fort Worth, Houston, and San Antonio, Texas

Salt Lake City, Utah

Burlington, Vermont

Norfolk, Richmond and Roanoke, Virginia

Seattle and Tacoma, Washington

Huntington, West Virginia

Milwaukee, Wisconsin

Cheyenne, Wyoming

(If you are not in one of the areas listed, call (301) 722-9000.)

STATE AGENCIES ON AGING

State Agencies on Aging coordinate a number of services for older Americans. They provide information on services, programs and opportunities for senior citizens.

ALABAMA: Commission on Aging, RSA Plaza, Suite 470, 770 Washington Avenue, Montgomery, AL 36130-1851; (334) 5743; Fax: 334-242-5594.

ALASKA: Commission on Aging, Division of Senior Services, Department of Administration, P.O. Box 11011, Juneau, AK 99811-0211; (907) 465-3250; Fax: 907-465-4716.

ARIZONA: Aging and Adult Administration, Site Code 950A, Department of Economic Security, 1789 West Jefferson, Phoenix, AZ 85007; (602) 542-4446; Fax: 602-542-6575.

ARKANSAS: Division of Aging and Adult Services, Arkansas Department of Human Services, P.O. Box 1437, Slot 1412, Little Rock, AR 72203-1437; (501) 682-2441; Fax: 501-682-8155.

CALIFORNIA: California Department of Aging, 1600 K Street, Sacramento, CA 95814; (916) 322-3887; Fax: 916-324-1903.

COLORADO: Aging and Adult Service, Department of Social Services, 110 16th Street, Suite 200, Denver, CO 80202-4147; (303) 620-4147; Fax: 303-620-4191.

CONNECTICUT: Community Services, Connecticut Department of Social Services, Elderly Services Division, 25 Sigourney Street, 10th Floor, Hartford, CT 06106-5033; (860) 424-5277; Fax: 860-424-4966.

DELAWARE: Division of Services for Aging & Adults with Physical Disabilities, DDHSS, 1901 North Dupont Highway, New Castle, DE 19720; (800) 223-9074; Fax: 301-577-4793.

DISTRICT OF COLUMBIA: District of Columbia Office on Aging, 441 Fourth Street, NW, Suite 900 South, Washington, DC 20001; (202) 724-5622; Fax: 202-724-4979.

FLORIDA: Department of Elder Affairs, 4040 Esplanade Way, Tallahassee, FL 32399-7000; (904) 414-2000; Fax: 904-414-2004.

GEORGIA: Division of Aging Services, Department of Human Resources, 2 Peachtree Street, N.E., 18th Floor, Atlanta, GA 30303; (404) 657-5258; Fax: 404-657-5285.

HAWAII: Executive Office on Aging, 250 South Hotel Street, Suite 107, Honolulu, HI 96813-2831; (808) 586-0100; 800-468-4644 Ext. 60100 (in Hawaii); Fax: 808-586-0185.

IDAHO: Commission on Aging, 700 West Jefferson, Room 108, P.O. Box 83720, Boise, ID 83720-0007; (208) 334-3833; Fax: 208-334-3033.

ILLINOIS: Department on Aging, 421 East Capitol Avenue, Suite 100, Springfield, IL 62701-1789; (217) 785-2870; Fax: 217-785-4477.

INDIANA: Division of Disability, Aging and Rehabilitative Service, Bureau of Aging and In-Home Services, 402 W. Washington Street, Indianapolis, IN 46207-7083; (800) 545-7763; Fax: 317-232-7867.

IOWA: Department of Elder Affairs, Clemens Building, 3rd Floor, 200 Tenth Street, Des Moines, IA 50309-3609; (515) 281-5187; Fax: 515-281-4036.

KANSAS: Department on Aging, Docking State Office Building, Room 150, 915 S.W. Harrison, Topeka, KS 66612-1505; (913) 296-4986; (800) 432-3535 (in Kansas).

KENTUCKY: Department of Social Services, CHR Building, 5th West, 275 East Main Street, Frankfort, KY 40621; (502) 564-6930; Fax: 502-564-4595.

LOUISIANA: Governor's Office of Elderly Affairs, P.O. Box 80374, Baton Rouge, LA 70898-0374; (504) 925-1700; 800-259-4990 (in LA); Fax: 504-925-1749.

MAINE: Bureau of Elder and Adult Services, Department of Human Services, 35 Anthony Avenue, State House, Station 11, Augusta, ME 04333-0011; (207) 624-5335; Fax: 207-624-5361.

MARYLAND: Office on Aging, State Office Building, Room 1004, 301 West Preston Street, Baltimore, MD 21201; (410) 767-1102; 800-243-3425 (in MD); Fax: 410-333-7943.

MASSACHUSETTS: Executive Office of Elder Affairs, 1 Ashburton Place, 5th Floor, Boston, MA 02108; (617) 727-7750; Fax: 800-882-2003 (in MA); Fax: 617-727-9368.

MICHIGAN: Office of Services to the Aging, P.O. Box 30026, Lansing, MI 48909; (517) 373-8230; Fax:

517-373-4092.

MINNESOTA: Minnesota Board on Aging, 444 Lafayette Road, St. Paul, MN 55155-3843; (800) 882-6262; Fax: 612-297-7855.

MISSISSIPPI: Division of Aging and Adult Services, 750 State Street, Jackson, MS 39202; (601) 359-4925; Fax: 601-359-4370.

MISSOURI: Division of Aging, Department of Social Services, P.O. Box 1337, 615 Howerton Court, Jefferson City, MO 65102-1337; 573-751-3082; Fax: 573-751-8687.

MONTANA: Office on Aging, 111 North Sanders, Room 210, Helena, MT 59620; (800) 332-2272; Fax: 406-444-7433.

NEBRASKA: Department on Aging, P.O. Box 95044, 301 Centennial Mall-South, Lincoln, NE 68509-5044; (402) 471-4619; Fax: 402-471-4619.

NEVADA: Division for Aging Services, Department of Human Resources, 340 North 11th Street, Suite 203, Las Vegas, NV 89101; (702) 486-3545; Fax: 702-486-3572.

NEW HAMPSHIRE: Division of Elderly and Adult Services, State Office Park South, 115 Pleasant Street Annex Building #1, Concord, NH 03301-6501; (603)

271-4680; Fax: 603-271-4643.

NEW JERSEY: Department of Health and Senior Services, Division of Senior Affairs, 101 South Broad Street-CN 807, Trenton, NJ 08625-0807; (609) 292-3766; 800-792-8820 (in NJ); Fax: 609-633-6609.

NEW MEXICO: State Agency on Aging, La Villa Rivera Building, 228 East Palace Avenue, Ground Floor, Santa Fe, NM 87501; (505) 827-7640; 800-432-2080 (in NM); Fax: 505-827-7649.

NEW YORK: State Office For the Aging, 2 Empire State Plaza, Albany, NY 12223-1251; (518) 474-5731; Fax: 518-474-0608.

NORTH CAROLINA: Division of Aging, CB 29531, 693 Palmer Drive, Raleigh, NC 27626-0531; (919) 733-3983; Fax: 919-733-0443.

NORTH DAKOTA: Department of Human Services, 600 South Second Street, Suite 1C, Bismarck, ND 58507-5729; (701) 328-8910; 800-755-8521 (in ND); Fax: 701-328-8989.

OHIO: Department of Aging, 50 West Broad Street, 9th Floor, Columbus, OH 43215-5928; (614) 466-5500; Fax: 614-466-5741.

OKLAHOMA: Services for the Aging, Department of Human Services, P.O. Box 25352, Oklahoma City, OK 73125; (405) 521-2281; 800-211-2116 (in OK); Fax: 405-521-2086.

OREGON: Senior and Disabled, Services Division, 500 Summer Street, NE, 2nd Floor, Salem, OR 97310-1015; (503) 945-5811; 800-282-8096 (in OR); Fax: 503-373-7823.

PENNSYLVANIA: Department of Aging, 400 Market Street, 6th Floor, Harrisburg, PA 17101-2301; (717) 783-1550; Fax: 717-772-3382.

RHODE ISLAND: Department of Elderly Affairs, 160 Pine Street, Providence, RI 02903-3708; (401) 277-2858; Fax: 401-277-1490.

SOUTH CAROLINA: South Carolina Division on Aging, 202 Arbor Lake Drive, Suite 301, Columbia, SC 29223-4535; (803) 737-7500; 800-868-9095 (in SC); Fax: 803-737-7501.

SOUTH DAKOTA: Office of Adult Services and Aging, Richard Kneip Building, 700 Governors Drive, Pierre, SD 57501-2291; (605) 773-3656; Fax: 605-773-6834.

TENNESSEE: Commission on Aging, 500 Deaderick Street, Andrew Jackson Building, 9th Floor, Nashville, TN 37243-0860; (615) 741-2056; Fax: 615-741-3309.

TEXAS: Department on Aging, 4900 North Lamar, Austin, TX 78751-2399; (800) 252-9240; Fax: 512-424-6890.

UTAH: Division of Aging & Adult Services, Box 45500, 120 North 200 West, Suite 401, Salt Lake City, UT 84145-0500; (801) 538-3910; Fax: 801-538-4395.

VERMONT: Department of Aging and Disabilities, Waterbury Complex, 103 South Main Street, Waterbury, VT 05676; (802-241-2400; Fax: 802-241-2325.

VIRGINIA: Virginia Department for the Aging, 700 East Franklin Street, 10th Floor, Richmond, VA 23219-2327; (804) 225-2271; 800-552-3402 (in VA); Fax: 804-371-8381.

WASHINGTON: Aging and Adult Services Administration, Department of Social and Health Services, P.O. Box 45600, Olympia, WA 98504-5600; (800) 422-3263; Fax: 360-493-9484.

WEST VIRGINIA: West Virginia Commission on Aging, 1900 Kanawha Blvd., East, Holly Grove-Building 10, Charleston, WV 25305-0160; (304) 558-3317; Fax: 304-558-0004.

WISCONSIN: Bureau on Aging, Department of Health and Family Services, 217 South Hampton Street, Suite 300, Madison, WI 53703; (608) 266-2536; Fax: 608-267-3203.

WYOMING: Department of Health, Division on Aging, 117 Hathaway Building, Room 139, Cheyenne, WY 82002-0480; (800) 442-2766; Fax: 307-777-5340.

FOOD AND DRUG ADMINISTRATION PUBLIC AFFAIRS SPECIALISTS

There are more than 40 FDA public affairs specialists throughout the United States. These specialists respond to consumers' questions about the FDA and what it regulates, distribute publications on a variety of FDA-related topics, including health and nutrition. The public affairs specialists are located in the following FDA offices:

Northeast Region

Food and Drug Administration, One Montvale Ave., Stoneham, MA 02180; (617) 279-1675 (ext.184); Fax: (617) 279-1687.

Food and Drug Administration, 599 Delaware Ave., Buffalo, NY 14202; (706) 551-4461; Fax: (718) 965-5117.

Food and Drug Administration, 850 Third Ave., Brooklyn, NY 11232; (718) 965-5300 (ext. 5043); Fax: (718) 965-5117.

Mid-Atlantic Region

Food and Drug Administration, Waterview Corporate Center, 10 Waterview Blvd., 3rd Floor, Parsippany, NJ 07052; (201) 331-2926; Fax: (201) 331-2969.

Food and Drug Administration, U.S. Customhouse, Room 900, 2nd and Chestnut Streets, Philadelphia, PA 19106; (215) 597-4390; Fax: (215) 597-6649.

Food and Drug Administration, 900 Madison Ave., Baltimore, MD 21201; (410) 962-3731; Fax: (410) 962-2307.

Food and Drug Administration, Resident Inspection Post, 3820 Center Road, P.O. Box 838, Brunswick, OH 44212; (330) 273-1038 (ext. 114); Fax: (330) 225-7477.

Southeast Region

Food and Drug Administration, 60- 8th Street N.E., Atlanta, GA 30309; (404) 347-4001; Fax: (404) 347-1912.

Food and Drug Administration, 7200 Lake Ellenor Dr., Suite 120, Orlando, FL 32809; (407) 648-6922; Fax: (407) 648-6881.

Food and Drug Administration, 6601 N.W. 25th Street, P.O. Box 59-2256, Miami, FL 33159-2256; (305) 526-2800; Fax: (305) 526-2693.

Food and Drug Administration, 297 Plus Park Blvd., Nashville, TN 37217; (615) 781-5372; Fax: (615) 781-5383.

Food and Drug Administration, 4298 Elysian Fields Ave., New Orleans, LA 70122; (504) 589-2420 (EXT. 121): Fax: (504) 589-6360.

Midwest Region

Food and Drug Administration, 300 S. Riverside Plaza, Suite 550- South, Chicago, IL 60606; (312) 353-5863 (ext. 188); Fax: (312) 886-3280.

Food and Drug Administration, 1560 East Jefferson Ave, Detroit, MI 48207; (313) 226-6260 (ext. 149); Fax: (313) 226-3076.

Food and Drug Administration, Resident Inspection Post, 101 W. Ohio St., Indianapolis, IN 46204; (317) 226-6500 (ext. 13); Fax: (317) 226-6506.

Food and Drug Administration, 240 Hennepin Ave., Minneapolis, MN 55401; (612) 334-4100 (ext. 129); Fax: (612) 334-4134.

Food and Drug Administration, Resident Inspection Post, 2675 North Mayfair Road, Suite 200, Milwaukee, WI 53226-1305; (414) 771-7167; Fax: (414) 771-7512.

Southwest Region

Food and Drug Administration, 3310 Live Oak Street, Dallas, TX 75204; (214) 655-5315 (ext. 303); Fax: (214) 655-5331.

Food and Drug Administration, Resident Inspection Post, 1445 N. Loop West, Suite 420, Houston, TX 77008; (713) 802-9095 (ext. 15); Fax: (713) 802-0906.

Food and Drug Administration, Resident Inspection Post, 10127 Morocco, Suite 119, San Antonio, TX 78216; (210) 229-4531; Fax: (210) 229-4548.

Food and Drug Administration, 11630 West 80th Street, Lenexa, KS 66214; (913) 752-2141; Fax: (913) 752-2111.

Food and Drug Administration, 12 Sunnen Drive, Suite 122, St. Louis, MO 63143; (314) 645-1167 (ext. 23); Fax: (314) 645-2969.

Food and Drug Administration, Denver Federal Building, Building 20, Room B-1121, 6th Avenue and Kipling, Denver, CO 80225-0087; (303) 236-3018 9ext 318); Fax: (303) 236-3551.

Pacific Region

Food and Drug Administration, 1431 Harbor Bay Parkway, Alameda, CA 94502-7070; (510)337-6845 (ext. 1089); Fax: (510) 337-6708.

Food and Drug Administration, Resident Inspection Post, 4615 East Elmwood Street, Suite 200,

Phoenix, AZ 85040; (602) 379-4595 (ext. 225); Fax: (602) 379-4646.

Food and Drug Administration, 22201 23rd Dr. S.E., Bothell, WA 98021-4421; (206) 483-4953; Fax: (206) 483-4996.

Food and Drug Administration, Resident Inspection Post, 9780 S.W. Nimbus Ave., Beaverton, OR 97008-7163; (503) 671-9332 (ext. 22); Fax: (503) 671-9445.

HEALTH CARE FINANCING ADMINISTRATION REGIONAL OFFICES

Region I (CT, ME, MA, NH, RI, VT): Sidney Kaplan, Regional Administrator, JFK Federal Building, Room 2325, Boston, MA 02203; (617) 565-1188.

Region II (NY, NJ, Puerto Rico, Virgin Islands): Tom Kickman, Acting Regional Administrator, 26 Federal Plaza, Room 3811, New York, NY 10278; (212) 264-4488.

Region III (DE, District of Columbia, MD, PA, VA, WV): Maurice Hartman, Regional Administrator, 3535 Market Street, Room 3100, Philadelphia, PA 19104; (215) 596-1351.

Region IV (AL, FL, GA, KY, MS, NC, SC, TN): Rose Crum Johnson, Regional Administrator, 101 Marietta Tower, Room 701, Atlanta, GA 30323; (404) 331-2329.

Region V (IL, IN, MI, MN, OH, WI): Dorothy Burke Collins, Regional Administrator, 105 W. Adams Street, 15th & 16th Floors, Chicago, IL 60603; (312) 886-6432.

Region VI (AR, LA, NM, OK, TX): Ed Lessard, Acting Regional Administrator, 1200 Main Street, Suite 2000, Dallas, TX 75202-4348; (214) 767-6427.

Region VII (IA, KS, MO, NE): Joe Tilghman, Regional Administrator, Richard Bolling Federal Building, 601 East 12th Street, Room 235, Kansas City, MO 64106-2808; (816) 426-5233.

Region VIII (CO, MT, ND, SD, UT, WY): Mary Kay Smith, Regional Administrator, Federal Office Building, 1961 Stout Street, Room 522, Denver, CO 80294-3538; (303) 844-2111.

Region IX (AZ, CA, HI, NV): Beth Abbott, Regional Administrator, 75 Hawthorne Street, 4th Floor, San Francisco, CA 94105-3903; (415) 744-3507.

Region X (AK, ID, OR, WA): Nancy Dapper, Regional Administrator, 2201 Sixth Ave, Mail Stop RX 40, Seattle, WA 98121-2500; (206) 615-2306.

RURAL DEVELOPMENT OFFICES

AlABAMA: 4121 Carmichael Road, Sterling Center, Suite 601, Montgomery, AL 36106: (304) 279-3400

ALASKA: 800 West Evergreen, Suite 201, Palmer, AK 99645-6539; (907) 745-2176.

ARKANSAS: 700 W. Capitol St., P.O. Box 2778, Little Rock, AR 72203: (501) 324-6346.

ARIZONA: 3003 N. Central Ave., Suite 900, Phoenix, AZ 85012; (601) 280-8770.

CALIFORNIA: 194 W. Main Street, Suite F, Woodland, CA 95695; (916) 668-2090.

COLORADO: 655 Parfet St., Room E 100, Lakewood, CO 80215; (303) 236-2801

CONNECTICUT: 451 West St., Amherst, MA 01002; (413) 253-4302.

DELAWARE: 4611 S. Dupont Hwy., P.O. Box 400, Camden, DE 19934-9998; (302) 697-4300.

FLORIDA: 440 N.W. 25th Place, Gainesville, FL 32614-7010; (904) 338-3400.

GEORGIA: 335 E. Hancock Ave., Stephens Federal Building, Athens, GA 30610; (706) 546-2173.

HAWAII: 154 Wainuenue Ave., Federal Building, Room 311, Hilo, HI, 89701; (808) 933-3000.

IOWA: 210 Walnut Street, Federal Building, Suite 873, Des Moines, IA 50309; (515) 284-4663.

IDAHO: 3232 Elder Street, Boise, ID 83705; (208) 334-1301.

ILLINOIS: Illini Plaza, Suite 103, 1817 S. Neil St., Champaign, IL 61820; (217) 398-5235.

INDIANA: 5975 Lakeside Blvd., Indianapolis, IN 46278; (317) 290-3100.

KANSAS: 1200 SW Executive Dr., P.O. Box 4653, Topeka, KS 66604; (913) 271-2700.

KENTUCKY: 771 Corporate Plaza, Suite 200, Lexington, KY 40503; (606) 224-7300.

LOUISIANA: 3727 Government St., Alexandria, LA 71302; (318) 473-7921.

MAINE: 444 Stillwater Ave., Suite 2, P.O. Box 405, Bangor, ME 04402-0405; (207) 990-9160.

MARYLAND (Maryland RD offices are co-located with the Delaware offices): 4611 S. Dupont Hwy., P.O. Box 400, Camden, DE 19934-9998; (302) 697-4390.

MASSACHUSETTS: 451 West Street, Amherst, MA 01002; (413) 253-4302.

MICHIGAN: 3001 Coolidge Rd., Suite 200, E. Lansing, MI 48823; (517) 337-6635.

MINNESOTA: 410 Farm Credit Service Building, 375 Jackson St., St. Paul, MN 55101-1853: (612) 290-3058.

MISSISSIPPI: Suite 831 Federal Building, 100W Capital SF, Jackson, MS 39269: (601) 965-4318.

MISSOURI: 601 Business Loop 70 West, Parkade Center, Suite 235, Columbia, MO 65203; (314) 876-0976.

MONTANA: 900 Technology Blvd., Suite B, P.O. Box 850, Bozeman, MT 59771; (406) 585-2580.

NEBRASKA: Federal Building, Room 308, 100 Centennial Mall N., Lincoln, NE 68508; (402) 437-5551.

NEVADA: 1390 S Curry Street, Carson, NV 89703; (702) 887-1222.

NEW HAMPSHIRE: City Center, 3rd Floor, 89 Main Street, Montpelier, VT 05602; (802) 828-6002.

NEW JERSEY: Transfield Plaza, #22, Woodland Road, Mt. Holly, NJ 08060; (609) 265-3600.

NEW MEXICO: 6200 Jefferson Street, NE, Room 255, Albuquerque, NM 87109; (505) 761-4950.

NEW YORK: The Rural Development of New York State is administered from the State Office located at 441 S. Salina Street, Syracuse, New York. All other offices are divided into the following 3 regions:

Region A— Eastern New York Regional Office: P.O. Box 7145, Newburgh, NY 12550; (914) 564-6880.

Region B— Central New York Regional Office: 214 Oriskany Blvd., Whitesboro, NY 13492; (315) 768-3330.

Region C— Western New York Regional Office: 100 Main Street, Salamanca, NY 14779; (719) 945-5240.

NORTH CAROLINA: 4405 Bland Rd., Raleigh, NC 27609; (919) 790-2731.

NORTH DAKOTA: Federal Building, Room 208, 220 East Rosser, Bismarck, ND 58502; (701) 250-4670.

OHIO: Federal Building, Room 507, 200 North High Street, Columbus, OH 43215; (614) 469-5608.

OKLAHOMA: 100 USDA, Suite 108, Stillwater, OK 74074-2654; (405) 742-1000.

OREGON: 101 SW Main Street, Suite 1410, Portland, OR 97204; (503) 414-3300.

PENNSYLVANIA: One Credit Union Place, Suite 330, Harrisburg, PA 17110-9408; (717) 782-4878.

RHODE ISLAND: 451 West St., Amherst, MA 01002; (413) 253-4302.

SOUTH CAROLINA: 1835 Assembly Street, Federal Building, Room 1007, Columbia, SC 29201; (803) 765-5163.

SOUTH DAKOTA: Federal Building, Room 308, 200 4th Street SW, Huron, SD 57530; (605) 352-1100.

TENNESSEE: Suite 300, 3322 West End Ave., Nashville, TN 37203-1071; (615) 783-1300.

TEXAS: Federal Building, Suite 102, 101 S. Main, Temple, TX 76501; (817) 774-1301.

UTAH: Federal Building, 125 State Street, Room 5428, Salt Lake City, UT 84138; (801) 524-4063.

VERMONT: City Center, 3rd Floor, 89 Main St., Montpelier, VT
05602; (802) 828-6002.

VIRGINIA: Culpepper Building, Suite 238, Richmond, VA 23229-5014; (804) 287-1718.

WASHINGTON: Federal Building, Room 319, 301 Yakima St., Wenatchee, WA 98807; (509) 664-0202.

WISCONSIN: 4949 Kirschling Court, Stevens Point, WI 54481; (715) 345-7600.

WEST VIRGINIA: 75 High Street, Morgantown, WV 26505-7500; (304) 291-4032.

WYOMING: 100 East B, Federal Building, Room 1005, Casper, WY 82602; (307) 261-5271.

STATE UTILITY COMMISSIONS

State Utility Commissions regulate consumer service and rates for gas, electricity and a variety of other services within your state. These services include rates for telephone calls and moving household goods. In some states, the utility commissions regulate water and transportation rates. Rates for utilities and services provided between states are regulated by the federal government. Many utility commissions also handle consumer complaints.

ALABAMA: Public Service Commission, P.O. Box 991, Montgomery, AL 36101-0991; (334) 242-5207; 800-392-8050 (in AL).

ALASKA: Alaska Public Utilities Commission, 1016 West 6th Avenue, Suite 400, Anchorage, AK; (907) 276-6222; 800-390-2782 (in Alaska).

ARIZONA: Corporation Commission, 1200 West Washington Street, Phoenix, AZ 85007; (602) 542-3935; 800-222-7000 (in AZ).

ARKANSAS: Public Service Commission, P.O. Box 400, Little Rock, AR 72203-0400; 501-682-1453; 800-482-1164 (in Arkansas; complaints).

CALIFORNIA: Public Utilities Commission, 505 Van Ness Avenue, Room 5218, San Francisco, CA 94102; 415-703-3703; 800-649-7570 (in California; complaints).

COLORADO: Public Utilities Commission, 1580 Logan Street, Logan Tower—Office Level 2, Denver, CO 80203; (303) 894-2000; 800-888-0170 (in Colorado).

CONNECTICUT: Department of Public Utility Control, 10 Franklin Square, New Britain, CT 06051; (860) 827-1553; 800-827-2613 (in Connecticut).

DELAWARE: Public Service Commission, 1560 South Dupont Highway, Dover, DE 19901; (302) 739-4247; 800-282-8574 (in Delaware).

DISTRICT OF COLUMBIA: Public Service Commission, 450 Fifth Street, N.W., Washington, DC 20001; (202) 626-5120.

FLORIDA: Public Service Commission, 2540 Shumard Oak Boulevard, Tallahassee, FL 32399-0850; (904) 413-6140; 800-342-3552 (in Florida).

GEORGIA: Public Service Commission, 244 Washington Street, S.W., Atlanta, GA 30334; (404) 656-4512; 800-282-5813 (in Georgia).

HAWAII: Public Utilities Commission, 465 South King Street, Room 103, Honolulu, HI 96813; (808) 586-2020.

IDAHO: Public Utilities Commission, P.O. Box 83720, Boise, ID 83720-0074; (208) 334-3912; 800-377-3529 (in Idaho).

ILLINOIS: Illinois Commerce Commission, 527 East Capitol Avenue, P.O. Box 19280, Springfield, IL 62794-9280; (217) 782-7907.

INDIANA: Utility Regulatory Commission, 302 West Washington Street, Suite E-306, Indianapolis, IN 46204; (317) 232-2701.

IOWA: Iowa Utilities Board, Lucas State Office Building, 5th Floor, Des Moines, IA 50319; (515) 281-8821.

KANSAS: State Corporate Commission, 1500 SW Arrowhead Road, Topeka, KS 66604-4027; (913) 271-3166; 800-662-0027 (in Kansas).

KENTUCKY: Public Service Commission, 730 Schenkel Lane, P.O. Box 615, Frankfort, KY 40602; (502) 564-3940; 800-772-4636 (in Kentucky; complaints).

LOUISIANA: Public Service Commission, P.O. Box 91154, Baton Rouge, LA 70821-9154; (504) 342-6687; 800-256-2413 (in Louisiana).

MAINE: Public Utilities Commission, 242 State Street, Augusta, ME 04333; (207) 287-3831; 800-452-4699 (in Maine).

MARYLAND: Public Service Commission, 6 St. Paul Street, 16th Floor, Baltimore, MD 21202; (410) 767-8000; 800-492-0474 (in Maryland).

MASSACHUSETTS: Department of Public Utilities, 100 Cambridge Street, 12th Floor, Boston, MA 02202; (617) 727-3500.

MICHIGAN: Public Service Commission, 6545 Mercantile Way, P.O. Box 30221, Lansing, MI 48909; (517) 334-6445; 800-292-9555 (in Michigan).

MINNESOTA: Public Utilities Commission, 121 Seventh Place East, Suite 350, St. Paul, MN 55101-2147; (612) 296-7124; 800-657-3782 (in Minnesota).

MISSISSIPPI: Public Service Commission, P.O. Box 1174, Jackson, MS 39215; (601) 961-5400; 800-356-6430 (in Mississippi).

MISSOURI: Public Service Commission, P.O. Box 360, Jefferson City, MO 65102; (573) 751-3243; 800-392-4211 (in Missouri).

MONTANA: Public Service Commission, 1701 Prospect Avenue, P.O. Box 202601, Helena, MT 59620-2601; (406) 444-6199; 800-646-6150 (in Montana).

NEBRASKA: Public Service Commission, 300 The Atrium, 1200 "N" Street, Lincoln, NE 68509, or P.O. Box 94927, Lincoln, NE 68509-4927; (402) 471-3101; 800-526-0017 (in Nebraska).

NEVADA: Public Service Commission, 555 East Washington Avenue, Room 4600, Las Vegas, NV 89101; (702) 486-2600; 800-992-0900 (in Nevada).

NEW HAMPSHIRE: Public Utilities Commission, 8 Old Suncook Road, Building No. 1, Concord, NH 03301; (603) 271-2431; 800-852-3793 (in New Hampshire).

NEW JERSEY: Board of Public Utilities, Two Gateway Center, Newark, NJ 07102; (201) 648-2027; 800-621-0241 (in New Jersey).

NEW MEXICO: New Mexico Public Utility Commission, Marian Hall, 224 East Palace Avenue, Santa FE, NM 87501-2013; (505) 827-6940; 800-663-9782 (in New Mexico).

NEW YORK: Public Service Commission, 3 Empire State Plaza, Albany, NY 12223; (518) 474-2530; 800-342-3377 (in New York; complaints).

NORTH CAROLINA: Utilities Commission, P.O. Box 29510, Raleigh, NC 27626-0501; (919) 733-4249.

NORTH DAKOTA; Public Service Commission, State Capitol, 12th Floor, Bismarck, ND 58505-0480; (701) 328-2400.

OHIO: Public Utilities Commission, 180 East Broad Street, Columbus, OH 43215-3793; (614) 466-3272; 800-686-7826 (in Ohio).

OKLAHOMA: Corporation Commission, Jim Thorpe Office Building, 2101 North Lincoln Boulevard, Oklahoma City, OK 73105; (405) 521-2267; 800-522-8154 (in Oklahoma).

OREGON: Public Utilities Commission, 550 Capitol St. NE, Salem, OR 97310-1380; (503) 378-6611; 800-522-2404 (in Oregon).

PENNSYLVANIA: Public Utilities Commission, P.O. Box 3265, Harrisburg, PA 17105; (717) 783-7349; 800-782-1110 (in Pennsylvania).

RHODE ISLAND: Public Utilities Commission, 100 Orange Street, Providence, RI 02903; (401) 277-3500; 800-341-1000 (in Rhode Island).

SOUTH CAROLINA: Public Service Commission, P.O. Drawer 11649; Columbia, SC 29211; (803) 737-5100; 800-922-1531 (in South Carolina).

SOUTH DAKOTA: Public Utilities Commission, 500 East Capitol Avenue, Pierre, SD 57501-5070; (605) 773-3201; 800-332-1782 (in South Dakota).

TENNESSEE: Tennessee Regulatory Authority, 460 James Robertson Parkway, Nashville, TN 37243-0505; (615) 741-3668; 800-342-8359 (in Tennessee).

TEXAS: Public Utilities Commission, 7800 Shoal Creek Boulevard, Suite 400N, Austin, TX 78757; (512) 458-0100.

UTAH: Public Service Commission, 160 East 300 South, Salt Lake City, UT 84111; (801) 530-6716.

VERMONT: Vermont Public Service Board, 112 State Street, Montpelier, VT 05620-2701; (802) 828-2358.

VIRGINIA: State Corporation Commission, P.O. Box 1197, Richmond, VA 23209; (804) 371-9608; 800-522-7945 (in Virginia).

WASHINGTON: Utilities and Transportation Commission, P.O. Box 47250, Olympia, WA 98504-7250; (360) 753-6423; 800-562-6150 (in Washington).

WEST VIRGINIA: Public Service Commission, P.O. Box 812, Charleston, WV 25323; (304) 340-0300; 800-344-5113 (in West Virginia).

WISCONSIN: Public Service Commission, 610 North Whitneyway, Madison, WI 53705-2729; (608)

266-5481; 800-225-7729 (in Wisconsin).

WYOMING: Public Service Commission, 700 West 21st Street, Cheyenne, WY 82002; (307) 777-7427; 800-877-9965 (in Wyoming).

VETERANS BENEFITS ADMINISTRATION FIELD OFFICES

In addition to the following field offices, the Department of Veterans Affairs provides toll-free telephone service throughout the 50 states and Washington, DC.

ALABAMA: 345 Perry Hill Road, Montgomery, AL 36109; (205) 279-4866.

ALASKA: 2925 DeBarr Road, Anchorage, AK 99508-2989; (907) 257-4776.

ARIZONA: 3225 N. Central Ave., Phoenix, AZ 85012; (602) 640-2703.

ARKANSAS: Building 65, Ft. Roots,P.O. Box 1280, Little Rock, AR 72215; (501) 370-3800.

CALIFORNIA: Federal Building, 11000 Wilshire Blvd., Los Angeles, CA 80024; (310) 479-4011. 2022 Camino Del Rio North, San Diego, CA 92108; (619) 297-8220. 1301 Clay Street, Room 1300 North, Oakland, CA 94612-5209; (520) 637-1325.

COLORADO: 44 Union Blvd., P.O. Box 25126, Denver, CO 80225; (303) 980-2799.

CONNECTICUT: 450 Main Street, Hartford, CT 06103; (203) 278-3230.

DELAWARE: 1601 Kirkwood Highway, Wilmington, DE 19805; (302) 633-5410.

DISTRICT OF COLUMBIA: 941 N. Capitol Street, NE, Washington, DC 20421; (202) 208-1300.

FLORIDA: 1833 Blvd, Room 3109,Jacksonville, FL 32206; (800) 827-1000. 51 SW First Ave., Miami, FL 33130; (800) 827-1000. 144 First Ave. S., St. Petersburg, FL 33731; (813) 893-3115.

GEORGIA: 730 Peachtree Street NE, Atlanta, GA 30365; (404) 347-3057.

HAWAII: PJKK Federal Building, 300 Ala Moana Blvd., P.O. Box 50188, Honolulu, HI 96813; (808) 541-1560.

IDAHO: 805 W. Franklin Street, Boise, ID 83724; (208) 334-1647.

ILLINOIS: 536 S. Clark Street, P.O. Box 8136, Chicago, IL
60680; (312) 353-3922.

INDIANA: 575 N. Pennsylvania St., Indianapolis, IN 46204; (317) 226-7921.

IOWA: Federal Office Building, 210 Walnut Street, Des Moines, IA 50309; (515) 284-4268.

KANSAS: 5500 E. Kellogg, Wichita, KS 67218; (316) 688-6827.

KENTUCKY: 545 S. Third Street, Louisville, KY 40202; (502) 582-5817.

LOUISIANA: 701 Loyola Avenue, New Orleans, LA 70113; (504) 582-6410.

MAINE: 475 Stevens Avenue, Portland, ME 04101; (800) 827-1000.Togus, ME 04330; (700) 833-5095.

MARYLAND: 31 Hopkins Plaza, Baltimore, MD 21201; (410) 962-2385.

MASSACHUSETTS: JFK Federal Building, Government Center, Boston, MA 02203; (617) 565-2541.

MICHIGAN: McNamara Federal Building, 477 Michigan Avenue, Detroit, MI 48226; (313) 226-4162.

MINNESOTA: Federal Building, Fort Snelling, St. Paul, MN 55111; (612) 725-3113.

MISSISSIPPI: 100 W. Capitol Street, Jackson, MS 39269; (601) 965-4875.

MISSOURI: 601 E. 12th Street, Kansas City, MO 64106; (800) 827-1000.400 S. 18th Street, St. Louis, MO 63103; (314) 589-9893.

MONTANA: Fort Harrison, MT 59636; (700) 585-7730.

NEBRASKA: 5631 S. 48th St., Lincoln, NE 68516; (402) 437-5047.

NEVADA: 1201 Terminal Way, Reno, NV 89520; (702) 784-5556.

NEW HAMPSHIRE; 275 Chesnut Street, Manchester, NH 03101; (603) 666-7746.

NEW JERSEY: 20 Washington Pl., Newark, NJ 07102; (201) 645-3562.

NEW MEXICO: 500 Gold Avenue SW, Albuquerque, NM 87102; (505) 766-3369.

NEW YORK: Clinton Avenue and North Pearl Street, Albany, NY 12207; (800) 827-1000. 111 W. Huron Street, Buffalo, NY 14202; (716) 551-5275. 245 W. Huston Street, New York, NY 10014; (212) 807-3420. 100 State Street, Rochester, NY 14614; (800) 827-0619. 344 W. Genesee Street, Syracuse, NY 13202; (800) 827-1000,

NORTH CAROLINA: Federal Building, 251 Main Street, Winston Salem, NC 27155; (919) 631-5434.

NORTH DAKOTA: 655 First Avenue N., Fargo, ND 58102; (701) 237-2637.

OHIO: 36 E. 7th Street, Suite 210, Cincinnati, OH 45202; (800) 827-1000. 1240 E. Ninth Street, Cleveland, OH 44199; (216) 522-4950. 200 N. High Street, Room 309, Columbus, OH 43215; (800) 827-1000.

OKLAHOMA: Federal Building, 125 S. Main Street, Muskogee, OK 74401; (918) 687-2153.

OREGON: Federal Building, 1220 SW 3rd Avenue, Portland, OR 97204; (503) 326-2414.

PENNSYLVANIA: VA Regional Office and Insurance Ctr., 5000 Wissahickon Avenue, Philadelphia, PA 19101; (215) 951-5301.

RHODE ISLAND: 380 Westminster Mall, Providence, RI 02903; (401) 528-4427.

SOUTH CAROLINA: 1801 Assembly Street, Columbia, SC 29201; (803) 765-5608.

SOUTH DAKOTA: 2501 W. 22nd Street, P.O. Box 5046, Sioux Falls, SD 57117; (605) 333-6845.

TENNESSEE: 110 9th Avenue S., Nashville, TN 37203; (615) 736-5367.

TEXAS: 1114 Commerce Street, Dallas,TX 75242; (800) 827-1000. 6900 Alameda Road, Houston, TX 77030; (713) 794-3678. 1205 Texas Avenue, Lubbock, TX 79401; (800) 827-1000. 3601 Bluemel Road, San Antonio, TX 78229-2041; (800) 827-1000. 1400 N. Valley Mills Dr., Waco, TX 76799; (817) 757-6777.

UTAH: 125 S. State. P.O. Box 11500, Salt Lake City, UT 84147; (801) 524-5975.

VERMONT: White River Junction, VT 05001; (700) 829-5323.

VIRGINIA: 210 Franklin Road SW, Roanoke, VA 24011; (703) 857-2109.

WASHINGTON: 915 Second Avenue, Seattle, WA 98174; (206) 220-6127.

WEST VIRGINIA: 4640 Fourth Avenue, Huntington, WV 25701; (304) 529-5786.

WISCONSIN: Building 6, 5000 W. National Ave., Milwaukee, WI 53295; (414) 382-5035.

WYOMING: 2360 E. Pershing Blvd., Cheyenne, WY 82001; (700) 328-7435.

Index